Daybreak Woman
∧∨∧∨

Daybreak Woman

AN **ANGLO-DAKOTA** LIFE

Jane Lamm Carroll

MINNESOTA
HISTORICAL
SOCIETY PRESS

mnhspress.org

The Minnesota Historical Society Press is a member of the Association of University Presses.

Manufactured in the United States of America

10 9 8 7 6 5 4 3 2 1

♾ The paper used in this publication meets the minimum requirements of the American National Standard for Information Sciences—Permanence for Printed Library Materials, ANSI Z39.48–1984.

International Standard Book Number
ISBN: 978-1-68134-166-8 (paper)
ISBN: 978-1-68134-167-5 (e-book)

Library of Congress Control Number: 2020943552.

This and other Minnesota Historical Society Press books are available from popular e-book vendors.

Interior book design by Wendy Holdman.

In tribute to the remarkable and influential women in my own life:
my grandmother, Ruth Alice Burns
my mother, Grace Jordan McGinniss
my sister, Julia Anne Lamm
and my daughter, Brigit Burns Carroll

Contents

Introduction

Lake Huron, 1836

The power of the Dakota had always dwelt in the land, from the great forest to the open prairies. Long before the white man ever dreamed of our existence, the Dakota roamed this land.

WAŊBDI WAKITA

In 1836, Daybreak Woman—Aŋpao Hiyaye Wiŋ to her Dakota kin, Jane Anderson Robertson to her British Canadian relatives—faced a critical juncture. For the first time in her life, she could choose where, with whom, and how she would live. A marriage proposal made these choices possible.

Lake Huron

Daybreak Woman was twenty-six years old. She had lived the first half of her life with her mother, Margaret Aird, Maḣpiya Ḣota Wiŋ (Grey Cloud Woman II), in Mni Sota Makoce, the homeland of the Santee Dakota. The second half she had spent with her British Canadian father, Thomas Anderson, on Lake Huron in Canada. Now her father was planning to move to establish a new Indian agency, taking her stepmother and four younger Anderson siblings with him. She could go with them, but at the time she was also being courted by a Scots immigrant, Andrew Robertson, who asked her to marry him.

The only known portrait photograph of Daybreak Woman—Jane Anderson Robertson—taken about 1890. *Minnesota Historical Society collections*

Robertson's proposal presented Daybreak Woman with two unprecedented opportunities: a chance to start her own family and the means to
return to Mni Sota Makoce to reunite with her mother and the Dakota
society she had left behind as a girl. She told Andrew she would marry
him, but only if he promised to take her home, and he could not refuse
her. Her decisions to marry a Scotsman and to return to her mother's
people proved pivotal in Daybreak Woman's life, and they are essential
to understanding the nature of her cultural identity and standpoint as an
Anglo-Dakota woman.* That she chose to go back to Mni Sota Makoce
after such a long separation from Dakota society, after spending so many
years in a mission school and living as an Anglo-American woman in her
father's second family, is evidence of the robust persistence of her Dakota
identity as well as her strong bonds to her mother and grandmother that
were integral to that identity.[1]

Mni Sota Makoce, Homeland of the Dakota

The Dakota homeland comprises most of what is now the state of Minnesota, the northern part of Iowa, western Wisconsin, and west into the
Dakotas past the Missouri River. Here the Dakota have lived for unknown
generations, since their creation; Mni Sota Makoce, the land where the
waters are so clear they reflect the clouds, is their place of origin. For the
Dakota, this homeland and its natural resources are gifts, manifestations
of the Great Mystery. As one white missionary explained in 1823, "The
Dacotas have no tradition of having ever emigrated from any other place,
to the spot upon which they now reside; they believe that they were created by the Supreme Being on the lands which they at present occupy."
The Dakota people and culture are inexorably embedded in Mni Sota
Makoce; their history, stories, values, and spiritual beliefs are enshrined
in specific places in the homeland.[2]

The Dakota are the people of the Oceti Šakowiŋ, the Seven Council
Fires, made up of seven major groups—four of which lived and live in
what is now the state of Minnesota. These four groups, who came to be
known as the Eastern or Santee Dakota (or Santee Sioux), occupied particular but fluid territories, across which they socialized, married, and
lived as one people with a shared language, culture, spirituality, and way
of life. In the 1700s, Dakota people lived throughout what is now northern

---

*A woman of British or British-American and Dakota heritage.

Minnesota, as well as farther south. By Daybreak Woman's time, the most eastern of the Seven Council fires was the Bdewakaŋtuŋwaŋ (Mdewakanton), whose bands lived in villages along the Mississippi River and the Lower Minnesota River. Just to the west and south were the Waḣpekute, while farther west on the prairies and the Upper Minnesota River lived the Waḣpetuŋwaŋ (Wahpeton) and the Sisituŋwaŋ (Sisseton).[3]

A Daughter of the Fur Trade

Daybreak Woman lived as far east as the eastern shore of Lake Huron in Canada and as far west as eastern South Dakota; in between, she lived in what are now the states of Wisconsin, Michigan, and Minnesota. Her first language was Dakota, and her second was English. She was born in 1810 on the Minnesota River at a trading post, and her life began there because the fur trade had, for many generations, created places along the region's waterways where Euro-Americans and Indigenous people came together to trade. Fur trade society comprised people of multiple cultures—Indigenous, French, British, and, later, Euro-Americans, as well as people of mixed European and Indigenous ancestry.[4]

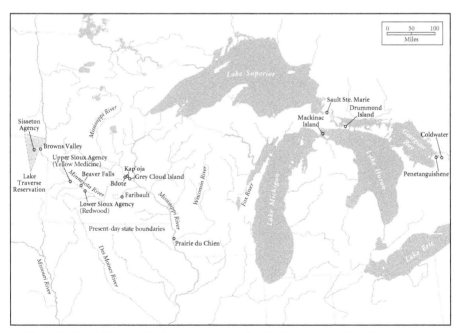

Places Daybreak Woman lived, 1810–1904. *Map by Matt Kania, Map Hero, Inc.*

Daybreak Woman lived the first fifty years of her life in communities composed mostly of Indigenous and Euro-Indigenous people in which Euro-Americans were the minority. However, by the 1850s this society was rapidly disappearing as thousands of Euro-American settler-colonists poured west across the Mississippi River to settle in Mni Sota Makoce. The Dakota communities Daybreak Woman had always known continued to exist for a time on the Dakota reservations on the Minnesota River created in 1851, but they were destroyed in 1862 by the forced exile of Dakota from the state after the US–Dakota War. In the ensuing decades, Dakota people who survived the traumatic calamity of 1862 and its genocidal aftermath rebuilt their lives. Some, including Daybreak Woman and her children, became part of reestablished Dakota communities on reservations in South Dakota and Nebraska, while other survivors eventually returned to Mni Sota Makoce to reconstitute communities in their Native homeland.

A Minnesota Story of Euro-American Colonization

Daybreak Woman was both Anglo and Dakota, a woman born of two cultures who embodied and embraced aspects of both societies. This book tells her story and that of the four generations of her Anglo-Dakota family starting with her Dakota grandmother and ending with Daybreak Woman's own death in 1904. The story continues today through her many, many descendants.*

This family's story must be placed within the broader context of the history of the Euro-American colonization of North America and its devastating impacts on Indigenous peoples and cultures. Colonization was a multifaceted process that persisted across centuries and eventually resulted in Euro-American social, cultural, political, and territorial domination of the entire continent and the Native peoples who lived on it. This process varied in its speed and intensity, depending on time and place; it moved via multiple fronts simultaneously, by economic, social, cultural, political, and legal means as well as by physically violent means (i.e., wars, genocide). Remarkably, despite centuries of this violent and genocidal colonization experience, many Indigenous peoples across North America

---

*See Appendix 2 for more on the Santee Dakota and the fur trade as well as women in Dakota culture. See Appendix 3 for more on Anglo-Dakota daughters and families in nineteenth-century Minnesota.

have managed to survive and endure and have conserved and revitalized their Native cultures, including the Santee Dakota of Mni Sota Makoce.

As Anglo-Dakota people, Daybreak Woman and her children—and, to a lesser extent, her mother—were both the progeny of and actors in the Euro-American colonization of Mni Sota Makoce. They were people rooted in two cultures, and they lived their lives accordingly. As Anglo-Dakota people, they embodied and modeled acculturation, moving easily between Euro-American and Dakota societies, but also living in particular ways because they were both Anglo and Dakota. In living near and working among the Dakota people, as teachers and farmers employed by the government, they encouraged their Dakota neighbors to adopt farming and literacy (in both the Dakota and English languages), because they saw those aspects of Euro-American culture as beneficial to Dakota people in the changing world wrought by colonization, a world in which it was increasingly difficult for Native people to survive as they had previously. Daybreak Woman and her children also became Christians, but, unlike their missionary friends, they did not think Christianity required converts to scorn or abandon other Dakota ways and values.

Replacing an Obsolete Narrative

In this biography I present Daybreak Woman and her family story within the broader context of Dakota history, Minnesota history, and the Euro-American colonization of North America. My fundamental aim in writing this book is to put Dakota and Euro-Dakota people firmly at the center of the story of Minnesota's past. In the last two decades, both Dakota and non-Dakota historians have worked to unearth and restore the Dakota to their rightful place in the story of the state and region's past, challenging the long-dominant historiographical narrative in which the Dakota people, their society, and their culture were largely ignored, stereotyped, misrepresented, or assumed to be irrelevant to Minnesota's story, except during the US–Dakota War of 1862. This book is part of that endeavor.

The long-established historiographical paradigm that Minnesota history begins with significant Euro-American settlement (1850s) and statehood (1858) has masked the rich multicultural history and experiences that preceded and succeeded statehood. This now obsolete but still firmly rooted master narrative of the state's history ignores evidence showing that for over a century prior to 1858, Indigenous people and Euro-Americans interacted socially, economically, and culturally as a result of the fur trade in the region, creating vibrant and influential communities comprising people of French, British, Indigenous, and Euro-Indigenous ancestry. By 1858, Indigenous and Euro-Indigenous people still made up more than half of the region's population, yet they have either been ignored or grossly underrepresented in the dominant narrative of Minnesota's past. With regard to the Dakota, the obsolete premise is that Dakota and Euro-Dakota people—pre-statehood, post-statehood, and post–Dakota War; and throughout the twentieth century, for that matter—are irrelevant to the history of Minnesota. My aim in this book is to contribute to the ongoing effort to replace this premise with a more inclusive, comprehensive, and accurate story of Minnesota's past.[5]

Women's History and the Masculine Historical Record— Or, Why Daybreak Woman?

Some people, including some historians, may wonder why Daybreak Woman is a worthy subject for a biography. She was not famous, wealthy, or extraordinarily accomplished for a woman of her time; she did not achieve notoriety outside the small communities in which she lived; she was not a "pioneer" or a "first" in taking on male roles; she was not a public figure; she was not even related to famous men. She was just an "ordinary" woman. But this is exactly why she is important as a focus of historical query. Most people in the nineteenth century, and especially women, were not famous, wealthy, or extraordinary. History isn't just about the few; if we want to understand how most people lived in the past and how most experienced the events and developments of their time, we need to study the individual lives of the unexceptional majority of people.

The purpose and work of women's history could be described in large part as a gigantic, never-ending reclamation project—we work like archeologists to reclaim a place for women in the past. We do that by digging up their stories and bringing them to light, including, and I would argue most importantly, the stories of ordinary women, in all their diversity. Daybreak Woman may not have been an extraordinary woman in the way she lived her life, but nevertheless she lived through and participated in significant and cataclysmic social developments in the region that resulted from Euro-American colonization and that deeply affected her and her family's lives, as well as those of her Dakota relatives and friends. Her experiences and those of her family over the course of the nineteenth century tell a unique story that reveals what the broader social changes of the era meant for ordinary people.

Writing a biography of a nineteenth-century Anglo-Dakota woman who was not famous, affluent, or otherwise notable is a daunting challenge. It's like putting together a puzzle for which many of the pieces are lost, broken, misshapen, or discolored, while having no idea what the final picture should look like—and knowing it's impossible to complete. Every historical account is only an approximation of the past, and the strength of a historical interpretation generally depends on the depth and breadth of the evidence upon which it is based. Writing about women in the nineteenth century is especially difficult due to the sparsity of the written record. In the early to mid-nineteenth century, many Euro-American women and most Dakota women were illiterate, although white middle-class girls and women were increasingly being educated. Even literate women rarely wrote accounts of their own lives, and not many of them tried to preserve their writing for posterity. In addition, records left by women were less likely to be preserved by their families or others because they were deemed of less interest or importance than those left by men. Most of society considered history to be something written about only certain kinds of men and certain subjects. Until the late twentieth century, most professional historians were men who shared this narrow definition of history and ignored women. Thus, women are virtually invisible in the written historical record created before the twentieth century, in texts, sources, and historiography. Finally, only in the last fifty years have significant numbers of professional historians worked to restore women to the written record and to employ gender as a lens for interpreting the past.[6]

For all of these reasons, I encountered significant challenges in attempting to reconstruct Daybreak Woman's life. Although she was educated and literate in both Dakota and English, she left no written account of her own life and experiences, and only a very few of her letters have survived, buried in the personal papers of men associated with her family or in the government record. Consequently, almost everything we can know about her comes from sources created by others, mostly men, who typically either neglected to record her presence or experiences or had little to say about her when they did. Indeed, outside of government and legal records in which her name appears, the vast majority of what we can know about Daybreak Woman in the written record is based in accounts written by or about the white men in her family—her grandfather James Aird, her father, Thomas Anderson, her husband, Andrew Robertson—as well as her son, Thomas Robertson. To a lesser extent, the Dakota men on Daybreak Woman's maternal side of the family, the chiefs Wapaha Ṡa (Wabasha), are also documented in the written historical record because they were important leaders among the Santee Dakota.

Fortunately, the history of Daybreak Woman's early life and marriage, as well as her Anglo-Dakota genealogy, was preserved by her eldest son, Thomas, and recorded in his "Reminiscences" in the 1910s, about a hundred years after his mother's birth. As with any autobiographical account, this memoir must be read critically, considering that he wrote it as an account for his children, and so was constructing his story for them. Moreover, the events that comprise the bulk of the memoir occurred more than fifty years earlier. Thomas's reminiscences offer disappointingly little detail about Daybreak Woman. He also says little about his younger siblings or the family's affairs. Thomas omits any mentions of his first wife, Niya Waṡte Wiŋ, rendering her virtually invisible in the written record of the family's story (as he was the only member of the family to leave an account). This omission highlights one of the central challenges for historians attempting to write about nineteenth-century women—an overdependence on sources written by men, which tend to neglect or erase women and focus almost exclusively on the authors themselves (and sometimes on other men). As another example, Daybreak Woman's father, Thomas Anderson, says little about his wife Grey Cloud Woman (Maḣpiya Ḣota Wiŋ) or their life together in Mni Sota Makoce in his memoir. Anderson does acknowledge his children with Grey Cloud Woman and recalls that he sent for them to live with him and be educated in Canada, but otherwise ignores his Dakota children, although they spent more than fourteen years with him.

One of the greatest challenges I have encountered in attempting to construct a coherent biography for Daybreak Woman has been to keep her continuously at the center of her own story, given the paucity of evidence for certain periods and details of her life. Where there are gaps in evidence about her experiences or activities, I have focused on members of her family (mostly her children or her husband) or on others who lived in proximity to her (friends, neighbors) to try to re-create her story. In these places in the narrative I ask the reader *to keep her in mind.* Even though she temporarily steps out of focus, we should think of her as there, in some way—as either physically present or as intimately connected to the people or experiences that are described, and therefore involved in and affected by them. The men in her family loom large in her story because much of what we can know about her comes from what they wrote or what was written about them, and it requires imagination to re-create Daybreak Woman's life from those sources. Additionally, it is important to remember that Daybreak Woman never lived apart from her family, except for a few years as an adolescent when she stayed at the mission school on Mackinac Island. It is thus impossible to tell the story of her life without also telling the stories of the people she lived with and with whom she was most closely socially bound, especially her mother, father, maternal grandparents, husband, and children.

The reader will find there are a few occasions in the narrative when I suggest how Daybreak Woman *may have felt* or what she *may have thought* about significant events or changes in her life, even when there is no evidence of what she actually felt or thought at the time. I do this when her story seems to call out for empathy and connection, when to not do so seems like a denial of her humanity and a silencing of her historical presence. However, in those places in the narrative, I make clear when I am speculating.

Telling a Dakota Story

Telling Daybreak Woman's story requires negotiating not only the limits and biases of the dominant male gaze but also the racial and cultural prejudices of the dominant Euro-American culture embedded in most of the primary and secondary sources (the historiography) related to the Dakota written by non-Indian people, mostly white men—and in myself, as a white woman.

Writing Dakota history requires "reading between the lines" of the non-Dakota sources in an attempt to unearth the most accurate portrayal of the Dakota experience as well as a Dakota perspective. Writing a complete and accurate account of any aspect of Dakota history requires incorporating all the extant available Dakota sources (accounts created by Dakota people themselves). However, not all Dakota sources are available to non-Dakota historians; Dakota families and communities have deep traditions of oral history, much of which has not been shared outside the community, which means there are very likely aspects of this history to which I have not had access as a non-Dakota historian. Given that limitation, I have attempted to write as complete a history as possible by relying on and integrating all the relevant available Dakota sources, learning as much as possible about Dakota history and culture, learning from and consulting with Dakota experts and descendants, and using sources provided by the Tribal Historic Preservation Office at the Sisseton Wahpeton Oyate Tribal Archives.[7]

It is not possible for me, a non-Dakota historian, to present a Dakota account of Daybreak Woman's story, nor do I claim to be doing so. The purpose of this book is to offer one interpretation of her life, written from my standpoint as an Anglo-American woman of the twentieth and twenty-first centuries, based on my expertise as a professional historian. For more than twenty-five years my teaching and scholarship has been grounded in US history, eighteenth- and nineteenth-century women's history, nineteenth-century Minnesota history, and the history of European colonialism and slavery in North America. For more than ten years I have conducted extensive research on the lives and cultural identities of Anglo-Dakota women and their families in Minnesota in the 1800s, and I have published their stories in journal articles. (See Appendix 3 for more about this research.) This work is meant as a contribution to the revisionist historical literature of the region that attempts to put Dakota and Euro-Dakota people back into Minnesota's history as central actors and influencers. I do not claim that this work is definitive, because that is never possible, and it has its limitations, as any work of history does. The purpose of this book is to put women and Dakota people back into the narrative of Minnesota history and contribute to the ongoing effort to replace the master historical narrative that silenced them. Regardless of its historiographical purpose, readers will find this an interesting story about people of mixed ancestry that puts a woman at its center and provides a unique window into the region's complex multicultural history.[8]

People of European and Dakota Ancestry in Nineteenth-Century Minnesota

Primary among Dakota cultural values is that an individual's greatest responsibility is to be a good relative, a good member of the community; a good person is one who does what is best for the family, the band, the people—the oyate. Kinship is the central organizing principle and essential cultural value of the Dakota; kinship rules dictate what it means to be a good person, a civilized person. A civilized person lives by the rules of kinship, the most important of which are "civility, good manners, and a sense of responsibility toward every individual." Moreover, Dakota kinship is expansive, comprising relatives beyond the small nucleus of parents and their children. The Dakota family is an extended one, in which a child's father's brothers are seen as additional fathers and a mother's sisters as additional mothers, while a father's sisters are aunts and a mother's brothers are uncles. The children of one's parents' siblings are considered brothers and sisters. This extended and inclusive family is known as the tióśpaye. In addition, Dakota values hold that *mitakuye owasiŋ*—we are all related.[9]

In the eighteenth and early nineteenth centuries in Mni Sota Makoce, French and British traders entered into and adapted to Dakota society. To operate successfully, traders had to speak the Dakota language and establish kinship bonds to secure their position. They married Dakota women, which assured them trade but also required them to abide by Dakota kinship rules of reciprocity, especially the values of generosity and sharing. Some established lifelong marriages with Dakota women, many were married for years if not decades, while others entered marriages of very short duration. These traders and their Euro-Dakota children became part of the tióśpaye. The children of Dakota women were Dakota in the eyes of their Dakota kin, regardless of their paternity; Dakota kinship is inclusive, not exclusive.

To the Dakota, people of mixed ancestry were simply their relatives; they would not have had any reason to distinguish them as otherwise, except that over the course of the early nineteenth century, Euro-American colonization created and exacerbated cultural and social distinctions among the Santee Dakota. By the late 1850s, this created an untenable social and economic situation on the Minnesota River reservations in which such distinctions became evident and, for some, divisive. Up to that point, people of Dakota and European ancestry, depending on their individual and family circumstances, had the social space to identify culturally in a variety of ways and to live their lives accordingly. From the Euro-American perspective, people sorted themselves on a spectrum that spanned from identifying and living solely as Dakota to total assimilation into Euro-American society. People of mixed ancestry were diverse in their cultural identities, and many of them identified and lived as people who comprised *both* cultures, as did Daybreak Woman.[10]

However, as the US government established a larger presence in Mni

Sota Makoce and more Euro-Americans moved into the region, they labeled people of mixed ancestry using racialized terms, most commonly as "mixed-bloods" or "half-breeds." Increasingly through the early 1800s, Euro-Americans (whites) referred to Euro-Indigenous people in racially categorized ways that eventually became pejorative when used by whites, most especially the term "half-breed," which became a slur that connoted tainted (non-white) blood in an American society that was becoming ever more deeply racialized. In order to clearly establish themselves as racially superior to anyone of non-European descent, Euro-Americans obsessed about the biological ancestral composition (i.e., the "blood") of human beings, and claimed that those with "purely" white blood were superior to all others. This racist ideology was used to justify the continuation of slavery as well as the denial of citizenship, constitutional rights, and social and legal equality to all non-whites in the United States.[11]

In the 1850s in Mni Sota Makoce tensions and conflicts mounted between Dakota people and whites as a result of Euro-American colonization, and it became increasingly difficult for those who identified as both Dakota and European to continue seamlessly uniting both cultures in their lives without encountering social conflict. When the treaties of 1851 reduced the geographical extent of Dakota territory to just two reservations on the Minnesota River, the social space for people of mixed ancestry also dramatically contracted. Some never moved to live on the reservations, remaining where they had lived for decades in what would become the cities of St. Paul and Minneapolis and in other places along the Mississippi and Minnesota Rivers such as Mendota, Bloomington, and Shakopee. Depending on where they lived and who their neighbors were, Euro-Dakota people in these places felt varying degrees of social pressure to mute their Dakota identities in what was rapidly becoming a white-dominated society that was deeply prejudiced against Indigenous people.[12]

Meanwhile, on the reservations, Euro-American acculturation policies and practices began to divide the Dakota oyate, as some people adopted some aspects of Euro-American culture, especially farming and Christianity. As most people on the reservations struggled just to survive, the economic disparities between people who acculturated and those who did not became more evident as well. Agents gave more food and supplies to those who farmed and adopted white dress. This caused division and occasional open conflict. As tensions among Dakota people, government officials, and the traders increased, Euro-Dakota people on the reservations continued to work for the government and in the traders' stores. With the explosion of the 1862 US–Dakota War, many Euro-Dakota people found themselves in a precarious status, still viewed as relatives and friends by many Dakota people, but seen by others, especially many who led and prosecuted the war, as traitors complicit in the Euro-American colonization process that was destroying the Dakota way of life.

Terminology

In this book, I try to be as specific as possible when identifying a person's heritage, because those people of mixed ancestry who identified with both cultures would have seen themselves primarily as French-Dakota or Anglo-Dakota (or Scots-Dakota, or English-Dakota). Secondarily, some saw themselves as part of a broader category of "mixed bloods," a term which they sometimes used to refer to themselves or others. This was also the term most commonly used in government documents to refer to mixed-ancestry people. Some mixed-ancestry people also referred to themselves and others as "half-breeds." However, because "half-breed" came to be used by whites as a racial slur, I do not use it in this book. I also do not use the term "mixed-blood" because it is also a term based on nineteenth-century racist ideology. To emphasize the importance of cultural identity in shaping the lives of human beings, I use the terms *Euro-Dakota* or *mixed ancestry* to identify people of both European and Indigenous ancestry, with the frank acknowledgment that these are not terms that people of the nineteenth century would have used. *Indigenous, Native American,* and *Native* are used synonymously in this book, with preference given to the first term. The terms *Euro-American* and *white* are used interchangeably. Although first-generation European immigrants primarily identified culturally with their particular homelands, all Euro-Americans eventually came to see themselves as white, as opposed to those people of non-European ancestry.[13]

The term *settler* in the context of the Euro-American colonization of the North American continent is a fraught one, laden with colonial assumptions that were used by whites to justify taking Indigenous lands. Euro-American colonizers claimed that although Indigenous people occupied the lands, they did not "settle" it or "civilize" it in the way of Europeans, and so they "wasted" it. This supposedly justified the colonists taking the land for themselves. As an alternative, I use *settler-colonists.*

This term indicates a particular kind of colonization, one in which the colonizers remove the original people from the land and take it for themselves. Although the Euro-American immigrants who came into Mni Sota Makoce saw themselves as entitled to settle on the land, in fact they were invading colonizers taking over the Dakota homeland.[14]

What's in a Name?

Aŋpao Hiyaye Wiŋ, Daybreak Woman, Jane Anderson Robertson had three names because she was both Dakota and Anglo-American. Her English name, Jane, was one of the most popular names for girls in England in the nineteenth century. To those who spoke only English, she was always Jane or Jennie, a common nickname for Jane in the nineteenth century.

Names hold significant cultural and social meaning for the Dakota and are very important to Dakota identity. There is nothing in the written record to explain why she was given her formal Dakota name, Aŋpao Hiyaye Wiŋ. In Dakota culture, the use of one's formal name is reserved for ceremonial use and it is considered disrespectful to use a person's formal name casually. In everyday life, Dakota people addressed (and often still address) each other using kinship terms such as daughter, mother, sister, aunt, niece. Jane Anderson Robertson was rooted in both cultures and moved back and forth between both societies over the course of her life, so in this story she is Daybreak Woman, the English version of her Dakota name.[15]

Names of other Dakota people appear in historical records variously, as phonetic translations made by speakers of English and as English translations only. When possible, those phonetic translations are corrected in this book to more accurate Dakota spellings. Because it is not possible to back-translate with certainty, some Dakota individuals are named here with only the English translations of their names.

Dakota Orthography

The Dakota language existed solely in oral form until the 1830s. In that decade, Presbyterian missionaries Stephen Riggs, Samuel and Gideon Pond, and Thomas Williamson, working for the American Board of Commissioners for Foreign Missions, came into Santee Sioux territory to bring their religion to the Dakota. As they worked to persuade Dakota people to adopt Christianity, the missionaries, in conjunction with a group of Dakota elders and leaders, created a written form of the Dakota language. They then translated Bible verses, Bible chapters, hymns, and prayers into

Dakota. The missionaries decided the best approach to gaining Christian converts would be to first teach the Dakota to read and write in their own language before attempting to teach them English. In 1852, these efforts resulted in the publication of the *Grammar and Dictionary of the Dakota Language*, edited by Stephen Riggs. This was the Dakota orthography that Daybreak Woman, her husband, and their children knew, taught, and used themselves throughout the nineteenth century, so it is the style most historically appropriate for this biography.[16]

Audience

Professionally, I am both a scholar and an educator. I intend this book to be read both as a work of historical scholarship and as an interesting story that appeals to a much broader audience, beyond scholars and experts. While historians of nineteenth-century Minnesota will find much that is already familiar to them in its pages, I expect that many more of the book's readers will discover much that is new and illuminating about the region's past. Most importantly, I hope readers will learn something from Daybreak Woman's story, as I have.

1. Mississippi River, 1812–1823

Prairie du Chien

They wanted to know how I became part Sioux. I told them my grandmother's name was Mahpiyahotewin, Grey Cloud Woman [I] and that at one time she was married to an Englishman who kept a trading post on the east side of Lake Traverse, at a point called Witahutiyahoe. They knew her right away and said she had fed many of them the winter of the great famine when so many of them had starved to death getting back from their winter hunt, and some of them even claimed relationship.

THOMAS ROBERTSON, 1918

In the late 1700s and early 1800s, Prairie du Chien, located 450 river miles above St. Louis at the confluence of the Wisconsin and Mississippi Rivers, was the primary fur trade depot of the Upper Mississippi River region. It was situated in the southeastern section of Mni Sota Makoce, the Santee or Eastern Dakota homeland; the easternmost bands of the Santee Dakota, the Bdewakaŋtuŋwaŋ, lived in villages on the Mississippi that ranged from the Upper Iowa River north to the Minnesota River at Bdote. The Dakota closest to Prairie du Chien were the people of the Kiyuksa band, led by Wapaha Ša (Red Leaf, or Wabasha), whose villages in the late 1700s were located at three sites: one on the Upper Iowa River, one at Lake Pepin, and one at Wapaha Ša's Prairie (currently the site of Winona, Minnesota). In the late 1700s and early 1800s, Bdewakaŋtuŋwaŋ women married British, French, and Euro-Indigenous fur traders, establishing reciprocal kinship relationships between the traders and the Dakota. Bdewakaŋtuŋwaŋ women who married traders lived with their husbands and children in Prairie du Chien when they were not at their trading posts on the rivers and lakes of Mni Sota Makoce.[1]

Wapaha Ša had several wives and eight children—two sons and six daughters. Five of his daughters married French or French-Indigenous men engaged in the fur trade. One, Maȟpiya Ḣota Wiŋ, Grey Cloud

Wapaha Ša's village on the Mississippi, about 1845. *Watercolor by Seth Eastman, Minnesota Historical Society collections*

Woman, married a Scots trader, James Aird. Grey Cloud Woman had one daughter with Aird, Margaret, who like her mother was called Maȟpiya Ȟota Wiŋ. Grey Cloud Woman II married a British Canadian trader, Thomas Anderson. In 1810, they had a daughter, Jane Anderson. To her Dakota kin, she was Aŋpao Hiyaye Wiŋ, Daybreak Woman.

Until she was twelve, Daybreak Woman lived in the fur trade society that had flourished for over a century in the western Great Lakes and Upper Mississippi River region. Founded upon the strong intercultural kinship ties established by intermarriage between Euro-American traders and Indigenous women, this society was characterized by intercultural exchange, interdependence, accommodation, and cultural syncretism. It included French, British, and American traders and their employees, soldiers stationed at nearby forts, and Dakota, Ojibwe (Chippewa), Sauk (Sac), Meskwaki (Fox), Menomonie, Ho-Chunk (Winnebago), Báxoje (Iowa), and other Indigenous peoples. In addition, Euro-Indigenous people, the progeny of marriages and alliances between Euro-Americans and Native women, made up a significant portion of the population. The fur trade and the society it created were first nurtured and dominated by the French and their Indigenous allies in the seventeenth century, then controlled by the British who pushed the French out of North America in 1763 after the French and Indian War. Although British traders took control of the trade, most of their employees continued to be French or French-Indigenous, and the nature of the society did not change significantly as British traders, clerks, and merchants became involved. The British continued to control the trade in the region even after the American Revolution; it was not until after the War of 1812 that the Americans pushed the British out and took over the trade.[2]

Prairie du Chien

Prairie du Chien, considered neutral ground by surrounding Indigenous nations, was a major rendezvous site for the fur trade from the mid-eighteenth century, and perhaps earlier. As a fur trade depot in the western Great Lakes/Upper Mississippi region, Prairie du Chien ranked second in importance only to Mackinac (originally Michilimackinac), established in 1679 by the French at the junction of Lake Michigan and Lake Huron. Prairie du Chien's location on the Upper Mississippi River near the mouth of the Wisconsin River made it important to the trade; goods

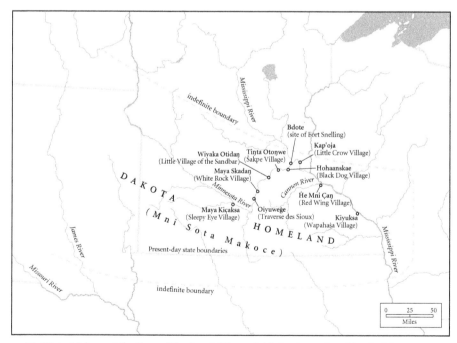

Mni Sota Makoce at the time of Daybreak Woman's birth, about 1810. *Map by Matt Kania, Map Hero, Inc.*

were transported to and from Mackinac via the Wisconsin and Fox Rivers to Green Bay, then across Lake Michigan through the Straits of Mackinac and across Lake Huron to Montreal. Alternative routes to and from Prairie du Chien were downriver to St. Louis or New Orleans and up the Mississippi through its headwaters to Lake Superior.[3]

In the mid-eighteenth century, Prairie du Chien became a meeting place for traders who dispersed from there to their wintering posts on the Upper Mississippi and its tributaries. In the spring, these traders met Indigenous hunters to exchange furs and trade goods, and from there the furs were shipped back to Montreal via Mackinac. The site grew in importance, and by the 1770s, some French-Canadians began to purchase land and live there permanently. These first residents came up the Mississippi from several French settlements below St. Louis. Mostly French voyageurs, the employees (engagés) of the fur trade, they settled and combined agriculture with contractual fur trade employment for their livelihoods. The village of Prairie du Chien was laid out according to the French colonial system, whereby each villager owned a town lot for a house as well as a narrow but long strip of land, or farm lot, that stretched behind the village. Some of the villagers erected barns on their farm lots, and there were narrow paths along each farm lot to allow access.[4]

By 1773, the main village at Prairie du Chien was centered on a long island not far from the east bank of the Mississippi River, cut off from the mainland by a swamp called the Marais de St. Feriole. In the 1780s and 1790s, French-Canadian and British traders who operated out of Montreal or Mackinac began to settle there. The village lots ran perpendicular from the river on the west to the marais on the east. The villagers' farm lots extended from the river or the marais east across the prairie to the river bluffs.

In 1810, there were three distinct villages making up the settlement, mainly divided by class based on ranking in the fur trade. The traders and merchants with the most wealth, mostly British and French-Canadians, with a few Americans, lived in the main village on the island closest to the Mississippi. To the north, separated from the main village by a Catholic cemetery, was the Upper Village, composed of French voyageurs (the laborers of the trade) and their families; on the mainland was St. Feriole, where more voyageurs' families lived. The wealthiest residents owned multiple farm lots and sometimes more than one village lot.[5]

Most of the men who lived in Prairie du Chien, whether French, British, or American, had Indigenous wives (of many different tribes) and

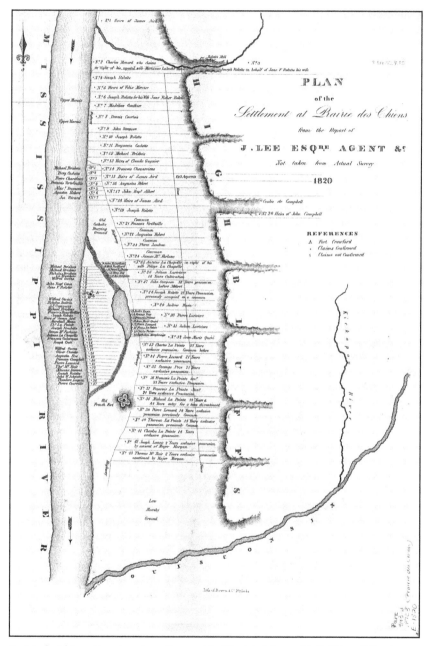

Prairie du Chien, 1820. *American Geographical Society Library Digital Map Collection, University of Wisconsin–Milwaukee Libraries*

Euro-Indigenous children. One visitor to Prairie du Chien in 1805 estimated that about half the population "had Indian blood." Nicolas Boilvin,
the newly appointed US Indian agent, reported in 1811 that of the about
one hundred families living there, only about twelve were "white." An 1815
visitor to the village noted that "all the people speak English, French and
Indian languages, all imperfectly." In 1817, Stephen Long, on an expedition
for the US government, noted that the inhabitants were primarily French
or Indigenous. Henry Schoolcraft, who visited that same year, described
Prairie du Chien as consisting of about eighty log buildings arranged in
two streets on the river with the "old shabby look of all antique French
towns on the Mississippi."[6]

Agent Boilvin also noted in his report that Prairie du Chien "is surrounded by numerous Indian tribes who wholly depend upon it for their
supplies. It is annually visited by at least six thousand Indians, and hitherto they have resorted to the Canadian traders for goods." While it was
true that people of various Native groups came to rendezvous at Prairie
du Chien once or twice a year, those whose territories were closest in proximity and who associated most frequently with Prairie du Chien's traders,
merchants, and voyageurs were the Eastern (Santee) Dakota, Sauk, Meskwaki, Ho-Chunk, and Menomonee. The Santee Dakota, whose hunting
territory extended along the east and west sides of the Upper Mississippi
River and whose villages were strung out along both the Mississippi
and Minnesota Rivers, had been closely associated with traders out of
Mackinac since the early 1700s. By the 1750s, there were at least one dozen
French traders operating posts among the Dakota on both the Mississippi
and Minnesota. Many of these traders entered into marriages "à la façon
du pays" (according to the Native customs of the country) with Dakota
women; such kinship relationships were central to the operation of the
fur trade from its beginning and were understood to incur benefits and
responsibilities on both sides. As the British, and later the Americans,
erected forts and garrisoned troops at fur trade centers, including Prairie
du Chien, some officers and soldiers also married Dakota women.[7]

Although traders operated out of their permanent homes in Prairie du
Chien, some living arrangements changed with the seasons. In late spring
and early summer, clerks, traders, and Indigenous people rendezvoused
to deliver furs gathered over the winter, trade, and settle accounts. In late
summer, the traders formed a canoe convoy to take the furs to Mackinac, and they returned with trade goods, supplies, and occasionally new

employees in the fall. Sometimes, more prosperous traders sent clerks to wintering locations or contracted with smaller traders to go farther into Native territory for the winter and trade for furs. However, frequently traders were "wintering partners" who went themselves into the interior posts for the winter rather than dispatching others. The Native wives and children of traders went with them to their interior posts.[8]

Dakota women, like other Indigenous women, played essential economic, social, and cultural roles in the North American fur trade. Their marriages to white traders deepened and fortified trade relationships with their Native communities, establishing kinship ties that demanded loyalty and reciprocity on both sides. Through these marriages, Dakota women helped establish the peaceful relationships and mutual understanding necessary to keep the fur trade operating. Dakota women ensured themselves, as well as their families and communities, access to desired trade goods, while their kinship ties ensured the traders a steady flow of furs provided by the labor of Dakota men. Thus, both the Dakota people and the white traders saw such unions as mutually beneficial.

Although Dakota women married French, British, American, and Euro-Indigenous traders so that their extended families and their communities could benefit from the fur trade, such practical economic and social aims did not necessarily preclude personal ambition, romantic sentiment, sexual attraction, a disposition to acculturation, or affection as factors affecting an individual woman's decision to marry a trader. Dakota women were not forced into marriage, and marriages were fluid in Dakota society—women were free to leave marriages, and men often had multiple wives. Women did not have to marry at all, if their parents could support them. As in most other North American Native communities, Dakota mothers retained control over their children regardless of their marital status. They also had extensive autonomy over their own bodies, their labor, the food they gathered and produced, and everything they manufactured—which included the family's shelter, household goods, tools, and clothing. Dakota girls were raised to be spirited and independent, and as women the centrality of their vital economic contributions to the communal subsistence lifestyle of their communities gave them significant autonomy and authority in the tiośpaye and Dakota society. While a woman's commitment to her tiośpaye undoubtedly was a primary consideration in her decision whether or not to marry a trader, the choice of whom to marry (and for how long) was ultimately hers to make. Such autonomy and agency in deciding whom

Dakota woman scraping a hide, 1840s. Women's labor in hide preparation was essential to the fur trade. *Drawing by Seth Eastman, Minnesota Historical Society collections*

to marry and the conditions of marriage were evident in the decisions of both Daybreak Woman and her mother.[9]

Prairie du Chien residents made their living through the fur trade and also through agriculture, raising livestock, milling, and investing in real estate. Most of the villagers had farm plots, and the soil was fertile; villagers traded or sold crops, vegetables, fruit, and livestock to their neighbors, including the local Indigenous population, and, after 1813, the British and Americans garrisoned at the fort. In 1811, Nicolas Boilvin reported that the villagers "raised considerable quantities of surplus produce, particularly wheat and corn. They annually dispose of about 80 thousand weight of flour to the traders and Indians, besides great quantities of meal.... All kinds of vegetables flourish in great perfection ... [and] Different fruit trees have lately been planted and promise to grow well." A visitor in May 1818 noted that the plum and cherry trees were in full bloom and people were planting their corn, and by July they were harvesting their wheat. Several Prairie du Chien residents built and operated mills to grind the village's wheat and corn. These were all horse-drawn except for one water-powered mill, erected in 1817. All of the mills were located a few miles outside of the village on the mainland.[10]

Early-nineteenth-century Prairie du Chien society was close-knit; its population was small, and many of its inhabitants were related to one another. Most worked together in the fur trade, they lived close together, and all were dependent on their neighbors for food, supplies, employment, labor, support, news, and entertainment. There were no resident clerics or churches, Catholic or Protestant, until the 1830s. A Catholic priest came through in 1817 and performed baptisms and marriages for many of the Catholic villagers and their children, but none returned for many years. Skilled labor was in short supply, and anyone with trade skills, experience, or formal education was in demand. Willard Keyes, a Vermonter who arrived in 1817 and stayed two years, found almost continuous employment in the village as a carpenter, artisan, mill operator, schoolteacher, and, finally, lumberjack. Daybreak Woman's grandfather James Aird employed Keyes to build a schoolhouse, to make a bolting chest, and to operate his horse mill for several months. When he wasn't living at one of the two mills he operated, Keyes rented rooms from several villagers, a common practice for those passing through town. In the summer of 1818, the villagers also hired Keyes to teach the first school in English in the settlement.[11]

By 1820, there were 492 inhabitants of Prairie du Chien, 361 civilians and 131 at the fort. The population decreased during the winter months, as traders and clerks were out at wintering posts. However, in spring and especially summer, it increased as boats brought visitors and sometimes new residents from downriver, upriver, and Mackinac. Fleets of canoes carrying Indigenous visitors arrived periodically; they camped nearby and frequented the village for days or weeks, sometimes playing lacrosse on the prairie on the mainland. During the summer, boats from St. Louis regularly delivered supplies, food, liquor, and wine. The arrival of boats from downriver and the return of canoes from Mackinac were causes for celebration and inebriation. In October 1814, James Aird brought a barrel of high wine—highly distilled spirits that needed to be cut with water—back from Mackinac, which he tapped and, according to the fort's commander, "was very obliging, it being an article not common in this place, in making almost a general business of it, till there was no more." Excessive drinking became a problem for some. In 1818, Ramsay Crooks, who visited Prairie du Chien to persuade Aird to join the American Fur Company, reported that Aird was "drinking heavily."[12]

Leisure hours in Prairie du Chien, especially Sundays and holidays, were spent playing ball games, racing horses, eating, and congregating at the tavern or a neighbor's to drink. Keyes, a New England Protestant, looked askance at the failure of the village's mostly Catholic inhabitants to keep the Sabbath. On his first Sunday in Prairie du Chien, he was shocked to see people "galloping about on French ponys playing at ball, billiards, etc., so that the Sabbath appears to be a day of recreation and amusement among them." He noted that Sundays were days of "riot and drunkenness" when there were "lots of drunken people in town." Christmas and New Year's Day were occasions for feasting and a "drunken frolic" at the tavern—in which he participated, despite his previous disapproval. The traders and clerks who stopped at Prairie du Chien on their way to and from Mackinac usually spent several days to a week socializing and relaxing before moving on. Thomas Anderson, a British Canadian trader and Daybreak Woman's father, recalled nightly parties of eating and drinking, and as for keeping the Sabbath, he recalled, "we sometimes kept Sunday, but whether on the right day was doubtful."[13]

Grey Cloud Woman (Maȟpiya Hota Wiŋ) and James Aird

Daybreak Woman's maternal grandmother, Grey Cloud Woman I, was a daughter of Wapaha Ša (Wabasha, Red Leaf), a prominent Dakota leader whose influence spanned from the 1740s to 1800. Wapaha Ša and his band first established kinship ties with the French, but during and after the French and Indian War (1756–63), they became closely aligned with British traders. By the time of the American Revolution, Wapaha Ša was firmly pro-British, so much so that he received a commission as an officer in the British Army and subsequently joined several other Indigenous nations of the region to fight against the Americans. The leader's main role during the war was to protect Prairie du Chien, but in 1789, he also led an Indigenous assault on the Spanish garrison at St. Louis. Despite their victory in the American Revolution (1775–84), the Americans were unable to end the dominance of the British over the fur trade in the region. Throughout the late 1700s and early 1800s, the Santee Dakota continued their close affiliation with British and French traders, cemented by kinship ties established through marriages to Dakota women. A number of Wapaha Ša's daughters married traders working out of Prairie du Chien, among them Grey Cloud Woman I (Maȟpiya Hota Wiŋ), who married the Scotsman James Aird.[14]

Aird had been trading with the Santee Dakota since at least 1779. In 1785, the Mackinac Company, a newly organized consortium of French-Canadian and British traders, organized its Sioux Outfit and sent traders out to six wintering stations among the Dakota on the Mississippi and Minnesota Rivers. The Sioux Outfit assigned Aird to Wapaha Ša's band. Grey Cloud Woman married Aird sometime in the late 1780s or early 1790s. He used Prairie du Chien as his base for trading, and he moved there permanently with Grey Cloud Woman by 1793, when their only child, Margaret (Grey Cloud Woman II), was born.[15]

By the late 1810s, Aird was the largest property owner in Prairie du Chien. The Aird house was situated in the middle of about eighteen houses that ranged along the first street in the main village, facing the Mississippi River. The family also owned several farm plots and two additional village plots that they rented to others. Most of the houses in Prairie du Chien were of log construction plastered over with mud and covered in tree bark, although a few frame houses were in place by 1805. There is no record of whether the Airds had a log or frame house, but since James Aird was a prosperous trader, their home's interior would have been well furnished and comfortable. Their closest neighbors to the north were Joseph Rolette, his wife, Margaret (Grey Cloud Woman's sister), and their children. Their longtime next-door neighbor to the south was one of Prairie du Chien's few American residents, Marshall Mann, who ran a tavern and inn for more than twenty years.[16]

Aird was one of the traders who usually wintered at interior posts rather than sending out employees. Grey Cloud Woman would have gone with him to these posts, especially in the early years of their marriage; actively helping him in the trade in later years, she may have chosen to remain in Prairie du Chien with their daughter. For many years, Aird traded on the Upper Minnesota River and in the spring brought the furs to Prairie du Chien. From there he traveled up to Mackinac to trade the furs and purchase supplies for the next year. By July or August, Aird returned to Prairie du Chien and stayed until the fall, when he would leave again to travel upriver to a winter station. Sometimes, he ventured even farther west to trade. In 1804–05, he was on the Upper Missouri River and the Big Sioux River, where he encountered the Lewis and Clark expedition. He wintered on the Upper Missouri River through 1811, then began trading again on the Upper Mississippi and the Minnesota River. In the winter of 1814–15, at the age of fifty-eight, Aird was on the Minnesota River trading with the Dakota, and three years later he was still trading on the river.[17]

Like most of their neighbors, the Airds supported themselves not only through the trade but also by agricultural ventures and investing in real estate. Their multiple farm lots presumably grew crops or produce or were rented to others. James Aird also had a horse-drawn grain mill built in 1818. He hired the Vermonter Willard Keyes to live at the mill and operate it for him. Aird also invested in real estate and, in May 1818, purchased all of Joseph Rolette's property in the village for $9,000. However, the two men disagreed almost immediately about the transaction and within a few weeks were in arbitration. Aird sued Rolette for breach of contract, and this legal dispute resulted in the first recorded trial at Prairie du Chien.[18]

According to Bernard Brisbois, another neighbor, Aird died at Mann's tavern in 1819 after choking to death on a wild rice hull. Grey Cloud Woman and her daughter inherited all of the property, some of which they sold almost immediately to neighbors. Then, in 1821, they sold the family's village lot with their house to the American Fur Company (AFC). They must have either rented another house in the village or arranged with the AFC to stay in their house as tenants, as they did not leave Prairie du Chien until 1825. These land sales sustained the family for several years.[19]

Little is known about Grey Cloud Woman before her marriage to Aird. Sources vary widely on the year of her birth, but most likely she was born in the mid- to late 1770s at Wapaha Ša's Prairie. Many of her Dakota kin lived in Prairie du Chien, and her father, her brother (who became Wapaha Ša II in 1806 and died in 1836), and other relatives were frequent visitors. Four of her sisters who married Euro-American men lived in the village with their families. In addition, other traders married Dakota and French-Dakota women who may have been related to Grey Cloud Woman. One prominent Scots-Dakota family in Prairie du Chien were the Campbells, whose patriarch, Archibald, had married a Dakota woman known as Ninse, with whom he raised five children. Another important family was that of the French-Canadian Jean Baptiste Faribault and his French-Dakota wife, Pelagie. By 1820, many of the eldest children of Prairie du Chien's first residents, including the Airds' only daughter, Grey Cloud Woman II, were married adults with their own children.[20]

Thomas Gummersall Anderson

Daybreak Woman's father, Thomas Anderson, first arrived in Prairie du Chien in 1800. A twenty-year-old British Canadian, he came to the village to begin his career as a fur trader. After five years working as a clerk in a store in Montreal, Anderson had resolved to go west and live a more adventurous life. His bourgeois (boss) supplied him with the usual clerk's outfit for the Mississippi fur trade: one coat, one pair of pants, four shirts, four pairs of socks, four blankets for bedding, a gun, shot and a powder horn, cooking utensils, a small tent, and provisions that included salt, pepper, tea, sugar, biscuits, and boiled ham. He also received an annual wage of $200. He traveled from Montreal to Mackinac as a passenger in large birchbark canoes, about forty feet long, five feet wide, and three feet deep, filled with provisions and trade goods and paddled by a team of voyageurs. At Mackinac, he and his bourgeois arranged to travel into Upper Mississippi country via Lake Michigan. At Green Bay, Anderson engaged an interpreter and a steersman for his own canoe and then started the tedious voyage of numerous portages up the Fox River and down the Wisconsin. About two weeks after leaving Mackinac, he finally arrived in Prairie du Chien. He described it as "a little village of about 10 or 15 houses" comprising mostly French-Canadians carrying on trade with Indigenous people. "Without exception," he noted, "the villagers were kind and hospitable, and prided themselves on their honesty and punctuality in paying their debts, and keeping their engagements."[21]

Anderson did not linger in Prairie du Chien; he left after only a few days for his assigned wintering post with the Sauk, downriver. The next year, he wintered on the Des Moines River among the Báxoǰe, and in 1802–03, he was trading with the Ho-Chunk on the Rock River. He then spent three years stationed at Milwaukee, trading with the Kickapoo and Potawatomie. As he did not speak any of these groups' languages, he hired an interpreter to accompany him to each post. Anderson began trading with the Santee Dakota in the winter of 1806–07, when he lived at a post on the Minnesota River about fifty miles from its junction with the Mississippi. After two years there, he moved even farther upriver to Lac qui Parle, where he wintered for two more years. There he allied himself with Red Thunder (Wakiŋyaŋ Duta) and his band, who camped nearby. As game was scarce and both trader and customers faced starvation, they joined forces and shared what food they had stored or could gather or

kill, including horses and diseased buffalo. The Dakota called Anderson
Wiyotaŋhaŋ (the Meridian Sun). He admired them, noting that they were
"cleanly," had "the best regulations as a tribe" and "the best bow and arrow
men," and were the "swiftest pedestrians." He also was impressed by their
ability to abstain from food for long periods of time.[22]

Grey Cloud Woman II (Maḣpiya Ḣota Wiŋ), Margaret Aird

Daybreak Woman's mother, Grey Cloud Woman II (Margaret Aird), was
a child of seven years old in 1800 when Thomas Anderson first arrived
in Prairie du Chien. She grew up surrounded by cousins, aunts, and uncles and the Euro-Indigenous children of neighbors. Her first language
was Dakota and her second French, and she may have either spoken or
understood English because it was her father's first language. There was
no school in the village when she was a child. Although it is possible her
father taught her how to read and write in English or French, there is no
evidence of her literacy in any language.

As a child, Grey Cloud Woman II would have known Anderson as a
man who passed through Prairie du Chien twice a year, like many others
in the trade, en route to Mackinac or his posts. He associated with all of
the traders in town, including her father; Anderson worked for Aird at one
point in these early years. His primary language was English, and it is not
clear to what extent, if any, he spoke French when he entered the fur trade.
Anderson did not begin trading with the Dakota until 1806 and did not
speak their language. As a trader, it was clearly in Anderson's interest to
marry Grey Cloud Woman, for through her parents he became well connected to both sides of the business. Why she chose to marry Anderson
we cannot know, as her reasons for marrying were not recorded by her or
her grandson in his memoir.

Several years after he had been trading with the Dakota in Mni Sota
Makoce, sometime around 1808, Grey Cloud Woman II married Thomas
Anderson. She was about fifteen; he was thirteen years older. There is
contradictory evidence for the birth years of their children. Their eldest
child, Angus Malcolm, was born about two years before Jane (Daybreak
Woman). Sometime before 1814, the couple seem to have had another
child—either their first or third, named Marion or Mary—who died as
an infant. Although Daybreak Woman consistently claimed later in her
life that she was born in 1810, on an 1837 register for treaty claimants, she

identified herself as twenty-five years old and Angus said he was twenty-seven, which would indicate he was born in 1809 or 1810 and she in 1811 or 1812. On a later census, Daybreak Woman's given age suggests she was born in 1809.[23]

In the memoir he wrote in the late 1800s, Thomas Anderson says little about his Dakota children and even less about his Dakota wife. In recalling his life as a fur trader, he makes only two references to Grey Cloud Woman II and never calls her, or their children, by their names. Of his marriage he says, "following the custom of the country, which I had hitherto resisted, I took to live with me a little half-breed." "Half-breed" was the common term used by whites in the nineteenth century for people of Euro-Indigenous heritage; reflecting the era's prevalent racism, it suggests that mixed people were inferior to whites. His use of "little" may suggest that she was physically diminutive, but it also may refer to her youth at the time they married.[24]

Daybreak Woman (Aŋpao Hiyaye Wiŋ), Jane Anderson

Daybreak Woman was born at a fur trading post at Patterson's Rapids on the Minnesota River, about 225 river miles upriver from the Mississippi and not far from the mouth of the Yellow Medicine River. This post had been in almost continuous use since 1783, when Charles Patterson first established it. James Aird and Patterson were partners in the 1780s; in subsequent years, Aird spent many winters trading on the Upper Minnesota, likely at this post. Daybreak Woman remembered visiting her grandfather at Patterson's Rapids at least once, probably in late summer or fall 1814, the last year he wintered on the Minnesota. She said she was born there on August 4, 1810.[25]

That year, Thomas Anderson was working in concert with other British and Euro-Indigenous traders to circumvent US restrictions on foreign traders. Anderson, Aird, Robert Dickson, Joseph Rolette, and several others filled seven boats with trade goods and slipped them by a blockade set up around the American garrison at Fort Mackinac. That winter, Anderson and Grey Cloud Woman, now with both their son, Angus, and their new child, Daybreak Woman, were trading on the lower St. Croix River near its junction with the Mississippi. In the spring of 1811, Anderson's trading partners decided that he should man a post at Pike Island (Wita Taŋka) at Bdote, the confluence of the Mississippi and Minnesota Rivers.

Since the family would stay there through the next season, Grey Cloud Woman and Anderson planted a garden, including corn and potatoes.[26]

Pike Island was ideally situated for commerce with the Bdewakaŋtuŋwaŋ Dakota. Their villages lined both rivers. In the Dakota language, the confluence of two rivers is known as a bdote; for many Dakota people, the confluence of the Mississippi and Minnesota Rivers is a place of special significance—*the* Bdote, the place the Dakota people came to from the stars, to begin to live on earth. As a little child, Daybreak Woman would have met many Dakota people coming to and going from the post, including her own relatives, and the family was positioned to easily travel to Prairie du Chien, where her grandparents lived. For the next three years, they kept a post on Pike Island, and in the summers, the family traveled up the rivers to hunt deer or buffalo with their Dakota friends. Every year, Anderson traveled to and from Mackinac via Prairie du Chien, while Grey Cloud Woman and the children lived with the Airds until he returned.[27]

The year 1814 was the last for Thomas Anderson as a fur trader in Mni Sota Makoce. By then, the British and Americans were two years into the War of 1812. Since the beginning of the war, most of the French-Canadian and British traders in the Great Lakes and Upper Mississippi region, including those at Prairie du Chien, had been actively working on behalf of the British, mainly by convincing surrounding Indigenous groups, including the Santee Dakota, to join the British in their fight against the Americans. Early in the war, the British and their allies had taken Fort Mackinac. Prairie du Chien, due to its strategic location on the Upper Mississippi, became a contested site as well.[28]

As Anderson traveled north to Mackinac in 1814, he learned along the way that the Americans had built Fort Shelby at Prairie du Chien. When he arrived, he immediately raised a volunteer militia of fur trade employees to descend on Prairie du Chien and oust the Americans. The British commander at Mackinac made him a captain and ordered him to lead his "Mississippi Volunteers," armed with three gunboats and mounted artillery, to Prairie du Chien. By the time he reached the village, he had garnered hundreds of warriors from various Indigenous groups who agreed to fight the Americans. Anderson was also able to persuade most of the Santee Dakota to fight for the British, as many of their fathers had during the Revolutionary War.

In July 1814, the fur traders' militia and its Indigenous allies took

Fort Shelby from the Americans with little bloodshed. Two months later, American gunboats came upriver to retake it, but Anderson's men successfully fought them off, escorting the American prisoners from the garrison and those on the retreating American gunboats far enough downriver to protect them from reprisals by the Sauk. Anderson commanded the fort at Prairie du Chien, renamed Fort McKay, until May 1815, when the British surrendered the garrison after the Americans won the war. While many of the Canadian traders who had supported the British stayed at Prairie du Chien after 1815, Anderson left for good. Like his father, a New York Loyalist who had fought in the British Army in the American Revolution and then moved to Canada, Thomas Anderson was unwilling to live under American rule.[29]

In his memoir, he says that in 1814, "my little half-breed took off my little boy and girl to her friends, and I never saw her again." Anderson suggests that Grey Cloud Woman parted with him for no reason, but the Robertson family's story holds that Anderson was planning on returning to Canada permanently, and she refused to leave Mni Sota Makoce. He stayed for ten days with the Brisbois family at Prairie du Chien before returning to Mackinac.[30]

Anderson also claims in his memoir that after Grey Cloud Woman left him in March 1814, he did not see her again. This seems improbable. He returned to Prairie du Chien and lived at Fort McKay from July 1814 to May 1815. The fort was located adjacent to the main village where the Airds, Grey Cloud Woman, and Anderson's children were living; he could hardly have avoided seeing her for an entire year in such a small community. Moreover, in his own journal from this period, he documents contact on more than one occasion with Aird, his father-in-law. Anderson's final farewell to the Upper Mississippi and his Dakota family was in May 1815, when the war ended and he was ordered to evacuate Fort McKay and return to Canada with his men. Fifteen years after he had first arrived in Prairie du Chien as a novice fur trader, he left it as a captain in the British Army, never to return.[31]

From the spring of 1814, when she was about four years old, until 1823, when she was about thirteen, Daybreak Woman lived in Prairie du Chien with her mother and brother in the home of her grandparents. Late in her life, she recalled attending school in Prairie du Chien between 1820 and 1822, but she and Angus also attended the school taught by Willard Keyes in the summer of 1818. Most of the other students at Keyes's school with Daybreak Woman were Euro-Indigenous, and many of them were relatives, the children of Grey Cloud Woman's cousins. Daybreak Woman grew up in a bilingual home in which the Dakota language was primary and French or English was secondary. The other children she played with mostly spoke French, Dakota, or both languages. Keyes noted that only two or three of his pupils in a class of twenty could speak English, while most spoke French; he found it necessary to borrow an English-French dictionary to better understand them. Although she may have understood some English and may have spoken the language a little, Daybreak Woman was neither fluent nor literate in English after attending Keyes's school or any subsequent schools in Prairie du Chien. She would not learn to read and write in English for some years yet.[32]

Sometime after July 1821, Thomas Anderson contacted Grey Cloud Woman and asked her to send the children to him in Canada so he could provide them with an English education. In his memoir, Anderson says his second wife, Elizabeth, whom he married in 1820, "insisted on my sending for my two little Sioux children. Though she had one of her own, she felt bound to care for the others." Grey Cloud Woman consented, and in the summer of 1823, she sent Daybreak Woman and Angus to their father, who was living on Drummond Island in Lake Huron, just across the Canadian border from the United States.[33]

It was a common practice for fur trade society parents who had the means and connections to send their Euro-Indigenous children to schools in the east for a few years to obtain formal educations. Parents saw such an education as key to their children's economic and social advancement in fur trade society and recognized that it could also open opportunities for their children beyond fur trade society. Although this must have been deeply wrenching for Grey Cloud Woman, she would not have consented to separate from Angus and Daybreak Woman unless she had thought it was in their interest to do so. She must have decided that she could not provide them the formal education and the kind of lives she thought they should have to prosper in the world, while their father could. Grey Cloud Woman may have also been concerned about her ability to provide for the children in other ways. Her father had been dead for four years, and although he had left some property in Prairie du Chien, the family no longer had his income from the fur trade.

Grey Cloud Woman's situation was unusual, however, because she wasn't just sending her children away to school for a few years, expecting them to return to her—she was sending them to live with their father indefinitely. Although we don't know the terms of the arrangement she made with Anderson, it appears that she thought of it as a permanent situation; she was giving him custody of their children and sending them off to live in a new community, where she presumed they would live as adults. We cannot know what Daybreak Woman and Angus, children of thirteen and fifteen, thought about leaving their mother, their grandmother, and the only community they had ever known to live in a new place with a father they had not seen for eight years. They were likely frightened and sad, but perhaps also excited. They may not have seen the separation from their mother as permanent (or would not accept it as such), whatever Grey Cloud Woman's understanding of the situation.

Grey Cloud Woman was only twenty-two years old when her marriage to Anderson ended, and she was thirty when she sent the children to him in Canada. About a year after that, she married Hazen Mooers, an American trader from New York. She and her mother, the first Grey Cloud Woman, moved to live with him and trade at the source of the Minnesota River at Big Stone Lake and Lake Traverse.[34]

Soon, Grey Cloud Woman and Hazen Mooers had children, three girls. In the nineteenth century it was common for parents to name infants after previous children in the family who had died. Even though Daybreak Woman had not died, it seems her departure from Mni Sota Makoce was effectively like a death to Grey Cloud Woman. Because she did not expect to see her oldest daughter again, when she gave birth to her second child with Hazen Mooers, Grey Cloud Woman named the infant Jane.[35]

2. Lake Huron, 1823–1837

Drummond Island,
Mackinac Island, Coldwater

I have been long enough in the mission school to talk English language well. I never wrote a letter before I came here, nor did I know that I must have a new heart to go to heaven. . . . I feel very anxious that the gospel might be sent to my dear relations and Friends. They are in the region [of the] shadow of death. My own mother belongs to the Indian tribe of Sioux, she lives west of the Mississippi. I hope you will try to send the gospel to my relations and pray for them.

DAYBREAK WOMAN, 1830

There was some mystery about his life that we have never been able to solve, the key to which I have always believed was a seal or signet ring in which a peculiar stone was set and on which something was engraved that we could never make out. This seal ring was lost during the Sioux Outbreak in Minnesota in 1862. This is about all we know of father's early life.

THOMAS ROBERTSON

In the summer of 1823, Daybreak Woman left her Dakota kin and Prairie du Chien to live in Canada with her father and his second family. At the time they were residing in the town surrounding Fort Collier on Drummond Island in Lake Huron. The society she encountered there was very much like that of Prairie du Chien: a community dominated by the fur trade surrounding a garrison.

Only her father and perhaps a few others spoke her first language, Dakota. As in Prairie du Chien, the primary spoken non-Native language was French, although some would know other Native languages; soldiers at the fort spoke English. While she may have understood English, she did not speak it much when she first arrived. However, she must have learned to speak some English, even if poorly, prior to attending school, as it was the first language of the Anderson family household.[1]

Daybreak Woman—or Jane Anderson, as she would be known for the next fifteen years—and her brother, Angus, had to not only reacquaint themselves with their father but also get to know their father's second family. This included their stepmother, Elizabeth (Betsy) Hamilton Anderson; a two-year-old brother, William Samuel; a newborn sister, Louisa; and their stepmother's extended family, who were prominent members of Mackinac Island and Drummond Island society.

After living with this family on Drummond Island for five years, Daybreak Woman was sent to attend the Mackinaw Mission School on Mackinac Island—also on Lake Huron, but in the United States. Angus was sent to a boys boarding school at Sandwich, located on the Canadian side of the Detroit River (across from what would become the city of Detroit), where he received "a good English education." Both children came home to Drummond Island during school holidays. The Anderson family increased during these years with the birth of Gustavus in 1825 and Francis (Frank) in 1828.[2]

The communities on Drummond Island and Mackinac Island were closely connected to each other, shaped by and reflecting the shifting patterns of warfare, international trade, and Euro-American colonization in the region. Daybreak Woman was to learn much as she navigated her new life as an Anglo-Dakota girl whose father and new family were centrally situated in the multicultural fur trade and garrison societies of the two islands.

Drummond Island

In June 1815, after surrendering Prairie du Chien to the Americans, Thomas Anderson returned to Mackinac. During the War of 1812 the British had taken the island and occupied it for three years, but it was turned over to the United States in 1815.

Despite losing the War of 1812, the British were determined to maintain their lucrative North American trade and compete with the Americans. The southwestern tip of Drummond Island—forty-five water miles east of Mackinac and separated from the Upper Peninsula of Michigan by only a narrow strait—offered a prominent and strategic position for the new British fort. Located in the far northwestern corner of Lake Huron, the island sat at the intersection of several major Great Lakes fur trading routes. From it one could travel north to the St. Mary's River to access Lake Superior and the headwaters of the Mississippi River or head southwest to Lake Michigan and use the Green Bay route to reach the Mississippi; alternatively, one could travel east or south via Lake Huron to enter the American interior via other waterways.

The British moved to Drummond Island in 1815, erroneously assuming that it was far enough north to remain in Canada when the boundary commission set up by the Treaty of Ghent finally determined the international border. British traders and other British citizens who did not wish to remain on Mackinac Island under American rule followed the garrison to the island and reestablished the fur trade–based society they had known on Mackinac. As the two islands were relatively close, inhabitants of both traveled back and forth regularly; Native allies and trading partners could still conveniently visit them.[3]

Anderson obtained an appointment in the Indian Department of Upper Canada (part of the British Army at the time) as a storekeeper, interpreter, and clerk at the rank of army captain. He would work for the department for the next forty-three years. In September 1815, he moved to Drummond Island and took charge of all the stores for the fur post. The British garrison had moved a few months earlier and established Fort Collier on the eastern side of a peninsula on the southwesternmost tip of the island, near the mile-wide strait that separated it from Michigan Territory. The parade ground and main buildings of the fort faced the bay to the east, and behind them stood a high ridge of limestone rock upon which the British placed artillery to command the navigation of the strait, the main waterway between Lake Superior and the lower Great Lakes. With the help of his interpreter, Anderson built a log house, twenty-four by eighteen feet, with a clay chimney, a cedar-bark roof, three rooms, and a small outdoor kitchen. In 1816 he constructed another building devoted to the business of trade with Indigenous people.[4]

The location of the Drummond Island post was chosen probably as much for its convenience as a rendezvous site as for its military advantage. According to the Treaty of Ghent, the British were supposed to give up the Indigenous trade in American territory, but they did not. To convince their Indigenous allies that the British were still strong and relevant as trading partners, they planned an extensive (albeit unnecessary) system of fortifications on Drummond—even in the face of orders from their superiors in London to refrain from building until the boundary commission made its final decisions. The British government supplied the trading post at Drummond Island with vast amounts of trade goods, and when Indigenous visitors were on the island, they were fed and given gifts to maintain strong relations. For the British, a foothold near Mackinac was essential to retaining the Indigenous trade and influence in the Northwest Territory. Therefore, in the words of one historian, they "clung with great tenacity to the countries adjoining the straits of Mackinaw."[5]

Following the company of soldiers stationed at Fort Collier were about twenty-five Indian Department employees. In addition, between 300 and 450 civilians left Mackinac and moved to Drummond Island because they did not want to live under US rule and established a little town near the garrison. Several hundred Indigenous residents lived permanently or semi-permanently nearby, but their numbers increased to as many as 4,500 or 5,000 in the spring and summer during rendezvous times.[6]

Because the townspeople assumed they were settling permanently on the island, many built substantial houses and planted extensive gardens and orchards. The army constructed two broad graded and guttered roads lined with poplar trees leading from the fort and town to the other side of the peninsula. The town had several large surface cellars for storing food, a lime kiln, a sawmill, and a community bake house. The more prosperous residents built large houses, some with two stories and large stone fireplaces, but most of the civilians lived in large lodges made of a framework of poles that was covered on the roof and sides with cedar bark. By 1823, there were eighteen garrison buildings, including several large log structures comprising the barracks and commissary, as well as many smaller log buildings for other purposes, with the officers' quarters scattered across the fort grounds. Fort Collier and the town, located on the sunny slope facing southeast, looked out on a beautiful bay dotted with small islands. They were oriented toward the place the garrison and civilians had been forced to leave; it was the closest of all Drummond Island's natural harbors to Mackinac.[7]

In 1816, when Thomas Anderson had lived on Drummond Island for a year, he met his second wife, Elizabeth Hamilton. At the age of twenty-one, she had come to live with her grandfather, Dr. David Mitchell, one of the most prominent Mackinac residents who had followed the British garrison to its new location. The grandparents of Daybreak Woman's stepmother, and their connections at Mackinac, would be an important part of her life on Lake Huron.[8]

Mitchell was a Scots immigrant and British Army doctor who first came to Fort Mackinac—then known as Fort Michilimackinac and located on the mainland—in 1774. Five years later, when the British moved the fort and the garrison town to the more easily defended nearby island, Mitchell acted as deputy commissary and managed the move of both the garrison and town structures to the island, a task not finally completed until 1783.

In 1776, Mitchell married Elizabeth Bertrand, a French-Ojibwe woman raised among the Ottawa of L'Arbre Croche. He resigned his position as regimental surgeon in 1780 when he learned the unit was to be transferred; he did not want to leave Elizabeth and their three-year-old daughter, Louisa, the first of their twelve children. But he continued to earn an income as physician for the Indigenous workers and voyageurs hired to erect the new fort as well as for the soldiers at the fort.

In the late 1700s and early 1800s, David and Elizabeth Mitchell's large house on Market Street in the town on the bay below Fort Mackinac was the center of the island's "high" society, constituting French, British, and Euro-Indigenous traders and merchants as well as the British Army officers and their wives. The house was the largest on the island, with two stories and an additional high attic. Elizabeth hosted card parties twice a week, and her home was often the site of balls, dinners, tea parties, and fancy weddings. The Mitchell home had a large library, and all twelve of their children were sent to either Europe or Montreal to be educated. The couple, especially Elizabeth, became active and prominent in the fur trade, as did several of their sons. Their daughter Jessie married another notable fur trader, Lewis Crawford, who with David and others was active in recruiting Indigenous allies to fight against the Americans in the War of 1812. In fact, the two men participated in the attack that forced the Americans to surrender Fort Mackinac, on the mainland, to the British in 1812.[9]

The Mitchells acquired some of the best land on Mackinac for farming and operated one of the few farms that supplied hay, potatoes, corn, and oats. Located on the southwest side of the island, the farm also had its own big house with a wide porch. Elizabeth managed the farm, a fruit orchard, and an extensive vegetable and flower garden of almost three acres near their house in town. She had a housekeeper to oversee her many servants, as well as employees who worked in the gardens, on the farm, in the fur trade business, and in the Mitchells' retail store. Like the rest of Mackinac society, she mainly spoke French, and she was one of three prominent Euro-Indigenous female traders on Mackinac Island. The two others were Therese Schindler and Magdelaine LaFramboise, Elizabeth Mitchell's best friend. When David Mitchell, intensely loyal to the British government, left Mackinac in 1815 to live on Drummond Island with several of their sons, Elizabeth stayed behind to manage the farming and fur trade businesses. She visited her husband and sons regularly, and her sons also traveled back and forth frequently.[10]

When the Mitchells' eldest daughter, Louisa, was fifteen, she married a British soldier, James Hamilton, stationed at Fort Mackinac. The Hamiltons moved with the regiment to Niagara and finally back to London, where Louisa died in 1802. Their eldest daughter, Elizabeth (Betsy), born in 1795, was the only child of four to live to adulthood. In 1816, Betsy came to North America to live with her grandparents on Drummond Island. Four years later, David Mitchell officiated as justice of the peace at her wedding to Thomas Anderson, who was sixteen years older than his second wife. The Mitchell and Anderson families were closely associated by both blood and friendship, and Daybreak Woman came to know her stepmother's grandparents well. One of their sons, George, married her stepmother's best friend, Harriet. She also knew Betsy's aunt, Jessie Mitchell Crawford, who lived on nearby St. Joseph Island.[11]

During the five years Daybreak Woman lived on Drummond Island with her father and stepmother, she probably helped Betsy with her young children. William Samuel (who died in 1829) and Louisa (who died in 1824) were joined by Gustavus in 1825 and Francis (Frank) in 1828. Daybreak Woman did not attend school during these five years, and the long delay in her education is curious. As she herself admitted, she did not speak English well until she had been at the school for more than a year; perhaps her father thought she should first improve her language skills. She may also have been traumatized by the move from Mni Sota Makoce and perhaps took a long time to adjust to her new life. The family also may have been financially constrained; with Angus away at the school in Sandwich, perhaps they could not afford to educate Angus, their young son William, and Daybreak Woman all at once. Thomas and Betsy knew the leaders of the Mackinaw Mission School, which was founded in 1823. They sent William Samuel to live there for two years, from 1825 to 1827, and it was only in 1828, after he moved home and did not return to the school, that they enrolled Daybreak Woman.[12]

Mackinac Island

Mackinaw Mission School was part of another military and trading community that had relocated. By the early 1800s, Mackinac Island was known as the "great emporium of the west." Nine hundred miles from Montreal by water, it was the largest and most important fur trade business outpost in the western Great Lakes and Upper Mississippi region. Since the 1670s, the Straits of Mackinac had been the center of fur trade activities for the western interior. It began as Michilimackinac, a French mission located on the mainland on the strait linking Lake Huron and Lake Michigan in 1671. By 1715, it was fortified as a trading post by the French. The fur trade society that grew up there was primarily controlled by French-Indigenous traders even after the British defeated France in the French and Indian War and took their territory in North America in the 1760s.

After 1763, elite British traders joined the most prosperous French and French-Indigenous traders in dominating Mackinac society. Under both the British and American regimes, most fur trade employees continued to be French-Canadian or Euro-Indigenous. During the American Revolution, the British maintained control of Mackinac; in 1780, they moved the fort and town to the nearby island to better defend it from the Americans. Although the British lost the war, which ended in 1784, they did not evacuate the island until 1796, when, under the terms of Jay's Treaty, they finally left Mackinac Island and built a new fort and town on St. Joseph Island, about forty miles northeast. Mackinac's importance in the fur trade continued under the Americans.[13]

Fort Mackinac, built of stone and plastered with the lime that gave it a white appearance, sat atop cliffs about one hundred feet high. From the fort, one could look southwest to Lake Michigan or northwest to Lake Huron. The village sat on the beach below the cliffs on a natural harbor. In 1796, one visitor noted that it had two streets, each about three-quarters of a mile long, with eighty-nine houses and stores, some spacious and handsome with lime plaster on the exterior. St. Anne's Catholic Church was the only church, and there was no resident priest until 1830. At one end of town was an impressively large government house with a spacious garden. About 250 Euro-Indigenous and French-Canadian families involved in the fur trade made up the permanent population that lived in the village. Even though the British had taken over control of the trade in the 1760s, French remained the common language.[14]

Willard Keyes, who first saw Mackinac Island in 1817, described it this way: "the fort makes a handsome appearance, standing on high ground and completely whitewashed; the island is about 3 miles long and 1.5 miles broad; the fort stands on elevated ground and can command the whole island; the town is on the south shore on a small plain just under the fort, the houses are many of them built of logs and roofs covered with bark; however, their appearance is better inside than out; many of them are handsomely furnished . . . the inhabitants are a mixture of French, British and Indians of all sorts."[15]

The elite society of the island was composed of a small group of the most prosperous French, Euro-Indigenous, and British fur trading families as well as the fort's officers and their wives. During the summers, the population swelled to as many as 4,000 or 4,500 as people rendezvoused to conduct the annual business of the fur trade. In winter, the population was relatively small and the island very quiet; the only transportation was by dogsled, and the mail arrived only once a month. Elizabeth Baird, who grew up on the island during the 1810s and 1820s, recalled, "I was particularly fond of the island of Mackinac in the winter, with its ice-bound shore. In some seasons, ice mountains loomed up, picturesque and color-enticing in every direction. At other seasons, the ice would be as smooth as one would wish."[16]

After 1815, the American Fur Company increasingly dominated the fur trade on Mackinac Island. By the mid-1820s, it had built a large number of structures devoted to its business, including warehouses, boatyards, offices, and stores. By the late 1820s, the company monopolized the trade and had surrounded its establishment with a high fence, inside of which were a massive three-story store, a large storehouse, and a three-story trader's house and office. During the 1820s and early 1830s, steamboats traveled a regular Mackinac–Chicago–Detroit route. The main United States Indian Agency headquarters for the region was at Sault St. Marie, but the government also created a subagency at Mackinac with a staff of five, an Indian agency house, and a council house. The Americans also established a post office and a jail on the island.[17]

By 1828, when Daybreak Woman came to live at the mission school on Mackinac Island, there were about five hundred permanent residents comprising forty-eight families, plus a few hundred American soldiers stationed at the fort. British, French and Euro-Indigenous fur trade families still dominated Mackinac society. The English-speaking elite were the Stuarts (Robert and Elizabeth—he was the chief American Fur Company trader), William and Amanda Ferry (the missionaries who established the Mackinaw Mission School), several other prosperous trading families, and the fort's officers.

Many of the Americans on the island were members of a strict Presbyterian sect led by the Ferrys. The evangelical Presbyterian leaders of the mission school were caught up in the Protestant revival known as the Second Great Awakening, which swept the northeastern United States in the early 1800s. They believed that it was necessary for individuals to have an intense and personal conversion in order to truly be saved. From 1828 to 1830, the Ferrys led a Protestant evangelical revival during which not only students at the mission but other island dwellers were pressured to undergo this personal conversion. This prompted a response from Catholics on the island, led by some of the French-Indigenous and French-Canadian residents who resented the proselytizing of the Presbyterian missionaries. Baird, a French-Odawa Catholic, described the social rift that resulted:

In 1823–24, the Protestant Mission House was established as an Indian school, which many attended. Ottawa and Chippewa women were taken as servants and taught to work. The teachers were from the New England states. For a while the school seemed to prosper, but soon the efforts of the teachers were diverted to another channel. Proselytizing seemed to pervade the atmosphere of the whole establishment. Everyone seemed to feel it her duty to make a convert daily. For a while the Presbyterians had full sway; then the Roman Catholics took a decided stand against them. Certainly both denominations carried the feeling to great extent. It really seemed a religious war. One had to be either Presbyterian or Roman Catholic in those days; nothing else would be for a moment tolerated. This state of things lasted for several years.[18]

The Protestant missionaries had some success in 1828 and 1829 in bringing new converts into their faith. Thirty-three people joined their church after having the required intense conversion experience, confessing their sins, and declaring a new relationship with Christ. Twenty-five of these new church members were of Indigenous descent. One of them was Jane Anderson—Daybreak Woman—who, along with a number of other Mackinaw Mission students, was deemed saved by the Ferrys.[19]

Mackinaw Mission School

The Ferrys established the school for Indigenous and Euro-Indigenous children on Mackinac Island in 1823. For the first two years of its existence, they rented a part of a large house of Magdelaine LaFramboise, the affluent French-Odawa fur trader and friend of Elizabeth Mitchell, to board and teach students. In 1825, the Ferrys built a mission house on the east end of the island on twelve acres of land provided by the US government. The substantial building, consisting of three sections, was designed as a place for the work of the school as well as a home for its pupils and teachers. The school had a center section that had a very large dining room, about thirty-eight by twenty-one feet, on the first floor with an expansive dormitory for boarding students above it. Each of the building's wings was about thirty-two by forty-four feet. In the western wing, there were four rooms on each of two floors. The Ferrys, their children, and the

Mackinaw Mission House, about 1902. The building, with the addition of a third story, served as a hotel, boardinghouse, resort, and conference center through much of the nineteenth and twentieth centuries. *Library of Congress*

other missionary teachers lived in this section. In the identical eastern wing, four classrooms occupied the second floor, and below these were apartments for various purposes, including accommodating the tradesmen who were hired to teach skills to the male students.[20]

Between 1824 and 1837, about five hundred children, ranging in age from four to eighteen, attended the Mackinaw Mission School. There were four twelve-week terms per year, during which the students, taught in English, took classes in spelling, reading, writing, arithmetic, and geography. In addition to classroom instruction, the boys received vocational training from the mission's blacksmith, carpenter, tailor, and shoemaker. The mission also operated a farm on the west side of the island that was used to teach the students about gardening and to supply their own provisions. The girls learned sewing and housework skills. All the students were required to participate in frequent hymn singing and the reciting of psalms. Many of the male students became interpreters, traders, or clerks in the fur trade. Many of the girls married American officers at Fort Mackinac or Euro-American traders.[21]

Over the Mackinaw Mission School's fourteen years of existence, about 50 percent of students were French-Ojibwe or British-Ojibwe. About 20 percent had French or British fathers and Odawa mothers, and another 25 percent of the children, including Daybreak Woman, had Dakota, Cree, or Assiniboine mothers. Many of these children would have been baptized and raised as Catholics or bought up to believe in the spirituality of their mother's people—or, most likely, embraced both their Catholicism and Native beliefs. Whereas Catholicism allowed Indigenous and Euro-Indigenous people to practice such religious syncretism, the evangelical Protestants who founded the Mackinaw Mission did not. They expected their students to become like Protestant Americans, not only in their faith but also in their appearance and lifestyle. Thus, the Ferrys and the other missionary teachers put tremendous pressure on the students at the school to assimilate, not only spiritually but culturally.[22]

The Mackinaw Mission required all students to be bathed, groomed, and clothed like Euro-Americans. The children were given English names, taught the English language, expected to worship and speak in English. The Ferrys and the mission's other teachers viewed all Euro-Indigenous people as Indians and viewed all Indians as the same and culturally inferior; they did not distinguish among the various Native heritages of their students, nor did they acknowledge the distinctive culture of the Euro-Indigenous fur trade society in which most of these children were raised. Their main intent was to Americanize all their students—that is, to make them as much like non-Indigenous, Protestant Americans as possible. Thus, as historian Keith Widder explains, the Mackinaw Mission represents the Americanization of fur trade society that took place in the 1820s and 1830s after the American government took control of the western Great Lakes and Upper Mississippi region.[23]

Daybreak Woman attended the Mackinaw Mission School for four years, beginning in the fall of 1828 and ending in the spring of 1832. According to the school's records, she was either fourteen or fifteen years of age when she started. However, if she was born in 1810, as she later claimed, she would have actually been eighteen years old in 1828. If this is true, then she must have appeared younger than she actually was to the missionaries, or she (or her father) had misled them, fearing that her age might disqualify her. There were no students at the mission over age eighteen.[24]

During the time Daybreak Woman lived at the Mackinaw Mission, the total enrollment of the school ranged from 100 to 134 students. Most slept in the upper story over the large kitchen and dining room in sex-segregated dormitories with two to three sharing a bed. In the dining room they were also separated by sex and sat at long tables for three meals a day, using utensils and plates. Breakfast consisted of salt fish or salt pork, bread, and cooked potatoes. For lunch they ate fresh fish or pork, vegetables, bread, corn, and beans or peas. Supper was a lighter meal of mush or corn. Daybreak Woman later had little to say about her school experience, remembering only that she had been at the school with the Beaulieu girls. Julia, Elizabeth, and Sophia Beaulieu were the daughters of Bazel Beaulieu and his Ojibwe wife, Respected Sky Woman. They sent all five of their children to the Mackinaw Mission school.[25]

William and Amanda Ferry had been friendly with the Andersons since the former couple's arrival at Drummond Island in 1823. In his reminiscences, Thomas Anderson recalled several visits by the Ferrys to the island. Their plans to open the mission school as well as their friendship with the Andersons may have prompted Betsy Anderson to suggest that Thomas send for his Dakota children so that they could attend the school.[26]

A few letters from the Mackinaw Mission's teachers to Betsy Anderson have survived. They reveal the cultural prejudices and religious zeal of the missionaries but also their friendly relationship with the Andersons and their assessment of Daybreak Woman. This friendly relationship with the Andersons meant that Daybreak Woman was treated kindly and perhaps given more leeway than other students. When she first arrived at the school, as previously noted, she was unable to write in English. She first wrote home in 1830, after she had attended the school for a year and a half. However, one of her teachers, Eunice Osmer, wrote to Betsy Anderson in early October 1828, not long after Daybreak Woman (Jane) first came to the school, and gave this report:

I trust that Jane will have the unceasing prayers of her Parents that she may improve the privileges which she now enjoys for time and eternity. I observe that she is naturally fond of dress, and history, and rather irritable, the latter is perhaps the most conspicuous fault in her character, for this I often reprove her, and think she manifests some desire to be delivered from it. I have the impression that you wish us to restrain her as we would a child of our own. . . . You must not have too raised expectations of her, but I hope she will not disappoint your wishes. She is willing to be told when she is thought to be wrong, which is very much in her favor. She appears well contented.

The missionaries had already pressured Daybreak Woman to have a personal conversion experience and find God in the intense, personal mode that they deemed necessary for a Christian to find true salvation, but she was hesitant. In the same letter to Daybreak Woman's stepmother, Osmer says of her reluctance to convert, "We had hopes at one time that she would choose the good part which should never be taken from her, but like too many she is halting between two opinions. I have written this freely respecting her because you are her best friend and if you have any directions to give with regard to her you will not fail to let me know."[27]

Daybreak Woman herself refers to this early period at the mission school and the pressure she endured to develop an intense relationship with God in a letter she wrote eighteen months later. In it she describes her initial failure to find Christ that first autumn at the school despite intense pressure from the missionaries: "The first year that I came here when I saw the girls seeking Christ, and the Teachers talked to me, they told me that if I did not give myself to him who died for me, I must be forever miserable. And I thought it was high time for me to seek him. But

in a few weeks I left off seeking Christ." When she returned to the school
the following year, she could no longer resist the call to salvation and
describes the pressure she felt to find Christ in the way the missionaries
said that she should:

> But I never felt happy and last winter we had a revival at this place, and
> it pleased God to open my eyes to see my wretched state, and I could
> not sleep for many nights, and one Sabbath Mr. Ferry preached on
> this text . . . then I thought I would not leave seeking until I found the
> Savior, and I could not go to sleep that night, and Monday morning
> I came to school I could not study my lessons, except the Bible, and I
> felt as if I had the whole house on me, I put my head on the desk and
> I prayed to God. . . . [A]nd in the spring I joined the church and many
> other girls at the same time.[28]

Daybreak Woman had been at the Mackinaw Mission School about a
year and a half when Amanda Ferry wrote to Betsy Anderson, attaching
her letter to one written in January 1830 by Daybreak Woman to her stepmother. In it Ferry praises her academic and spiritual progress: "You must
be delighted with her improvement. This is her own composition, unaided
by anyone. From a wild giddy girl she has become [a most] faithful child
and we humbly trust a devoted servant to God. . . . [H]er parents must find
her a pleasant companion. . . . We all love her."[29]

The letters to Betsy Anderson from the teachers at the mission school
provide some of the only descriptions of Daybreak Woman's personality
and character that exist in the historical record. Although their word-
ing clearly reflects the expectations for young women of that era, the descriptions suggest that Daybreak Woman had an engaging, perhaps even
somewhat exuberant, personality ("a wild, giddy girl") and that she was
intellectually curious ("she likes history"); forthright in expressing her
thinking or feelings and perhaps often impatient with others ("she is often
irritable"); independent in her thinking ("she is halting between two opinions"); and generally liked ("we all love her"; "her parents must find her
a pleasant companion"). As she didn't leave her mother until the age of
thirteen and she didn't start school for five years after arriving in Canada,
she presumably developed these personality and character traits as a child
in Mni Sota Makoce and as an adolescent in the Anderson household.

In her letter of January 1830, Daybreak Woman addresses her stepmother as "My Ever Dear Mother" and notes that she is "very happy to hear from you." Of her teachers, she says, "They are very kind to me. I feel just as if I was at home." She sends her love to "my dear father" and asks Betsy to "kiss little Francis and Gustavus for me" and "also remember my love to Mrs. Mitchell and R. [Mitchell] and all my Friends." She closes with "I remain your affectionate Daughter." The tone suggests that she enjoyed affectionate and close relationships with her stepmother and Anderson siblings.[30]

There is little information, either in her early correspondence or in letters she wrote later in her life, that reveals the nature of Daybreak Woman's relationship with her father. Likewise, Anderson says little about her or Angus in his memoir other than to note that he sent for them, to state where they were educated, and to mention that both worked for him at the Coldwater Indian Agency as young adults. In his memoir, written in the late 1800s, Anderson is incorrect in identifying the number and sex of Daybreak Woman's children (his grandchildren), which indicates he did not correspond with her very much, if at all, once she returned to Mni Sota Makoce.[31]

In her January 1830 letter to her stepmother, Daybreak Woman also describes her spiritual development. Having been saved herself, she expresses concern about her father's spiritual welfare: "I feel anxious to know if my Dear Father thinks that he is the friend of God, the Bible says except a man be born again he cannot see the kingdom of God."[32]

Although Betsy Anderson was not an evangelical Protestant like Daybreak Woman's teachers at the mission school, her piety as a staunch Episcopalian appears to have exempted her from the kind of concern Daybreak Woman expressed for her father. Thomas Anderson had also been raised as an Episcopalian but perhaps was not as religiously demonstrative as his wife. The Episcopal faith was deeply important to the family—Gustavus Anderson would become an Episcopal priest. Despite her Mackinaw School mission experience, and later close association with the Presbyterian missionaries in Mni Sota Makoce, once the Episcopalians arrived in 1860, Daybreak Woman would quickly return to the fold of the Episcopal Church, the faith of her father and stepmother. This association would prove deeply significant.[33]

When Daybreak Woman left the mission school in the spring of 1832, she sailed across Lake Huron to rejoin the Anderson family, who had relocated to a place called Coldwater on Huron's far eastern shore.

Coldwater

When Amanda Ferry wrote her letter to Betsy Anderson in early 1830, the Anderson family was no longer on Drummond Island. In November 1828, the Indian Department and the British garrison had evacuated Drummond Island for a British post called Penetanguishene in southeastern Georgian Bay, on the eastern shore of Lake Huron. Six years earlier, in 1822, the boundary commission had determined that Drummond Island was part of the United States. The British took their time evacuating the island, officially surrendering the garrison to the Americans on November 14, 1828. That day the officers, soldiers, and Indian Department employees and their families, a total of ninety-one people (including fifteen women and twenty-six children), sailed on two boats across Lake Huron for five days in stormy weather to reach Penetanguishene. Among them were Thomas Anderson, his wife, and their children William Samuel (seven), Gustavus (three), and baby Frank. Betsy's grandfather, Dr. David Mitchell, as well as his sons Andrew and George and their wives, also moved to Penetanguishene. The elder Mitchell died there in 1832 at George's home. Most of the Euro-Indigenous voyageurs and their families who had followed the garrison from Mackinac in 1815 followed them again in 1829. The British government granted these loyal British subjects land in or near the naval post at Penetanguishene as compensation for the homes they had been forced to leave behind.[34]

Daybreak Woman stayed at the Mackinaw Mission School while the family traveled to their new home. It is likely that she was sent to the school in the fall of 1828 (after William Samuel was sent home) in anticipation of the move; the government employees on Drummond Island had known the location of the new post for some time. After her first term at school, she went home for a brief vacation to Drummond Island, where she said goodbye to the family before they moved to Penetanguishene. Returning to school for the winter term, she stayed through the spring of 1829 and thereafter took the long trip to see her family only during the summers.[35]

In early March 1829, just a few months after the family moved to Penetanguishene, William Samuel died. Daybreak Woman wrote of this sad event a year later when the Ferrys prompted her to write a letter to the American Board of Commissioners for Foreign Missions (ABCFM) as part of their school's progress report. She said: "I had a little brother named Samuel, he stayed in the mission three years, he was about five or six years old, he went home when I came to stay and about nine months after I arrived here my stepmother wrote to Mrs. Ferry about my brother's death—he caught cold while they were travelling, my father was not at home while my brother was sick."[36]

The Andersons had lost their second child in five years. Almost exactly one year later, their next child, Sophia, was born. The Anderson family lived at Penetanguishene for about a year and a half. During their first year there, Betsy Anderson's father, James Matthew Hamilton, his second wife, and their children emigrated from England to live nearby.[37]

In 1830, Thomas Anderson was summoned to York (now Toronto) by the chief superintendent of Indian Affairs and ordered to undertake the oversight of three bands of Ojibwe people living in two communities— one near the Coldwater River about twenty miles southeast of Penetan-guishene and another at the Narrows (now Orillia). The new Coldwater Indian Agency, located ninety miles north of Toronto, oversaw these two settlements.[38]

In the summer of 1830, Thomas moved the family to live in bark lodges on Matchedash Bay while he surveyed and had a road cut from Matche-dash to the new agency at Coldwater. Daybreak Woman's younger half sister Sophia Anderson recalled these early days in her reminiscences:

> Early in the summer of that year my father was sent to Matchedatch near the mouth of the Coldwater River to survey the land and find out if it would be suitable for an Indian Settlement.... Matchedatch was found unsuitable for the purpose intended, and my father was sent to Coldwater, then a wilderness. The soil was good and in every other way it appeared to be a suitable locality. A number of workmen were engaged and log houses were soon erected for the superintendent and the Indians, also a large school house for the Indian boys and girls.... Saw and grist mills were also erected.... My father and a party of Indians "blazed the trees" and afterwards cut the roads open between Coldwater and Orillia (about 14 miles).... [About sixteen] Comfort-able houses were built all along it for the Indians, each having several acres of land attached for them to cultivate.[39]

Soon after this, Anderson received a land grant from the government that consisted of several hundred acres along the Coldwater River stretch-ing from the village of Medonte to the south. On this grant, which he named "Clayfields" for its swampy grounds, Anderson built a log house for the family in 1830.[40]

Daybreak Woman finally left the mission school and Mackinac Island in the spring of 1832 and traveled across Lake Huron to reunite with the Anderson family at Coldwater. Betsy would bear two more daughters, Eliza (1832) and Martha (1836). Sadly, three of the family's children died very young: Louisa at age one in 1824, William Samuel at age eight in 1829, and Eliza at age three in 1835. In 1833–34, Daybreak Woman taught the girls in the Indigenous school at Coldwater. By the spring of 1834, her brother Angus had also finished school and was working as a clerk and storekeeper for their father at the Coldwater Agency.[41]

In the fall of 1833, Daybreak Woman met Andrew Robertson, who taught the boys in the agency school from September 1833 through December 1834. She was twenty-two and he was forty-two. Andrew was born on December 6, 1790, in Tinwald, Dumfries, Scotland, where he was listed on the burgess roll. He was the son of the minister of Tinwald, but his parents died when he was only three years old. His grandparents raised him in the village of Troque, Reidbank, Scotland. He attended Dumfries Academy and then Durham University, where he studied to become a doctor. He traveled to Russia and South America, and he spent three years on a whaling expedition as well. He was for some years the co-owner of a plantation in South America, but his partner sold the property during one of his absences and pocketed all of the money, leaving him broke. In 1831, he came to New York City, where he left all his possessions in a hotel while he went to Canada. The hotel burned down in a fire, and he lost everything he owned. In an interview late in her life, Daybreak Woman said that Andrew had practiced medicine for a time in Lower Canada, presumably prior to coming to Coldwater.[42]

In March 1835, Andrew left Coldwater to be the schoolteacher at the Sault St. Marie Indian Agency, on the far northeastern end of Lake Huron. His replacement at Coldwater, a Mr. Burkitt, was not successful. While Andrew was at Sault St. Marie, Thomas Anderson wrote two letters on behalf of the Ojibwe requesting Burkitt's removal and Andrew's return to Coldwater. In his second request to the chief superintendent of Indian Affairs, Anderson wrote: "The Indians of this place still object to Mr. Burkett's [sic] being employed by them as Teacher in the School; there are scarcely any children attending the School in consequence and they

Andrew Robertson, about 1855. *Minnesota Historical Society collections*

request that Mr. Andrew Robertson, to whom they appear much attached, may relieve him of that duty." Burkitt was dismissed in April 1836.[43]

Anderson may have been acting at the request of both the Ojibwe and Andrew himself, who was probably eager to be reappointed to Coldwater. Sometime between 1833, when he and Daybreak Woman met, and 1836, Andrew had developed a romantic attachment to her. They were married at Clayfields on May 23, a month after his return, by the Reverend George Hallen. The story in the Robertson family is that Daybreak Woman agreed to marry Andrew, twenty years her senior, after he promised to take her back to find her mother, Grey Cloud Woman. Although this story suggests that she may not have married him otherwise, he did have many attributes to recommend him as a husband. An acquaintance later in his life described him as "handsome, aristocratic, highly educated," and "charming in conversation and magnificent in hospitality" and said that "personal association with Mr. Robertson was not only a delight, but an education."[44]

By the time Andrew proposed marriage, Daybreak Woman would have known that her father had been ordered to scout for a new site for an Indian agency on Manitoulin Island, which meant she would have to leave Coldwater with her family. Angus had already returned to Mni Sota Makoce, and his departure undoubtedly fueled her own desire to go back and find her mother. Although she may have wanted to return to Mni Sota Makoce for some time even before Angus's departure, she could not safely do so as a young single woman. Traveling to Prairie du Chien meant a long trip of several weeks across Lake Huron and Lake Michigan, then down the Fox and Wisconsin Rivers to the Mississippi. The physical challenge of such an arduous journey would have been daunting, and traveling without a male companion was dangerous. Another likely obstacle was the expense. Perhaps her father refused to provide the funds, or perhaps he could not afford the cost. It is also possible he objected to her returning to live with her mother. However, she was a spirited and strong-minded woman determined to return to Mni Sota Makoce. Despite all the years she had spent in her father's society, her Dakota identity and her desire for the homeland of her childhood remained robust and compelling.[45]

At the age of twenty-five, Daybreak Woman must also have been ready to start her own life, independent of her father and the rest of the Anderson family. Although she was educated, she had few occupational options in Upper Canada. She may have been able to find work as a teacher, but teaching, like all "female" occupations, paid very low wages, and as a single woman she would not have been able to live independently. Marriage was the primary means of economic security for all nineteenth-century women who did not inherit wealth, for society made it virtually impossible for them to survive economically otherwise. In addition, Daybreak Woman felt great affection for her younger Anderson siblings—Gus, Frank, Sophia, and Martha—and seems to have liked children; she was ready to marry and start her own family.

Andrew and Daybreak Woman remained at Coldwater for more than a year after they were married, probably so that they could earn enough to finance their journey to Mni Sota Makoce. He continued as teacher through March 1837. He also acted as Coldwater's superintendent in Thomas Anderson's absences during the summers of 1836 and 1837, as the Anderson family prepared to move to the new Indian agency on Manitoulin Island. The last record of Andrew on the Coldwater Agency books is June 27, 1837, when he was paid sixty pounds for his labor. Shortly afterward, he and Daybreak Woman began their journey back to Mni Sota Makoce to find Grey Cloud Woman. She would never see her father again.[46]

Over the ensuing years Daybreak Woman stayed in some contact with several of her Anderson siblings, including Gustavus, to whom she wrote occasionally as late as the 1880s. Her attachment to her half brothers and sisters is reflected in the names she chose for her own children. She named six of her nine children for her Anderson siblings, including Gustavus, Francis, Mary Sophia (Sophie), Martha, William. She also named one son for her father, one for her brother Angus, and her eldest, James Wabasha, for her grandfather Aird and her great-grandfather Wapaha Ṡa.[47]

∧∨∧∨

In seeking to return from Canada and to find Grey Cloud Woman, Daybreak Woman chose a future associated with her Dakota kin and heritage rather than a future solely as an Anglo-American woman. She could have chosen a life with Andrew in eastern Canada or the United States, living in Euro-American society; the world in which her Anderson siblings lived as adults was available to her as a result of her education, her years in her father's household, and her marriage to an educated man from Scotland. Instead, she asked Andrew to take her home to the people and places of her childhood and to the mother she had not seen or communicated with for fourteen years. In 1837, Daybreak Woman stood at the proverbial crossroads of her life and made a clear choice about its direction. Her choice is a testament to her close bond with her mother as well as to the enduring strength of her Dakota identity.

3. Mississippi River, 1837–1853

Grey Cloud Island, Kap'oja

[My father and mother] traveled up the Mississippi in boats paddled by voyageurs. When they reached Mendota, they learned that Grandmother was at Little Rock. When they arrived at Little Rock, she was not at home. They were told that she was out with the other women of the village playing a game of Lacrosse.

THOMAS ROBERTSON

In July 1837, Daybreak Woman and Andrew Robertson, now married a little more than a year, left Lake Huron and set out to find Grey Cloud Woman. Their son Thomas recalled their tale of this journey as one involving "some thrilling experiences," including crossing Lake Michigan in a terrible storm and canoeing down the Fox River during another thunderstorm in a birchbark canoe. Thomas claimed his mother developed a fear of "big waters" on account of her dreadful experience on the storm-tossed waters of Lake Michigan, such that she "would never consent to go back to Scotland with Father."[1]

When they reached Prairie du Chien, they were told that Grey Cloud Woman II had married an American trader named Hazen Mooers and moved with him to his post on the Minnesota River. Daybreak Woman's grandmother, Grey Cloud Woman I, also had left Prairie du Chien to live with her daughter and son-in-law. In the 1820s and early 1830s, Mooers operated a trading post for the American Fur Company at Lake Traverse, near the headwaters of the Minnesota River. By 1837, he had moved downriver to a post at Little Rapids or Little Rock Creek, about one hundred miles up the Minnesota River from its mouth at Bdote and near the future site of Fort Ridgely.

Daybreak Woman and Andrew continued up the Mississippi to Bdote, where a trading depot known as Mendota (an anglicized version of Bdote) had developed across the river from Fort Snelling, built in the early 1820s.

There they were told they could find Grey Cloud Woman and Mooers at Little Rock Rapids. At Mendota they briefly reunited with Daybreak Woman's brother Angus Anderson, who had found employment as a clerk at Henry Hastings Sibley's American Fur Company trading post. From there the Robertsons continued up the Minnesota River to Little Rock, to find Mooers's trading post.[2]

Hazen Mooers was a New Yorker who began trading in Mni Sota Makoce in about 1818. He, like Thomas Anderson, had been employed by Grey Cloud Woman's father, James Aird. Prior to his marriage to Grey Cloud Woman, Mooers was married to a Dakota woman from Red Wing's village, with whom he had a son, John. In 1837, when the Robertsons first met Hazen Mooers, he was forty-eight years old and described by one visitor to the region as "a thin, good-looking man." Mooers was a popular trader among the Dakota because he honored kinship ties and their custom of reciprocity; he was especially favored among the Sisituŋwaŋ and Waȟpetuŋwaŋ, with whom he had traded on the Upper Minnesota River since the early 1820s. In fact, his generosity to the Dakota men with whom he traded got him fired: in 1835, his American Fur Company employer, Henry Sibley, removed Mooers from his Lake Traverse post for being too liberal with his credits to hunters. Subsequently, Mooers moved downriver to Little Rock and set up as an independent trader. There the family farmed and he traded with the local Dakota band, who were his relations through his wife.[3]

Shortly after Mooers established his post at Little Rock, an English visitor to the region, George Featherstonehaugh, encountered the family on his journey up the Minnesota River. Featherstonehaugh noted that the Mooerses were living in tents and described them as follows: "He [Mooers] has an Indian wife, a middle-aged bustling woman, and is building a house consisting of two rooms, one where they are to sleep and the other where he is to keep his goods. Mooers was in a canoe fishing with his children, and appears to be fond of them; they have more of their mother than their father in their faces." The children Featherstonehaugh describes were Daybreak Woman's three Mooers half sisters. In 1837, they were Mary (eleven), Jane Anne (ten), and Madeline (seven).[4]

Daybreak Woman must have been thrilled to finally be with her mother again, having sought a reunion for years, and Grey Cloud Woman's joy at the return of her daughter must also have been considerable. Grey Cloud Woman had sent away her then twelve-year-old girl in 1823, and after so many years of separation, she probably did not expect to see her again. Now the woman standing before her was twenty-seven, with an older husband by her side, and she was pregnant. Daybreak Woman's first child, James Wabasha Robertson, would be born a few months later. It must have been tremendously reassuring that her mother was with her to help bring her first child into the world.[5]

∧∨∧∨

During this time, Daybreak Woman's Bdewakaŋtuŋwaŋ relatives were navigating a period of great change. Over the previous decade, the Dakota bands living along the Mississippi had become increasingly desperate for food as the game in the area decreased dramatically. Since the 1820s, many from the Mississippi River villages had migrated west to live among relatives in the Minnesota River Valley, where game was more available. As the number of fur-bearing animals declined, the American Fur Company, which had a virtual monopoly on the trade in the region, cut back on credits given to hunters. Food and supplies were no longer extended on credit to most, leaving many desperate. Hunger became a regular and significant problem for the Bdewakaŋtuŋwaŋ Dakota.

During the 1830s, the Indian agent at Fort Snelling, Lawrence Taliaferro, began to give out government rations of food and fishing equipment and supplied some plows to encourage more extensive farming and less reliance on hunting and gathering. Most Bdewakaŋtuŋwaŋ Dakota resisted these efforts to become more dependent on farming, although under the leadership of Cloud Man (Maḣpiya Wiçaśṭa) and with Taliaferro's support, one group did move to a farming community established on Bde Maka Ska (known to whites as Lake Calhoun), about eight miles west of Fort Snelling. There they successfully cultivated sufficient crops to feed their population, which grew to several hundred by the late 1830s. The villagers, however, did not save most of their surplus crops and produce but, as was expected in Dakota culture, shared it with relatives from other bands or consumed it themselves after harvest. Some surplus was sold to soldiers and people living near the fort, but the farming experiment at Bde Maka Ska demonstrated that cultivating a significant amount of food did not necessarily mean that people would have sufficient food to get them through the winter and spring.[6]

The Bdewakaŋtuŋwaŋ Dakota population decreased dramatically

during the 1820s and 1830s due to starvation, disease (especially a small-pox epidemic in 1835), and the westward migration of many band members. These decreases and the increasing numbers of non-Indigenous people settling on the east side of the Mississippi combined to persuade Bdewakaŋtuŋwaŋ leaders, with Taliaferro's urging, to enter into treaty negotiations with the US government. In the Treaty of 1837, the Bdewakaŋtuŋwaŋ gave up five million acres of land east of the Mississippi River for $1 million that would be used to provide government aid of various sorts, including cash annuities, food, supplies, equipment, government teachers, farmers, and tradespeople. Starvation was no longer a threat, and their population increased in the following decade, nearly doubling by 1849. Relatives who had moved west due to the lack of food now returned to collect annuities and food rations. However, in the decade after the Treaty of 1837, the Bdewakaŋtuŋwaŋ also came under increasing pressure from the government to become like the invading settler-colonists—they were to abandon their way of life and beliefs by sending their children to missionary schools and becoming farmers.[7]

The treaty also provided a sum of money for payments to the mixed-ancestry relatives of the Bdewakaŋtuŋwaŋ Dakota. In August 1837, the prominent trader Jean Baptiste Faribault penned a letter to Henry Dodge, the governor of Wisconsin Territory, who was the 1837 treaty commissioner. This letter, which was signed by Angus Anderson, Daybreak Woman, the Mooerses, and other Euro-Dakota people, objected to the use of the term *half-breed* in the treaty, saying that it should have been *relations*. Faribault argued that *half-breed* was a generic term used by non-Indigenous people to describe all Euro-Indigenous people, and therefore a strict definition of the term, as in 50 percent Dakota blood, should not be used as a basis for assigning treaty payments to Bdewakaŋtuŋwaŋ relatives. He wrote, "We are all usually determined half-breeds, but are in fact quarter-breeds, nay many of us cannot say more than that we know we are of Sioux blood and consequently relations." Faribault's letter was apparently persuasive, for the final treaty stipulated that relatives that had at least one-quarter Dakota blood were to receive a share of the funds set aside for the "relatives and friends" of the Bdewakaŋtuŋwaŋ Dakota. On the record of claims under the 1837 Treaty, completed in 1838, Grey Cloud Woman (Margaret Mooers) is listed as "half blood"; "Jenny Robertson" (Daybreak Woman), Angus Anderson, and the three Mooers girls are all listed as "quarter blood."[8]

Grey Cloud Island

The Robertsons and Mooerses lived together in the Mooerses' log cabin at Little Rock during the fall and winter of 1837–38. As Hazen Mooers had been struggling to make a living at the Little Rock post, in the spring of 1838, the two families decided to move to an island in the Mississippi about eighteen miles below St. Paul. Andrew named their new home Grey Cloud Island, for Daybreak Woman's mother and grandmother.

Before the arrival of the Mooers and Robertson families, the island was the home of a Dakota band led by Wakaŋ Ojaŋjaŋ (Holy Light, also known as Medicine Bottle); no record survives of the Dakota name for the place. In the autumn of 1837, the band left the island because of the newly signed Treaty of 1837, which left it open for claims by the Mooerses and Robertsons.[9]

When the families came to Grey Cloud Island, they moved into two bark and willow lodges vacated by the Holy Light band the previous autumn and used a third lodge as a storehouse. They lived and worked side by side, planting corn, potatoes, and a large vegetable garden as well as the first wheat crop on the island. They also raised cattle and hogs and produced milk and butter. They sold their surplus produce and grain to the garrison at Fort Snelling and shipped their livestock and dairy products downriver to St. Louis via steamboats. In 1839, each family built a new log house with a stone chimney and three rooms looking out on the Mississippi. Sometime around 1840, John Mooers, Hazen's teenage son by his previous Dakota wife, came to live with the families as well.[10]

Grey Cloud Island was just five miles long and two miles wide, but the Mooerses and Robertsons shared it with several other families, establishing relationships that would become deeply significant. The Anglo-American trader Joseph Renshaw Brown and his French-Dakota wife, Susan Frenier Brown, arrived the same summer as the Mooerses and Robertsons. The Browns built a log house at the steamboat landing on the southern shore of the island, where they farmed and Brown opened a tavern and store. The Browns' first son, Angus Mitchell Anderson Brown, was named for Daybreak Woman's brother, who became a close friend of Joseph. Also living in the Brown household were Susan's mother, Winona Crawford, as well as Winona's son Gabriel Renville, her baby Francois, and her third husband, Akipa (Ta Caŋdahupa Hotaŋka). Brown helped Akipa build a cabin for his family, and Akipa also became a farmer. Several others moved to the site around the Brown family and built three houses: James Clewett (an English immigrant), Marcelle Courturier, Joseph Bourcier, and Pierre Felix, who was married to Rosalie Frenier (a relative of Susan Brown). The Browns lived on the island for about five years before moving west to live on the Upper Minnesota River.[11]

During these years, Angus Anderson was living and working at the Mendota trading post. In 1838 and 1839, he partnered with Joseph Brown and James Clewett to establish a grog shop—saloon—on the east bank of the Mississippi directly across from Fort Snelling in an area known as Rumtown. The three men owned the establishment but hired others to manage it and live there. Angus left or was fired from his position at the American Fur Company Mendota post; it appears he may have lost his job because of the grog shop, which the fort's surgeon blamed for increased drunkenness among the soldiers. Angus then partnered with Hazen Mooers to trade independently with the Dakota. In the summer of 1840, Angus traveled downriver to St. Louis to purchase supplies for the trade but never returned; he took ill and died of fever, perhaps cholera or typhoid.[12]

A year after losing her brother, Daybreak Woman lost her oldest child, James Wabasha, when he was only three years old. She was not at leisure to grieve; she had a toddler and an infant to look after: son Thomas, born in October 1839, and daughter Marion, born in the fall of 1840. Another son, whom she named for Angus, arrived in September 1842. Daybreak Woman suffered another loss in 1844, when her grandmother, Grey Cloud Woman I, the daughter of Wapaha Ṡa I, the sister of Wapaha Ṡa II, and the widow of James Aird, died at Black Dog's village near the mouth of the Minnesota River. Although her year of birth is not certain, she was likely in her midseventies when she passed.[13]

That same year, the Robertsons sold their hogs and cattle to the army at Fort Snelling and left the island. Daybreak Woman and Andrew moved just off the island onto a new claim on the east bank of the Mississippi at a place called Cave Spring. There Daybreak Woman gave birth to another son, Gustavus, in December 1844. The next year her fifth son, Francis, was born at Cave Spring as well. By 1845, Daybreak Woman was a very busy and likely exhausted mother to five children under the age of six.[14]

By November 1848, the rapidly growing family prompted Andrew to wonder about how his children would be educated. He wrote a letter from Cave Spring to Henry Sibley, now Minnesota's territorial representative in Washington, DC, asking him to establish a school for the Dakota and Euro-Dakota children in the region using the funds from the Treaty of 1837. Andrew requested a government school unaffiliated with the missionaries because many Dakota parents did not want their children under such religious influence. He wrote that, although the missionaries had tried for twelve years to convert the Dakota people, and were "talented" and "persevering," they had not been very successful. He also asked Sibley to look into the Lake Pepin allotments of land that were supposed to go to the relatives of the Dakota under the 1830 Treaty of Prairie du Chien. The reservation on the west side of Lake Pepin created for the Euro-Dakota by that treaty was never occupied; in the years after 1830, several attempts had been made to effect new treaties with provisions for converting the Pepin reservation land into payments, but all of these proposed treaties had failed in the US Senate. In 1848, Sibley and the territorial governor, Alexander Ramsey, submitted a new treaty to the Senate and over the course of 1849 and 1850 pushed for its ratification. However, this effort to pay the mixed-ancestry relatives of the Dakota for the 1830 reservation also failed.[15]

Daybreak Woman and Andrew squatted on government land at Cave Spring, intending to preempt it, but by 1849, they had hired a man to protect their claim and were on the move again. They farmed briefly at Cottage Grove, a few miles north of Grey Cloud Island; Daybreak Woman and the children seemed to have lived there for a time after Andrew began a new job as the government farmer at Kap'oja, Little Crow's village on the Mississippi (now South St. Paul). By 1849, the entire family had moved to Kap'oja. During this time, the man they had hired took their claim at Cave Spring for himself.[16]

Grey Cloud Woman and Hazen Mooers stayed on Grey Cloud Island for several years after Daybreak Woman and Andrew left. In 1846, their eldest daughter, Mary, married Joseph R. Brown's brother, John Wesley Brown. Mary and John Brown moved to live in Black Dog's village on the Minnesota River, not far from Bdote. That year, Hazen built a house for the rest of the family in Shakopee's village on the Minnesota River. A year later Grey Cloud Woman and Hazen joined their daughter Mary and her family in Black Dog's village, where Mooers took the job as government farmer. Joseph and Susan Frenier Brown left Grey Cloud Island about the same time as the Robertsons, moving up the Minnesota River to trade with the Sisituŋwaŋ and Wahpetuŋwaŋ.[17]

Little Crow's village on the Mississippi, about 1846–48. *Watercolor by Seth Eastman, Minnesota Historical Society collections*

Kap'oja

When the Robertsons moved to Kap'oja, His Scarlet People (Ta Oyate Duta) had been the band's leader for several years. He was the fourth hereditary leader of the band to be known as Little Crow, the name used by whites. In Dakota, Kap'oja (anglicized as Kaposia) means "light or swift of foot." The village had moved several times since the early 1800s; in the late 1840s, it was located in what is now South St. Paul. Little Crow was born in 1810, when the Bdewakaŋtuŋwaŋ Dakota had numbered about two thousand people living in six villages on the Mississippi and Minnesota Rivers, ranging as far south as Lake Pepin and as far north as Kap'oja. Little Crow was close to Daybreak Woman in age and was related to her through her mother. He became closely acquainted with the entire Robertson family and developed an especially close friendship with Andrew over the years.[18]

The inhabitants of Little Crow's village, located on the east bank of the Mississippi River about five miles south of the city of St. Paul and just north of the junction of the Mississippi and St. Croix Rivers, by this time comprised the northernmost Bdewakaŋtuŋwaŋ Dakota band. The village's close access to the St. Croix River to the east as well as its proximity to the mouth of the Minnesota River to the southwest made it a transportation nexus. It served as a staging area for hunting and gathering trips throughout the year and was occupied continuously from the late spring through the summer, when the women planted and harvested corn, squash, and beans. Travelers up the Mississippi in the early decades of the nineteenth century who passed Kap'oja observed about twelve permanent houses in the village, constructed of elm frames and covered with elm bark. These were very large structures, each accommodating as many as twenty-five people. At the houses' entrances were wooden platforms used for drying food and hides and for sleeping outside in the hot summer months.[19]

After the first frost in the fall, the Kap'oja band moved up the St. Croix and its tributaries, where they hunted deer through midwinter. In March, the band divided into hunting and sugar-making parties; the women col-

A Dakota summer lodge, about 1846–48. *Watercolor by Seth Eastman, Minnesota Historical Society collections*

lected sap from maple trees while the men hunted smaller game, such as muskrats and beavers. When spring thaw began, the band returned to Kap'oja, where the women prepared and planted their fields. Some of the men traveled west to trade and hunt buffalo and waterfowl and to fish on the Upper Minnesota River. During the summer, the band supplemented their diet by gathering wild foods such as berries, seeds, and wild turnips and other roots. In late September, they picked cranberries and harvested wild rice from the lakes in the region to the north, near the Rum River.[20]

Before 1837, Kap'oja was located on the east side of the Mississippi, near what is now called Dayton's Bluff; before that, it was a couple of miles downstream. After the land cession under the Treaty of 1837, Little Crow's band moved to the west side of the Mississippi. The former site of Kap'oja became the community of Pig's Eye, named for the French-Canadian Pierre Parrant, a former fur trader who was blind in one eye and was the first to have a whiskey shop there in the early 1840s. After the Dakota band left, Parrant, joined by several French-Canadian families, formed the nucleus of what would become the city of St. Paul. Little Crow's band sold firewood and traded game for supplies with the early St. Paul residents across the river. St. Paul grew rapidly during the 1840s, and Kap'oja was on the edge of the developing urban center.[21]

As a result of the 1837 Treaty, the Kap'oja band and the other Bdewakaŋtuŋwaŋ Dakota felt increasing pressure from US government officials stationed at Fort Snelling at Bdote and from Protestant missionaries to alter their way of life. They also were rapidly being surrounded by settler-colonists moving into what had been Bdewakaŋtuŋwaŋ territory on the east side of the Mississippi, with whom they had to compete for the area's resources. In the decade following the treaty, all of the Bdewakaŋtuŋwaŋ villages became more dependent on government annuities for subsistence. The government also appointed farmers to work and live at each village and to teach Euro-American-style agriculture to the Bdewakaŋtuŋwaŋ bands. The government's goal was to force the bands to give up their traditional, seasonal communal economy and become dependent on agriculture for their subsistence. In addition, both government officials and missionaries encouraged and pressured the Bdewakaŋtuŋwaŋ communities to adopt the religion, lifestyle, and gender roles of Euro-Americans—in other words, to abandon their Dakota culture and religion. The government's Indian agents pressured the leaders to send their band's children to the new schools established by missionaries in their villages, to adopt Euro-American clothing, to learn English, and to convert to Christianity.[22]

Before Andrew Robertson's appointment as government farmer to Kap'oja, several previous government appointees and missionaries had established schools and worked to teach Little Crow's band Euro-American agriculture, without much success. Schools established after 1837 at Kap'oja by the government and by Methodist missionaries were both closed by 1842, having had little impact. The situation changed when Ta Oyate Duta (Little Crow IV) became leader in 1846 and invited Thomas and Margaret Williamson, missionaries he had encountered on the Minnesota River at Lac qui Parle, to open a school at Kap'oja. The Williamsons had taught some of the Dakota at Lac qui Parle (many of whom were Little Crow's relatives) to read and write in the Dakota language. They had also translated the Bible into Dakota, and a small number of people at Lac qui Parle converted to Christianity.[23]

When the Robertson family moved to the village in 1849, Daybreak Woman and Andrew lived about a quarter mile south of Kap'oja. A few years earlier, Andrew had helped the Williamsons build their mission house, a large home with eleven rooms, just about a half mile from the Robertsons' house. The Williamsons and the Robertsons became close friends and associates. Thomas Williamson baptized all the Robertson children, and both Daybreak Woman and Andrew became members of his Presbyterian congregation.[24]

From the late 1840s through the early 1850s, Little Crow encouraged his band to send their children to the Williamsons' mission school, where the children were taught to read and write in the Dakota language. In the late 1840s, the Kap'oja school averaged about thirty pupils a day, with as many as fifty-four children attending regularly. However, the missionaries had less success converting Kap'oja band members to their faith; only about six new converts entered the church during these years. Beginning in 1848, some Dakota children boarded with the missionaries or other government workers at Kap'oja, presumably in an effort to accelerate their learning as well as their acculturation. Two of Little Crow's children boarded with the Williamsons for a year.[25]

In 1851, the six oldest Robertson children, five Williamson children, sixteen Dakota pupils, and about seven Euro-Dakota children attended the school. The teacher was Jane Smith Williamson, Thomas's sister, who arrived in 1846 to join her brother, Margaret, and their five children. Jane Williamson began studying Dakota so she could teach the children how to read and write in their own language. She also became good friends with some of the Dakota girls who were her students, including Daybreak Woman's eldest daughter, Marion Robertson.[26]

Daybreak Woman encouraged Marion to have as much interaction with the missionary women as possible. Marion seems to have gone back and forth between her own home and living with the Williamsons during these years. Daybreak Woman also hoped Marion might be able to live for a time with Nancy Aiton, another missionary who was stationed at Red Wing but was often at Kap'oja. The Williamsons regularly had five or six Dakota children boarding with them (most often girls), and in the early 1850s, the Robertsons often boarded Bdewakaŋtuŋwaŋ girls who were mission students as well. In 1851–52, Daybreak Woman was overseeing a household with five girls as boarders and her own seven children (her son William, known as Willie, was born in December 1850). The girls who boarded with the Robertsons were mostly from the Kap'oja band, but a few were from other Bdewakaŋtuŋwaŋ bands. Using funds provided by the 1837 treaty, the government paid the Williamsons and Robertsons to take on the Dakota boarders and teach them how to live like white people. Girls were taught Euro-American domestic skills, manners, and dress in addition to the reading, writing, and arithmetic they were taught in the schoolroom.[27]

In October of 1851, Jane Williamson traveled back east with other missionary families and took her niece Nancy Jane as well as Marion Robertson (age eleven) with her on the trip. Both of the girls contracted scarlet fever during their stay at Williamson's cousin's house in Ohio, but both recovered. Marion returned to Kap'oja in May 1852 with the Williamsons. A few months before their return, Jane Williamson wrote her missionary friend Nancy Aiton at Kap'oja that she had heard that Mr. Robertson was unwell. She said of Andrew, "I hope he too is well again, but almost would not. Good natured as Marion is she almost thinks it hard. They do not write us. How does her mother bear her absence." Jane Williamson, who felt great affection for Marion, was angry at Andrew and Daybreak Woman for neglecting to correspond and inquire after Marion's well-being. Away from her family for the first time in her life, Marion was likely homesick. But her parents were undoubtedly consumed with the care of their six other young children and their many boarders and likely were fully confident in Jane Williamson's care for their eldest daughter.

In 1852–53, Marion lived with friends of the Williamsons in Ohio, where she attended school. She was the only one of Daybreak Woman's children to be sent east for an education.[28]

At Kap'oja, the Robertsons were neighbors with another large Euro-Dakota family, the Campbells. Scott Campbell was Scots-Dakota, and his wife, Margaret, was French, Ojibwe, and Menominee. From the 1820s until the early 1850s, the family lived near Little Crow's village. The Campbell children, like their parents, were multilingual, speaking French, Dakota, English, and Menominee. Scott's father, like James Aird, was a Scots trader who married a Dakota woman and lived in Prairie du Chien; Scott was born there a few years before Grey Cloud Woman. The Aird and Campbell families knew each other well. In 1819, Scott became the government interpreter for Major Taliaferro at Fort Snelling. The two youngest of Scott and Margaret's nine children, Margaret and Marie, were about the same ages as Daybreak Woman's two oldest. The Campbells were closely related to Little Crow.[29]

Andrew was very busy as a government farmer at Kap'oja. The annual report for the farming effort in 1849–50 reveals that he plowed 6.5 acres for corn and harvested 3.3 bushels, with about one-third of the crop saved for winter. He also cut rails for fencing the fields, but these were all swept away in a spring flood (as were the Robertsons' garden and fence). He also put up thirty-five to forty tons of hay and assisted Little Crow in building a log house as well as several small storehouses.[30]

In June 1849, Daybreak Woman's mother was fifty-six years old and living in Black Dog's village with her husband, Hazen, and two youngest daughters, Jane Anne (now twenty-three) and Madeline (twenty). Also in the village was her oldest Mooers daughter, Mary, with her young family. Five years earlier, in the same village, Daybreak Woman's grandmother, the first Grey Cloud Woman, had died at an advanced age. Grey Cloud Woman II, Margaret Aird Anderson Mooers, was not as long-lived. Just one month after the 1849 census, she died, surrounded by all four of her daughters. The cause of her death is not documented. Losing her mother must have been a blow to Daybreak Woman; since their reunion, mother, daughter, and their families had been intimately associated, living for many years together, then side by side on Grey Cloud Island, and afterward separated by only a short canoe ride between Kap'oja and Black Dog. However, with so many children of her own, as well as her boarders, Daybreak Woman could not stop long to grieve. At the time of her mother's death, she was thirty-seven years old with six children under the age of ten—Thomas, Marion, Angus, Gustavus, Francis (Frank), and Mary Sophia (Sophie)—and she was pregnant with her seventh child, William.[31]

The Treaties of Mendota and Traverse des Sioux

In 1851, the Santee Dakota were forced by poverty, starvation, and the greed of settler-colonists, fur traders, and politicians to enter into treaties to sell most of their homeland. Influential American Fur Company trader and Minnesota territorial delegate to Congress Henry Sibley and Governor Alexander Ramsey worked with fur traders and a number of influential Euro-Dakota relatives of the bands to exert pressure on the Santee Dakota to sign treaties giving up their territory in Minnesota. The strategy adopted by politicians and traders to obtain a treaty was to negotiate first with the Waȟpetuŋwaŋ and Sisituŋwaŋ, who were suffering starvation and were more desperate than the eastern bands, thinking that once the western bands signed, the Bdewakaŋtuŋwaŋ and Waȟpekute would be under greater pressure to negotiate. The treaty talks that followed and the treaties themselves were transparently about greed for money, greed for land, and "naked conquest." As historian Rhoda Gilman explains, "If no treaty were signed, white men would swarm into the land anyway, and should the Dakota try to drive them out, some pretext would be found to send in troops." This pattern in US policy with respect to Indigenous peoples was well established, having been used by the government against Indigenous nations in the Ohio Valley, Illinois, and Wisconsin.[32]

Traders worked closely with Sibley to both manipulate treaty negotiations and ensure that the trade debts they claimed the Dakota owed them were paid directly out of the treaty funds. Traders sought the repayment of debts going as far back as the 1820s. Sibley himself was in financial ruin and had a significant personal interest in obtaining treaty funds, as many Dakota and their Euro-Dakota relatives owed him money. Sibley worked to unite the mixed-ancestry relatives of the Dakota as well as the traders in support of the treaties, then use them to put pressure on the Dakota to accept the treaty terms. Sibley's close associates Joseph R. Brown and Martin McLeod, who both had deep family ties to the Waȟpetuŋwaŋ and Sisituŋwaŋ bands through their Dakota wives as well as years of trading among the Dakota, were also key players in this endeavor.[33]

In July 1851, the Sisituŋwaŋ and Waȟpetuŋwaŋ bands negotiated a treaty with the US government at Traverse des Sioux, the site of a Sisituŋwaŋ village on the Minnesota River, located about seventy-five miles above the river's mouth. The Sisituŋwaŋ and Waȟpetuŋwaŋ sold lands in central Minnesota as far west as the Red River and Sioux River that had been reserved to them under a previous treaty. The Upper Sioux Reservation created along the Upper Minnesota River extended ten miles on either side of the river from Yellow Medicine to Lake Traverse. Under the terms of the treaty, the bands were to be paid an annuity for fifty years, with an initial amount invested in schools, mills, blacksmith shops, plowing, fencing, and housing. An additional amount of money was provided to the Dakota leaders to pay for the costs of removal to the reservation and subsistence for the bands until they began to receive their annuities. Because the subsistence fund was to be paid directly to the leaders, the traders and their Euro-Dakota allies schemed to wrest the funds immediately from the Dakota leaders.[34]

After Dakota leaders signed the treaty at Traverse des Sioux, they were directed to an "upended barrel," where Brown sat with another paper they were told to sign. The document, the traders' paper, pledged them to pay their bands' debts and also assigned funds to be paid to traders and mixed-ancestry individuals out of the treaty fund set aside for the leaders to cover the removal costs and subsistence. According to Gilman, some of the Dakota "obviously knew what the paper was and approved; others were in the dark." The document was not read or explained at the treaty council—even though the Indian agent, Nathaniel Maclean, requested that this be done, his request was ignored by the treaty commissioners. The Dakota who were left "in the dark" did not understand that they were agreeing to hand over their treaty funds directly to the traders.[35]

Negotiations for the Treaty of Mendota, with the eastern Bdewakaŋtuŋwaŋ and Waȟpekute bands, began at the end of July. The Bdewakaŋtuŋwaŋ were the most experienced of the bands in dealing with the US government, having previously negotiated the Treaty of 1837. They were also not as economically desperate as the western bands, as they had received annuities from that treaty, although they were still owed a substantial sum of money by the government. Little Crow and Wapaha Śa, speaking for the band, told the treaty commissioners at the outset that they would not negotiate a new treaty until they were paid the money still owed them. The commissioners immediately offered them $30,000 in cash, but the Bdewakaŋtuŋwaŋ maintained their resistance, and negotiations continued for over a week. Some of the younger Bdewakaŋtuŋwaŋ warriors were adamantly opposed to a treaty, as were some of the younger Sisituŋwaŋ and Waȟpetuŋwaŋ men at Traverse des Sioux. At Mendota, the young warriors threatened to kill any leader who signed the treaty. But in the end, Little Crow and the other Dakota leaders understood that the settler-colonists would take their land regardless of any treaty and their people would be left with nothing. On August 5, Little Crow declared he would be the first to sign the treaty, even if he were shot on the spot. Other Bdewakaŋtuŋwaŋ and Waȟpekute leaders lined up behind Little Crow to sign the treaty.[36]

The US Senate didn't ratify the treaties until June 1852, almost a year after they were signed. Meanwhile, Dakota watched angrily as whites swarmed onto their land almost immediately after the signing. As settler-colonists crossed to the west side of the Mississippi onto Dakota territory not yet officially sold, the commandant at Fort Snelling did nothing to remove the squatters. Politicians and government officials also did nothing, expecting that the increase in white squatters would put more even pressure on Dakota to accept the treaties as negotiated.[37]

In amending the treaty prior to ratification, the Senate eliminated the two reservations as well as a tract of land that had been set aside for the mixed-ancestry relatives of the bands. The Dakota had to agree to these amendments for the treaty to become final, but many leaders were rightly incensed at the loss of the reservations and refused. Governor Ramsey feared that open conflict might result between the Bdewakaŋtuŋwaŋ and white squatters, so he appealed to the administration to grant the Dakota temporary occupation of the reservations under the president's authority. While waiting for an official approval of this appeal, Ramsey proceeded to assure the Dakota people that they would have their reservations and worked with traders and politicians to persuade the Dakota to sign on to the amended treaty and to pay the traders their claims. When Waȟpetuŋwaŋ and Sisituŋwaŋ leaders proved adamantly opposed to handing over funds to the traders, Ramsey used violent coercion to get what he wanted. Ramsey simply arrested the leaders who refused to sign the traders' papers and replaced them with others who complied. When the Bdewakaŋtuŋwaŋ likewise opposed giving treaty funds directly to the traders, Ramsey withheld the annuities due to them under the Treaty of 1837. Ultimately, Sibley helped reach a compromise with the Bdewakaŋtuŋwaŋ that gave the leaders some of the cash and set aside the remainder for Sibley to pay the traders.[38]

Missionaries, including Thomas Williamson, and a few other white allies of the Dakota people spoke out against the injustice of eliminating the reservations. The missionaries wanted the reservations to focus on Christianization efforts, which they thought would be impossible without concentrating the Indigenous population. Government officials expected to consolidate Dakota people on reservations to prevent conflicts with settler-colonists and to establish "civilization" programs; their idea was to force the Dakota people to become like whites by undermining their traditional communal practices and forcing them to embrace individual capitalism. By allotting land to individuals or nuclear families, promoting single-family households as the basic unit of economic production, government officials and missionaries alike hoped to destroy the Dakota communal subsistence way of life and their expansive definition of family, which extended far beyond white notions.

Such were the intentions of the government officials and missionaries on the Minnesota River reservations during the 1850s. However, Dakota people responded in varied ways to these pressures and until the late 1850s many were able to resist these efforts of forced assimilation fairly successfully; they continued to practice their communal subsistence lifestyle for a time before settler-colonists reached the Upper Minnesota River in large numbers. They continued to hunt, fish, and gather wild foods on land taken from them in the 1851 treaties. Although settler-colonists reached the southeastern border of reservation lands by 1854, the "Big Woods" area north of the Minnesota River, as well as several valleys south of the river, were more sparsely settled by white migrants until 1858. So, for a time after the establishment of the Minnesota River reservations, many collected their treaty annuities but continued to live as they had prior to the treaties.[39]

4. Minnesota River, 1853–1860

Yellow Medicine Agency, Redwood Agency

The farmer had a mixed blood for a wife who was educated in Canada. She was a pleasing woman and very interesting in giving her reminiscences of life among the Dakotas. The farmer boarded the men employed, and his wife, assisted by an Indian woman, did the cooking. The house was well kept and I never heard any fault with the cooking.

JARED DANIELS

You talk well and use fine language and that's all.... You then promised that we should have this same land forever, and yet now you want to take half of it away.

LITTLE CROW, 1858

In the summer of 1853, Daybreak Woman's husband and their eldest son, Thomas, now fourteen, left the family behind in Kap'oja and traveled up the Minnesota River to the newly created Dakota reservations. Andrew and Hazen Mooers had earned the government contracts to establish the two agencies for the reservations: one for the Sisituŋwaŋ and Waĥpetuŋwaŋ at the Yellow Medicine River (the Upper Sioux Reservation) and one for the Bdewakaŋtuŋwaŋ and Waĥpekute at the Redwood River (the Lower Sioux Reservation). Also on the journey were Mooers's son John and a number of hired men. The group traveled upriver on three steamboats. The new Minnesota River reservations, called the Upper Sioux and Lower Sioux Reservations (or Agencies), were created by the Treaties of Mendota and Traverse des Sioux in 1851. As a result of these treaties, the Santee Dakota were forced to give up their lands west of the Mississippi River and south of the Minnesota River, twenty-four million acres, in exchange for annuity payments, government support, and two ten-mile-wide strips of land that ran for 140 miles along the northern and southern banks of the Upper

Minnesota River. These lands were not clearly designated as reservations—the Dakota held them only "at the president's pleasure."

One of the boats stopped where Fort Ridgely would be built, while the others continued on as far as the mouth of the Redwood River, the site of what would become the Lower Sioux or Redwood Agency. There the Mooers and their men disembarked to start construction on the agency buildings. The Robertsons continued upriver eighteen miles to the second agency site, the Upper Sioux Agency, located at the mouth of the river known to the Dakota as Peji Huta Zizi K'api, Where They Dig the Yellow Medicine.[1]

Yellow Medicine Agency

That first summer, the two Robertsons and their men employed five yoke of oxen, two wagons, and a plow to start breaking land for agricultural fields at the village of Running Walker (Iŋyaŋg Mani) near the Yellow Medicine Agency site. They also built a gristmill on the Yellow Medicine River. Meanwhile, downriver, the Mooerses supervised the construction of a sawmill and other buildings at Redwood Falls. That fall, Andrew and Thomas returned to Kap'oja to spend the winter with Daybreak Woman and the rest of the family. John Mooers returned to Shakopee, where he was the government farmer, and Hazen returned to his residence in Black Dog's village.[2]

In the spring of 1854 Andrew, Thomas, and the Mooers men returned to the agency sites to continue building. At Yellow Medicine, Andrew and Thomas constructed a house for the family to live in, as Andrew had been appointed the government farmer for the Yellow Medicine Agency. By the end of the summer, the house was completed, so Andrew brought Daybreak Woman and the rest of the children upriver to their new home. Their house was located just four miles upriver from Daybreak Woman's birthplace at Patterson's Rapids. One other log building housed the rest of the agency's employees.[3]

The following year, John Mooers and his French-Dakota wife, Rosalie, moved their family of three young children into two log cabins near the Redwood Agency, where they would live until 1862. Daybreak Woman's half sister, Jane Anne Mooers, who had epilepsy, also lived with John's family. By this time, Hazen Mooers had married for a third time and had a new young daughter. After completion of his government contract, he moved to a new home downriver near Fort Ridgely. Daybreak Woman's

youngest half sister, Madeline Mooers, died sometime after 1851 and before the family's move to the Minnesota River reservations.[4]

Yellow Medicine Society

At Yellow Medicine, the Robertsons were once again neighbors to the
Williamsons, who had moved there in 1852 to establish a new mission.
Thomas Williamson named it Pajutazee, using a version of the river's
Dakota name. It was located about three miles northwest of the Yellow
Medicine Agency, where Daybreak Woman and her family lived. Another
Presbyterian missionary, Stephen Riggs, and his wife, Mary, established
a separate mission about thirty miles beyond Pajutazee at Lac qui Parle.
After a fire destroyed the Lac qui Parle mission station in 1854, the Riggses,
with fifteen Dakota families, moved to a new farming mission he called
Hazelwood, about six miles north of the Yellow Medicine Agency. The
American Board of Commissioners for Foreign Missions paid for a small
sawmill there, and Stephen Riggs helped the Dakota farmers build frame
houses and fence fields. The government provided funds to buy oxen and
to pay the farmers for improvements to the land. By 1854, some of the
Hazelwood farmers had adopted white clothing. Several Dakota farming
villages developed at the Yellow Medicine Agency, one under Running
Walker, another comprising relatives of Joseph Renville at Lac qui Parle,
and yet another under Cloud Man at Patterson's Rapids.[5]

The Williamsons and Robertsons resumed their close association at Yellow Medicine. A short time after Daybreak Woman and Andrew moved the
children up to the agency, they sent Sophie, then six, to live in the Williamson household, as her sister Marion had done at Kap'oja. Sophie learned to
read and write in both Dakota and English during these years. She lived
with the Williamsons until her mother and father moved the family down
to the Redwood Agency in 1857. Daybreak Woman also lived with the Williamsons in February and March of 1855, when she became seriously ill.
Thomas Williamson reported to his superior that "Mrs. Robertson has been
sick for most of the winter and has been with us for several weeks while she
slowly recovers." As her last child, Martha, would be born in the autumn of
that year, it could be that Daybreak Woman was suffering from her pregnancy. She was forty-five years old, and Martha was her ninth child.[6]

Thomas Williamson's regard for Andrew and Daybreak Woman are
evident in his correspondence with the mission board. In March 1855, he
described Daybreak Woman as "educated at Mackinac" and "an excellent

woman." He described Andrew as a Scotsman by birth, educated in England, "superior in writing and making calculations. He is kind and polite
and feels no little interest in the welfare of the Indians."[7]

Jared Daniels, another neighbor with whom Daybreak Woman and
Andrew would become close friends, arrived in the summer of 1855 to fill
the position of agency physician. Daniels found three log buildings at the
agency, one for the farmer and his family (the Robertsons) as well as the
government employees who were boarders, one for the blacksmith and
his family, and one for the blacksmith shop. The agency buildings were
located on the north bank of the Yellow Medicine River, about two miles
from its mouth at the Minnesota River. The agency sat on what Daniels
described as "a horseshoe shaped piece of bottom land surrounded by
high bluffs" and comprised about ten acres. On the opposite side of the
Yellow Medicine River were three log trading posts that sat in front of
high bluffs covered with trees. When Daniels arrived, the plum trees that
lined the road down the bluff to the agency were in bloom, and it was all
pleasingly picturesque. Daniels boarded with the only white family living
at the agency, the family of the blacksmith Ford, in the attic of their house.
Although the Fords were white, Mrs. Ford spoke Dakota fluently.[8]

Andrew introduced Daniels to the Dakota families living near the
agency, to the government employees, and to the missionaries. In his reminiscences, Daniels describes Andrew as "a Scotchman educated at Oxford,
[who] had travelled in many countries. He spoke French, and Spanish fluently. He was a large, broad-shouldered man six feet two inches in height,
and a weight of 245 pounds. He was kind and generous with the urbanity
of deportment, and conversation that fitted him for the most polished
society." The next summer, Daniels married and brought his wife to the
agency, where they lived until 1861, when they moved downriver to the
Redwood Agency.[9]

Daniels's account of his first days at Yellow Medicine also provides a
window into the nature of Daybreak Woman's life there. He describes the
Robertson house as the center of agency society in these early years—a so-
ciety that was culturally heterogeneous, composed of French-Canadians,
Europeans of various nationalities, Anglo-Americans, Dakota and
Euro-Dakota people. Daniels's description and assessment of the Yellow
Medicine society reflect attitudes typical among white Americans of the
nineteenth century who were startled to find themselves living in a com-

munity where people of various ethnicities and cultures interacted on more equal terms than the prejudices of "civilized" white society usually allowed.

> At the farmer's house there was a dance every two weeks that served for amusements as like could not have been witnessed in any city or country. Among the employees there were two Germans, one Irishman, and two Canadians with "fiddles." . . . For partners the dusky maidens of camp were bro't down with their mothers and taken back after the close. . . . The dining room was cleared for use, and put in order, with two lamps on brackets either side, and a table at the end on which the fiddler was perched. . . . Under the eyes of the chaperone, the farmer and his wife, these amusements were conducted with as much propriety as tho' they were all civilized people.[10]

Daniels also provides the only detailed description in the historical record of Daybreak Woman in her middle age. He depicts her as "educated," "pleasing," "interesting," and a good cook. Undoubtedly, Daniels thought his assessment highly complimentary for a mixed-ancestry woman; he makes clear that in a number of important ways, Daybreak Woman meets white society's standards for respectable womanhood.[11]

Several months after Jared Daniels arrived at the Yellow Medicine Agency, Daybreak Woman gave birth to her last child, Martha Catherine Robertson (Mattie). When baby Martha was born, Thomas was sixteen, Marion fifteen, Angus thirteen, Gustavus eleven, Frank nine, Sophie seven, and Willie five. Martha came into the world on the Minnesota River, just a few miles from where her mother was born.

While caring for all her children, Daybreak Woman also fed the twelve government laborers who worked at the agency. For this labor and her work as the housekeeper for the government farmer, Daybreak Woman earned $20 per month. By this time, Thomas was also able to contribute to the family income, working occasionally as a translator for Indian agent Charles Flandrau. Andrew, as government farmer at Yellow Medicine, earned $500 per year and was supervising thirty-one government employees at the agency, including Dr. Daniels, Mr. Ford, a sawyer, a miller, and two carpenters. These employees comprised six Germans, nine French-Canadians, five French-Dakota, a few Swiss immigrants from the Red River community at Pembina, an Irishman, and a Scotsman.[12]

In the winter of 1856, Charles Flandrau, the new Indian agent, set out from his headquarters at the Redwood Agency to visit Yellow Medicine for the first time. Jared Daniels's brother, Dr. Asa Daniels, the Redwood Agency physician, brought his wife and baby and accompanied Flandrau the thirty miles upriver. A blizzard hit just after they arrived, making it impossible to leave the Upper Sioux Agency for ten days. Their extensive visit provided an opportunity for both of the Daniels families, Flandrau, and the Robertsons to become well acquainted.

In his memoir, Flandrau dismisses Daybreak Woman, with a common derogatory reference to her as a Native woman. But he has much to say about Andrew, whom he found intriguing, entertaining, and a person one would not have expected to find on the Minnesota frontier in the 1850s.

> The upper agency was in charge of my chief farmer, a Scottish gentle-man by the name of Robertson. He was a mystery which I never unraveled,—a handsome, aristocratic, highly educated man about seventy years of age, with the manners of a Chesterfield. He had been in the Indian country for many years, had married a s——, and raised a numerous family of children, and had been in the employment of the government ever since the making of the treaties. I always thought he was once a man of fortune, who had dissipated it in some way, after traveling the world over, and had sought oblivion in the wilds of America.

While the blizzard raged, Flandrau says Andrew was creative and resource-ful in providing his guests with delicious dishes of exotic game day after day as they waited out the storm: "He gave us every day a dinner party composed of viands unknown outside the frontier of North America. One day we would have the tail of a beaver, always regarded as a delicacy of the border; the next, the paws of a bear soused.... Then again, roasted muskrat, which in the winter is as delicate as a young chicken; then fricas-seed skunk, which, in season is free from all offensive odor, and extremely delicate,—all served with *le riz sauvage* [wild rice]. In fact, he exhausted the resources of the county to make us happy." However, it was Daybreak Woman who was creative and resourceful—and did the work. She knew the recipes, processed the ingredients, and cooked or supervised the cook-ing of the dishes that Flandrau deemed delicious.[13]

Flandrau also praised Andrew for entertaining everyone by producing fiddlers for dancing and evening assemblies at which he would read Shakespeare and poetry by Robert Burns. He remembered his time with Andrew as "not only a delight, but an education. He had been everywhere, knew everything. He was charming in conversation and magnificent in hospitality."[14]

During these years one of the Yellow Medicine Agency's government employees, Alexander Hunter, a carpenter, also became close to the family— perhaps because, like Andrew Robertson, he was a Scots immigrant. Hunter nearly died in the winter of 1857 in a fierce blizzard. Flandrau describes the event in his report:

> Two of the teams belonging to the upper establishment were returning from St. Paul with provisions when they were overtaken by a storm between Redwood and Yellow Medicine, and the snow compelled them to camp at Patterson's Rapids. The storm continued the next day, and the men, fearful that the cattle would suffer, attempted to go through and drive the cattle before them, with the mail and their blankets tied upon their horns. They pushed on all day, but the fury of the storm bewildered them, and they wandered about all the night without knowing where they were. The next day, Sunday the 11th of February, Mr. Robertson, being apprehensive that something had happened, sent out a detachment to search for them and found one, Alexander Hunter, within three miles of the Yellow Medicine River very badly frozen and wandering about in a frantic condition. He was immediately cared for and the search continued for the other man, who was found a mile or two from there in a state of exhaustion, and also very badly frozen.

Soon after the men were rescued it became apparent that their severe frostbite made amputations necessary to save them from gangrene. Jared and Asa Daniels operated on the men together. The Danielses amputated all of Hunter's toes, which made it very difficult for him to walk and impossible for him to run, but he survived the ordeal.[15]

Although his official position was government farmer, Andrew Robertson effectively acted as a subagent at Yellow Medicine under Flandrau, who seems to have rarely visited the Upper Sioux Reservation, preferring to direct affairs from the Redwood Agency. The two men frequently corresponded. John Mooers and others, including Little Crow, often carried correspondence between the two agencies. On at least one occasion,

Flandrau entrusted Mooers with carrying the entire cash payroll from Redwood to Yellow Medicine so that Andrew could pay the agency employees. Andrew reported regularly on developments and events at Yellow Medicine, provided information about his own supervision of work at the agency, requested funds, provisions, and equipment of the agent, and supervised and recorded the payment of annuities to the Upper Sioux Reservation bands. He also acted as an intermediary between the Dakota people and Flandrau, reporting to the agent their concerns, complaints, and mindset. In November 1856, Andrew reported ominously what his Dakota contacts were telling him: "The son of the chief of this village came in yesterday from the Big Woods part of the Minnesota River. He reports the whole country filled with white people. He also states that near Long Lake he thinks they are within the reservation."[16]

Although his band lived at the Redwood Agency, Little Crow had many relatives and friends at Yellow Medicine. Correspondence from 1857 reveals that he visited the Upper Agency frequently. Moreover, the Robertsons and the Williamsons were his friends from Kap'oja. Little Crow relied on Andrew to relay his requests to the Indian agent, as revealed in Andrew's letter of April 1857 to Flandrau: "I anticipated your wishes about Crow's sick wife—she has already had whatever was proper for her and will now have more according to your order, of which I apprised Crow. He expressed great disappointment that the letter did not contain an order of slaughter of an ox for him."[17]

The Euro-American population boom in Minnesota Territory started after the 1851 treaties and accelerated swiftly in 1855. Even before the treaties were finally ratified by the US Senate in the fall of 1852, at least five thousand white squatters had poured into the Dakota homeland west of the Mississippi River. After the treaties were finally ratified, the land taken from the Santee Dakota was still not legally open to settlement, for under federal preemption law the land could not be legally occupied or claimed until it had been officially surveyed. Nevertheless, Euro-American settler-colonists continued to flood in, settling illegally on unsurveyed public lands. In August 1854, at the urging of Minnesota officials, Congress passed a law to allow squatters in Minnesota the privilege of preemption. This set off a land boom. Between 1854 and 1857, the white population of Minnesota Territory jumped from 32,000 to over 150,000. The Minnesota River acted as the main navigable artery of colonization, facilitating the immigration of settler-colonists into the region as well as commercial development. Steamboats plied the river continuously; as many as 292 moved up and down the Minnesota in 1857 alone.[18]

In 1854, the Robertsons gained the means to acquire some land for themselves. That year, the US Congress finally approved legislation that allowed the mixed-ancestry relatives of Bdewakaŋtuŋwaŋ Dakota to claim their share of the Lake Pepin reservation created by the Treaty of 1830. The law allowed for payments in government "scrip," or vouchers, which could be used to purchase public land anywhere. Over the course of 1856 and 1857, Andrew and Daybreak Woman worked to establish her claim and those of her children to the government scrip. In 1856, Andrew's sworn statement was entered on the US government's "Mixed-Blood Claimants Roll," legally documenting Daybreak Woman's Bdewakaŋtuŋwaŋ heritage and that of each of their children to establish their entitlement to the scrip. Obtaining this would prove vital to the Robertson family's future financial security.[19]

Redwood Agency

In 1857 Joseph R. Brown replaced Charles Flandrau as the Indian agent assigned to the reservation. Brown, the Robertsons' former neighbor on Grey Cloud Island, wanted to open the government schools that had been promised in the 1851 treaties but were not yet established. He appointed Andrew superintendent of schools for both reservations, a position that paid better than government farmer and would allow the family to move downriver to the Redwood Agency. Andrew was anxious to move the family to Redwood for greater security after conflicts between one Dakota band and settler-colonists in southern Minnesota earlier that year had led to killings on both sides.

The Spirit Lake Massacre, as it came to be called by whites, was not one event, but a series of violent clashes between settler-colonists and a band of Dakota led by Iŋkpaduta. They had refused to sign on to the 1851 treaties and to live on the reservations, continuing to subsist as they always had in southern Minnesota. During the course of the conflict, a small group of Iŋkpaduta's band took some settler-colonists captive. Abby Gardner, one of the white women taken, was rescued by some Dakota men from the Upper Sioux Reservation. They brought her to the Yellow Medicine Agency, where Daybreak Woman took care of her. When she recovered, Andrew, Thomas, and Paul Maza Kute Mani (known as Little Paul), the

Dakota man mainly responsible for her rescue, accompanied her to St. Paul. The Robertsons' personal connection to Gardner, whose captivity and rescue became a well-known story across the state, undoubtedly increased Andrew's anxiety about the family's safety at Yellow Medicine, which was remote from white communities and Fort Ridgely. Andrew decided that the Williamsons' Pajutazee mission, where his and Daybreak Woman's daughter Sophie was boarding, was too isolated and insecure. Jane Williamson recalled, "When the sad news of the Spirit Lake Massacre reached us, her [Sophie Robertson's] father took her home, saying the mission was on the frontier and without defense."[20]

In the fall of 1857, Daybreak Woman and her family left the Yellow Medicine Agency and moved to the Redwood Agency. There, as at Kap'oja and Yellow Medicine, Daybreak Woman, Andrew, and their oldest children were dependent almost entirely on the government for their livelihood. As the school superintendent, Andrew taught the first government school at Yellow Medicine in 1857–58. Daybreak Woman, Thomas, and Angus were appointed as teachers in the government school at Redwood. As bilingual people, the Robertsons were well positioned to teach their Dakota pupils; they followed the Williamsons' teaching model, which was to instruct students to read and write in Dakota first before teaching them English. Instruction in other subjects, such as arithmetic, would have been in Dakota as well. All of Daybreak Woman's children were not only bilingual but literate in both languages. Over the next five years, her sons held jobs as government interpreters, clerks, and assistants, and her daughter Marion would marry one of the agency carpenters. In addition to teaching at the government school, Thomas found employment at trader Alexis Bailly's store.[21]

At Redwood, the Robertsons' house was located on the council square, where about fourteen agency buildings were clustered around a common green. These included the doctor's house, where Asa Daniels lived. Also on the square were the agency office and warehouse; the carpenter and blacksmith shops and the houses for the carpenters, the blacksmiths, and their families; a boardinghouse; government workers' quarters; the home of the government farmer and interpreter; and several other houses. Next door to the Robertsons was the home of the Campbell family.[22]

The Campbells had been neighbors of the Robertsons at Kap'oja, and the first generation of Campbells, Archibald and Nince, had been neighbors of the Airds at Prairie du Chien. Joe (Antoine Joseph) Campbell, grandson of Archibald and the oldest son of Scott Campbell, took over the care of his mother and his younger siblings after his father died in 1850. The entire family moved to the Lower Sioux Reservation. There, Joe's wife, Mary Anne Dalton, ran a boardinghouse, and Joe and two of his brothers worked for Andrew Myrick at his trading post. By the late 1850s, Joe's four younger brothers had all married Dakota or Euro-Dakota women and were living near the Redwood Agency. The Campbell family was large: Joe, Mary Anne, seven children, Margaret Campbell (Joe's mother), three of Joe's brothers, a Dakota sister-in-law, and her two children.[23]

Also living in the council square were Philander Prescott, his Dakota wife, Naġi Owiŋna (Spirit of the Moon or Mary Keeiyah), and their three youngest children, Lawrence, Julia, and Sophia. Philander and Naġi Owiŋna had been married thirty-five years and had two grown, married children who were living on their old homestead in what would become the city of Minneapolis. Prescott had long been associated with the Bde-wakaŋtuŋwaŋ Dakota, having worked as a trader, government farmer, and interpreter in various Dakota villages since the 1820s. He had been superintendent of government farming at the Redwood Agency since 1853. The Prescotts lived just a few houses away from the Robertsons, and the two families became close at Redwood.[24]

Another Euro-Dakota family, the Faribaults, lived about two miles from the agency. David Faribault was the son of Jean Baptiste Faribault and a French-Dakota woman, Pelagie, who, like the Campbells, had been neighbors of Daybreak Woman's grandparents in Prairie du Chien. Nancy McClure Faribault was the daughter of an American army officer, Lieutenant McClure, and Winona, the daughter of Walking Shooting Iron (Maza Kute Mani). After McClure died, Winona married Antoine Renville, the son of Joseph Renville. Nancy lived with her mother and Renville for ten years at Lac qui Parle and attended Williamsons' and Riggses' mission schools there in the 1840s. After her mother died, Nancy married David during the 1851 treaty negotiations at Traverse des Sioux. They had a farm at Redwood and traded with the Dakota bands on the reservation.[25]

Celia Campbell Stay, Joe Campbell's daughter, remembered the Redwood Agency community as it was in 1862:

> Lower Sioux Agency was a neat little village built on top of the hill twelve miles west of Fort Ridgely. . . . A belt of timber [was] on one side facing the river and on the other prairie. The [Indian] Department

buildings were all commodious and painted white—four buildings—
one was boarding house run by old Joe and his wife—four rooms—
housed German cooks, hired men and hired girls.

Opposite and a little below was John Nairn's carpenter shop; a few
yards up the road was a warehouse or granary combined, next the
house we lived in, further up another where a carpenter's family [the
Nairns] lived at one end, Robertson's at the other end, opposite was
Dr. [Jared] Daniels' cottage just built and next going down the road
again was the other and last white house where the doctor [Philander
Humphrey] lived, back of them was a hewed log stable, a ravine ran
along ending just north of the boarding house, there was two root
houses and an ice house on its north side and a fine spring enclosed,
to the north was LaBathe's store and kitchen, all log cabins, next
Myrick's new frame store, kitchen and stables and ice house; across
from the ravine a few rods was Louis Roberts' stores, a log one and a
frame one, log kitchen and stables, going east of there a road took past

The stone warehouse built at Lower Sioux Agency in 1861, as it looked in 1897.
Photograph by Edward A. Bromley, Minnesota Historical Society collections

Robinettes log house, then Petit Jeanis boarding house, opposite was
Forbes store and new kitchen.[26]

As Joseph R. Brown was now the Indian agent for the reservations, his
family was also living at Redwood. The Browns and Robertsons were once
again neighbors and became closely associated, as they had been on Grey
Cloud Island twenty years earlier. A number of the Brown and Robertson
children developed close friendships, including Frank Robertson and
Samuel Brown, who in the early 1860s were classmates at the Seabury Mission Episcopal School for boys in Faribault. The younger children in both
families were of the same age and played together, and Daybreak Woman
and Susan Frenier Brown renewed their friendship. The Robertsons' close
association with the Browns was important to the economic security of
Daybreak Woman's family during these years, because they could rely on
Joseph Brown to employ them. The relationship of the two families would
become even more consequential in later decades as a result of the intermarriage of four of the Robertson and Brown children.[27]

When the Robertsons moved down to Redwood in 1857, there were
forty-five Dakota families living in houses with small agricultural plots
and many also had stables. By 1862, there were nearly two hundred brick,
frame, and log houses spread along the bluffs of the Minnesota River from
ten miles above the Redwood Agency to almost ten miles below. Most of
the Bdewakaŋtuŋwaŋ Dakota congregated in six villages on the Lower
Sioux Reservation. Shakopee's band lived just north of Redwood River;
those of Little Crow, Big Eagle, and Mankato lived south of the Redwood
River (a few miles north of the agency); Travelling Hail's band was closest
to the agency; and the Wapaha Ṡa and Wakute bands lived just downriver.
Wapaha Ṡa III (Joseph Wabasha) was born about 1800 near Winona on
the Mississippi River. His father, Wapaha Ṡa II, was Daybreak Woman's
great-grandfather. Wapaha Ṡa had opposed the treaty of 1851, but once
he reluctantly moved his band to the new reservation he encouraged his
people to become farmers and Christians.[28]

Until the late 1850s, when large numbers of settler-colonists began
to take up land in the country surrounding the Minnesota River reservation, many Dakota on the Lower Sioux Reservation maintained their
traditional lifestyle, moving freely throughout the countryside to hunt
and gather and living only part of the year on the reservation. Sometimes
there was still good hunting in the Big Woods, located to the northeast

of the reservation. However, in the 1850s, those who lived by hunting and gathering increasingly came to depend also on the food cultivated on the reservation farms as game and wild food resources, already diminished prior to the treaties, were rapidly depleted. As a result of an increasing shortage of game and other wild food resources, conflicts occasionally developed between hunters and farmers. Those bands that continued to rely primarily on hunting and gathering for subsistence expected the farming bands to share their food with them, in keeping with traditional Dakota ways—to be good relatives. Occasionally, if food was not freely given, they took it, raiding the reservation farm fields. In July 1855, a small number of hunters, desperate to feed their hungry children, broke into the Redwood Agency warehouse and took the food stores.[29]

When Brown became Indian agent in October 1857, he was determined to turn more Dakota men into successful individual farmers. Previous agents had allowed the people to work the fields communally: each band had its own field, and the women cultivated and tended the crops of corn, beans, squash, and potatoes. The bands themselves decided how the food was allotted. Brown planned to move the bands on the lower reservation away from this traditional practice. Agency carpenter John Nairn said this plan was generally "not favored" by most of the Dakota, as it was fundamentally contrary to their culture. Brown obtained substantial government funds for his ambitious agricultural acculturation project. He used the funds to pay individuals directly in cash for their labor on the reservation, paying men to construct houses and other buildings. He also paid men to farm as individuals, and the opportunity to earn cash income persuaded a number to adopt this model.[30]

Brown had been engaged in economic, social, and personal relationships with the Santee Dakota since the 1820s, including his marriage to Susan, and he was sincerely convinced that his farming plan would benefit them. He thought the Dakota people could peacefully coexist with whites only if their communal ownership of the land ceased and they gave up hunting and gathering as means of subsistence. Like most government officials in the Indian agency service of his own time and long after, Brown thought it necessary to destroy Native culture in order to save Native people.[31]

Brown was also, like most Indian agents and other government appointees in the US Indian service, corrupt in his dealings, using the office to line his own pocket. Indeed, it was openly acknowledged at the time

that a job in the Indian service was a lucrative windfall, allowing appointees ample opportunities for embezzlement and fraud as a means to gar-
ner wealth. In 1861, complaints about Brown's corruption as well as that
of his successor, Thomas Galbraith, and other Republican appointees, including Clark Thompson, the superintendent of Indian Affairs for Minnesota, prompted a congressional investigation. In his report, the federal
investigator claimed that Brown had "committed numerous frauds and vi-
olations of the law" as agent. Evidence that he had skimmed a substantial
amount of funds as agent existed at Sacred Heart Creek, near the Upper
Agency, where by spring of 1861 he had built a large stone mansion for
Susan and their children with very expensive furnishings. Although his
salary during the four years he was agent was only $1,500 per year, Brown's
mansion cost $18,000 to build.[32]

The Treaty of 1858

The Spirit Lake conflict of 1857 spurred calls from whites for the removal
of all Dakota people from Minnesota. Meanwhile, other whites were
scheming to convince the Dakota to give up some of their reservation land.
Agent Brown reasoned that giving up some reservation land and turning
to individual ownership would enable Dakota people to stay where they
were; he argued that they needed another treaty to protect them from
removal since the reservations were not legally guaranteed under the 1851
treaties—the Dakota held lands only "at the president's pleasure." Brown
saw a new treaty as a means of forcing more rapid acculturation, but also
as a way to protect Dakota people from those who were calling for their
complete removal. Brown was serving his own interests in the matter as
well—he and others, including his predecessor, Flandrau, hoped to make
money from land speculation when new tracts were opened for purchase.
Also eager for a new treaty were the traders at Redwood, who wanted
Dakota debts to them paid out of treaty funds, as they had been in 1851.[33]

Brown and the superintendent of Indian Affairs in Minnesota at the
time, William Cullen, hatched a plan to take the older Dakota leaders and
those who were less resistant to acculturation on a trip to Washington to
meet with Indian Commissioner Charles Mix. Brown and Cullen never
suggested that a land cession would be an issue; rather, to Dakota leaders
they presented the Washington meeting as an opportunity to talk to the
government about its failure to fulfill the 1851 treaty promises and perhaps adjust them to the benefit of the Dakota people. The delegation of

Dakota leaders from both agencies thought they were going to get annuity payments still due to them under the 1837 and 1851 treaties; they also intended to present grievances about the late payments and about the poor quality and inadequate nature of provisions and supplies distributed on the reservation. Little Crow in particular prepared carefully for the meeting, creating a list of specific grievances and unpaid debts he planned to negotiate with the government.[34]

Agent Brown, his son Nathaniel, and Andrew and Thomas Robertson were among the delegation of whites and Euro-Dakota people who accompanied Little Crow and twenty-four other Dakota leaders to Washington, DC. In March 1858, they left the Redwood Agency, traveling first by sleigh, then by wagons and trains. The delegation was away through April, May, and June, returning via New York City. Andrew and Thomas took the Dakota delegation for a cruise on the Potomac River. Andrew also purchased (with government funds) clothing, combs, handkerchiefs, mittens, socks, cloth for leggings, shirts, blankets, moccasins, and a buffalo robe for the Dakota. Altogether the delegation spent three months in Washington and some time at the end of the trip in New York City sightseeing, going to theaters, enjoying the nightlife (saloons and restaurants), meeting dignitaries, and having photographs taken.[35]

The negotiations with the government did not go well for the Dakota representatives, and the treaty that resulted proved disastrous. The Dakota leaders entered the initial meeting with the commissioner thinking they were there to present their grievances and demand more from the government, but they were stymied and outmaneuvered over the course of a series of meetings that stretched out over several months. Eventually, after much delay, Commissioner Mix told the Dakota representatives that he expected them to sign away half their reservation lands. He mostly dismissed their grievances and the other issues they hoped to discuss. Mix stunned the Dakota leaders by telling them they did not have any legal right to their reservation lands and that they were only allowed to live on them because of the generosity of the president of the United States, their "Great Father." When Little Crow protested that they had been promised in the treaty that they could have their reservations forever, Mix showed them a copy of the amended 1851 treaty, pointing to the pertinent provisions that decreed the reservation as only existing at the pleasure of the president. A new treaty, he promised, would give the Dakota people permanent right to their remaining lands southwest of the Minnesota River,

Treaty delegation to Washington, DC, 1858. Standing: Joseph R. Brown, Antoine Joseph (Joe) Campbell, Caŋhpi Yuha (Has a War Club), Andrew Robertson, Hiŋhaŋ Duta (Red Owl), Thomas A. Robertson, Nathaniel R. Brown. Seated: Maŋkato, Wapaha Ṡa III, Henry Belland. *Photograph by Charles DeForest Fredericks, Minnesota Historical Society collections*

allotted individually in eighty-acre plots. In addition, they would be paid for ceded land (which Mix pointed out they did not really own anyway). If they did not agree, Mix suggested that the state of Minnesota could legally claim the land. It became clear very quickly that not only would the Dakota negotiators not be able to have their grievances addressed, but they were being forced to agree to the loss of more land.[36]

Little Crow, angry and frustrated by the government's manipulation and demands—especially Mix's claim that the Dakota people did not really own the reservation land under the 1851 treaty—responded by saying, "We had, we supposed, made a complete treaty, and we were promised a great many things, horses, cattle, flour, plows, and farming utensils, but now it appears the wind blows it all off and that we got words and nothing else." The only benefit to the Dakota, from Little Crow's point of view, was that money for the ceded lands would pay their debts and enable them to buy provisions. But the Dakota people were not even given a set price for their ceded lands; instead, they were told to wait to see what Congress decided to give them. They waited some time; the Senate did not ratify the 1858 treaty until March 1859 and waited until 1860 to designate a price for the land cession. In the end, the Dakota people themselves got very little. The government paid them only $267,000 (thirty cents per acre, which was only about one-twentieth of its worth), and almost all of this money went to pay trader debts.[37]

Not surprisingly, when Little Crow returned from Washington, he was not popular with many of his people on the reservation, for they had expected him to resolve existing grievances, not lose half of their land. Some angry young warriors talked of assassination, and Joseph R. Brown reported from the Lower Agency that Little Crow and the rest of the treaty delegation were "being accused of having spoken falsely to their young men." According to Big Eagle, Little Crow was always blamed for the part he took in the loss of half the reservation. Big Eagle recalled later:

> In 1858 the ten miles of this strip belonging to the Mdewakanton and the Wacouta [Waȟpekute] bands, and lying north of the river were sold, mainly through the influence of Little Crow. That year, with some other chiefs, I went to Washington on business connected with the treaty. The selling of that strip north of the Minnesota caused great dissatisfaction among the Sioux, and Little Crow was always blamed for the part he took in the sale. It caused us all to move to the south side of the river, where there was very little game, and many of our people, under the treaty, were induced to give up the old life and go to work like white men, which was very distasteful to many.

The treaty delegation returned to Minnesota in early July 1858. At Redwood, rapid changes had been taking place under Brown's acculturation plan. By the fall of 1858, more than forty-five frame houses had been erected, and most of these would be replaced by brick houses over the next two years. Dakota men cut lumber and did most of the construction. Brown also had a crew working along the Minnesota River, staking off individual land claims to be allotted to individuals, and the same work was underway at Yellow Medicine. By 1859, Brown had nearly doubled the amount of land cultivated, and farmers were harvesting large corn and potato crops. A growing number of Dakota men at Redwood were dressing like whites, cutting their hair, and pledging not to drink liquor. Brown rewarded these farmers by giving each two pairs of pants, two coats, two shirts, a yoke of oxen, and a cow. These gifts convinced others, and by 1859, more than two hundred men had joined the "pantaloons band," including leaders Wabasha, Mankato, and Wakute, who all lived in brick houses on small farms of two to three acres by 1860. Also by 1860, more than four hundred Bdewakaŋtuŋwaŋ and Waȟpekute, one-sixth of those living on the Lower Sioux Reservation, had become farmers; that year they harvested sixty thousand bushels of corn and twenty thousand bushels of potatoes.[38]

This rapid acculturation of some at Redwood was socially divisive, as those who continued to live a traditional Dakota lifestyle were angry that Brown denied them goods and provisions in favor of the farmers. Later, Big Eagle claimed the intratribal conflict generated at Redwood as a result of Brown's aggressive acculturation policies and focus on economic individualism was a major factor in influencing some traditionalists to turn to violence in 1862: "The farmers were favored by the government in every way. They had houses built for them, some of them even had brick houses, and they were not allowed to suffer. The other Indians did not like this. They were envious and jealous, and disliked them because they were favored. They called them 'farmers,' as if it was disgraceful to be a farmer. They called them 'cut-hairs,' because they had given up the Indian fashion of wearing the hair, and 'breeches men,' because they wore pantaloons."[39]

Heretofore Dakota men had proved their manhood as warriors and hunters; farming was seen as women's work and therefore not masculine. Many of the younger warriors disdained the farmers, whom they viewed as craven capitulators to white values and lifestyle. They despised them for selling their corn and potatoes to the government instead of sharing them with all those in need, violating Dakota values. Some of the young warriors began harassing the farmers, destroying their crops and killing their livestock. They extended this same harassment to the settler-colonists, who by the late 1850s were living in the vicinity of the reservation. Some traditionalists also became more hostile toward the Euro-Dakota in their midst, whom they now increasingly reviled as models and perpetrators of acculturation. Some of the younger men began forming soldiers' lodges to challenge the authority of some of the older leaders, whom they saw as too accommodating to white ways.[40]

In fact, most reservation farmers did not abandon their Dakota identities, values, or spiritual beliefs. Most who adopted farming did so out of economic necessity forced upon them by the treaties of 1851 and 1858, which made it impossible to survive on the reservation by traditional means. Moreover, by the late 1850s, the hunting grounds off the reservation were rapidly diminishing as newly established farms destroyed habitat. Hunger and starvation were real problems on the reservations by the mid-1850s, even when annuities and provisions were paid on time, in full, and unspoiled, and even when hunters could find game in the vicinity. For most of the Dakota farmers, adopting white agricultural practices as a means of survival did not alter their core identities or change their fundamental beliefs and values as Dakota people. While some of the farmers were Christian, most were not; Christian Dakota constituted a very small minority on the reservation. Although missionaries had been active among the Santee Dakota since the 1830s, their efforts had resulted in relatively few converts.

Among the people on the Lower Sioux Reservation, members of the bands led by Wapaha Śa, Wakute, Mankato, Little Crow, and Passing Hail were more likely than others to adopt farming as a primary means of subsistence. Wapaha Śa, Wakute, and Mankato also cut their hair and wore white clothing. Big Eagle joined the farmer band at Redwood in 1858 and conformed to some white ways, including wearing some white clothing, although he did so reluctantly, seeing it as a necessary means of economic survival. The bands most resistant to acculturation and farming included Shakopee's Bdewakaŋtuŋwaŋ band and the Waḣpekute band led by Red Legs.[41]

Little Crow encouraged farming among his own band but did not encourage changes that threatened to undermine Dakota traditional beliefs or values. After he returned to Redwood from Washington, he moved into a two-story log house and had government farmers break twelve acres for his four wives to cultivate. He refused to cut his hair, and the way he dressed varied according to audience and situation. He was friendly with the missionaries and sometimes attended their church services but did not give up his Dakota spiritual beliefs and rituals. Although he understood English, he did not speak it in public. However, at Kap'oja and at Redwood, he advocated education for Dakota children so they could position themselves successfully in the new society created by Euro-American colonialism.[42]

By the late 1850s, there were increasing conflicts between the Dakota bands living on the Lower Sioux Reservation and their white neighbors.

More and more settler-colonists were claiming land along the southern border of the reservation, and very few of them got along with their Dakota neighbors. Large numbers of Germans came into Minnesota starting in the mid-1850s, and many of them took land in the Minnesota River Valley. German immigrants tended to form tight communities, speaking German and keeping to themselves. Not only did they have no knowledge or understanding of the Dakota people, they tended to be suspicious of all Native people.

Many Dakota people came to dislike their German neighbors in particular because they rejected Dakota norms of hospitality and reciprocity. To their Dakota neighbors, the German farmers embodied the immediate threat that white colonization posed to their way of life, as the immigrants' homesteads sat on Dakota hunting grounds. Some came to despise the settler-colonists because they had taken the land and run off the game— and were unwilling to share what they had with others. That they were unwilling to share food when people were hungry was a particular affront to Dakota values. To many, the settler-colonists were intruders and aliens; they despised them, too, because they were farmers. The Dakota word *ia śica*, meaning bad speakers or bad language, was coined at this time, used derogatively in reference to the way these immigrants spoke.[43]

In the summer of 1858, the Dakota on the Lower Sioux Reservation became enraged when the northeast bank of the Minnesota River opened to settlement—before they had received payment for the sale of the land and before Congress ratified the treaty. The land office in Henderson registered the patents of a dozen German settler-colonists who took land on Beaver Creek, just across the river from Shakopee's village. The Dakota tried to drive them out, and by the spring of 1859, the commander at Fort Ridgely received a deluge of complaints from all sides: settler-colonists, Dakotas, and government employees. Initially, authorities decided to evict the settler-colonists, but they appealed to politician Henry Rice. He stopped it. After that, hundreds of whites flocked to the area, and by March 1860, five hundred families had taken land along and near the Minnesota River across from the lower reservation. The Big Woods to the east were also filling up; by 1860, cabins and fields were evident from the trails the Dakota took that led to their hunting grounds.[44]

With the loss of half of the Minnesota River reservation after 1858, most Dakota people became even more economically dependent on the government and were increasingly reduced to desperate poverty. This vulnerability gave the white men on the reservation more opportunity to sexually exploit Dakota women to an extent that had not occurred previously. By the late 1850s, government employees and soldiers stationed at Fort Ridgely were frequently "buying" Dakota women by the day for sex. Traders and other government employees used their positions and access to provisions and material goods to sexually exploit poor Dakota women continuously. The most notorious men at Redwood were James Lynd, a trader, and James Manger, the Redwood superintendent of farming, who used his power over distribution of goods to obtain sexual favors from the desperately poor (and whom Little Crow included in his list of grievances to Mix at the 1858 treaty negotiations).[45]

As the economic security of many Dakota people on the reservation deteriorated after 1858, the Robertsons had the security of government employment as well as government housing at the Redwood Agency. By the late 1850s, they were sharing half of their large house on the council square with the Scots immigrant John Nairn, his wife, Magdelene, and their young children. Nairn was the head carpenter at the agency and a close friend of Alexander Hunter, the young man whom the Robertsons had befriended at Yellow Medicine. Hunter followed the Robertsons to Redwood, where he continued to work as a reservation carpenter. During these years, he and Marion Robertson, who turned eighteen in 1858, were developing a closer relationship; they would later marry. Frank, who was twelve in 1858, attended a boys preparatory school one hundred miles to the southeast in Faribault. Daybreak Woman ran the full household, which included three children under age ten: Sophie, Willie, and Mattie.[46]

One month after home returning from Washington in 1858, Andrew and Thomas were off again on another government-sponsored excursion. That August, Special Indian Agent Pritchette came from Washington to travel to the James River in Dakota Territory to negotiate a treaty with the Drifting Goose band of Ihaŋktuŋwaŋna. Andrew, Thomas, and William Quinn (the government interpreter), as well as two Dakota guides, accompanied Pritchette to South Dakota. Thomas later remembered that Pritchette, who had no experience with the Dakota people, was "quick tempered and [of] an arbitrary turn of mind." He quickly got himself into trouble with the Yanktonai, trying to "bulldoze this small band into whatever he wanted to have done." Andrew, "seeing the way matters were drifting, and knowing well the disposition of the Indians," kept himself apart from the escalating confrontation, sitting on a rock some distance away from the council grounds. When the Dakota men took the party's horses and threatened to do worse, Pritchette ran to Andrew for help, but he refused, suggesting that Thomas might be able to restore calm. Thomas took gifts to the Dakota men and sat down with them, telling them he was part Dakota himself and his grandmother was Grey Cloud Woman, who had kept a trading post on the east side of Lake Traverse with her husband, an Englishman. They remembered her right away and remembered that she had kept many of them from starving to death during a winter of famine, and some of them claimed to be related to her. "The Old Chief then told the young men to let the horses go, as everything was all right."[47]

Andrew Robertson's Death

Daybreak Woman lost her husband of twenty-three years on May 11, 1859, when Andrew died of massive heart failure at the Redwood Agency. Just as marrying him had marked a significant crossroads in her life, so did his death. From all accounts, Andrew was a kind, generous, intelligent, knowledgeable, interesting, gregarious, and affable man who was admired and respected by Dakota people and whites alike. The emotional void created by his death must have loomed large for Daybreak Woman and their children. Also devastating for Daybreak Woman was the loss of her economic partner; she was now a widow with eight children ranging in age from four to twenty. She and Andrew had worked hard together to provide for their large family. For over a decade, Andrew's government employment at Kap'oja, Yellow Medicine, and Redwood had provided the family's stable financial base. Now that was gone.

Fortunately for the Robertsons, their old family friend Joseph R. Brown was still the Indian agent. Brown, sympathetic to her financial predicament, appointed Daybreak Woman superintendent of schools after Andrew died, which provided a short-term continuance of the salary the family depended on. She and Angus taught for a year in the agency schools. Thomas continued to work in Alexis Bailly's store at the agency, but when that job ended in 1860, he taught school for about six months. However, the family's economic future remained uncertain. As long as Brown was agent, they knew they could have work as government employees and could continue to live in the house on the council square, but Brown was a political appointee, and there was no guarantee that he would stay in his position or that the next agent would employ them.[48]

In his report of September 1859, Brown wrote of Andrew's death and its impacts on the agency:

In the death of Mr. Robertson, not only the school, but the cause of education, has suffered a loss that is truly irreparable. His removal has created a void that never can be filled, and the cause of education has lost a friend whose absence will be long felt by all connected with educational progress among the Sioux. After the death of Mr. Robertson, his school was necessarily closed temporarily; but it has again opened, under the control of Mrs. Robertson, his widow, assisted by her son Angus, and is now attended by an average of about twelve to fourteen scholars. . . . A good schoolhouse is also being erected at Wakutes' village for the accommodation of the bands of Red Legs, Wabashaw and Wakute. This school will be under the direction of Thomas A. Robertson, who, from the experience he obtained in the school of his father, is well fitted for the duties he has assumed.[49]

Andrew Robertson's grave at the Redwood Agency sits a short distance from the council square house where the family lived. The gravestone, a long, flat slab of white marble, was sent from New York via steamboat up the Minnesota River in 1860. Andrew was a Freemason; he must have joined the New York lodge of the secret society when he lived there for three years in the 1830s. The monument reads, "Sacred to the Memory of Andrew Robertson, Superintendent of Indian Schools, Born in Dumfries Scotland, December 6th, 1790, Died May 11th, 1859, Aged 68 years, 5 months and 5 days."[50]

Daybreak Woman was fortunate in having several adult and young adult children who were old enough to work and contribute to supporting the family. For the next decade, she and her older children worked to sustain each other and the youngest Robertsons.

5. Minnesota River, 1860–August 17, 1862

Beaver Creek, Redwood Agency

It was, as it were, a spark thrown into a pile of highly combustible matter, caused by the tardiness of—to put it mildly—government officials in carrying out solemnly pledged treaty stipulations and frauds perpetrated in connivance with some of the Indian traders.

THOMAS ROBERTSON

After her husband died, Daybreak Woman struggled mightily to support herself and her children, having lost the economic security she had known as a daughter in her father's household and then as Andrew's wife. Her economic struggle was typical of the vast majority of widows in the United States in the nineteenth century, most of whom lived in poverty unless they were supported by the men in their families. The American socioeconomic system made it very difficult for single women, whether never married or widowed, to support themselves and live independently. They were restricted to a handful of "female professions" that paid such low wages that most women could not earn enough income to maintain a minimal standard of independent living. Widows with children were the most disadvantaged in this patriarchal system, for they needed to earn more money than single women, yet employers usually preferred to hire younger women without children. Most widows, as well as married women with children who also needed wages, had to earn income in their homes, as seamstresses or laundresses or by taking in boarders.[1]

Although in 1860 she was a fifty-year-old widow with many children to support, Daybreak Woman was not without resources. Her four eldest were young adults (Thomas, twenty-one; Marion, twenty; Angus, eighteen; and Gustavus, sixteen) who could contribute to the family's subsistence. After Andrew's death, Thomas seems to have stepped into his father's shoes and acted as the patriarch of the family, partnering with his mother in making decisions for the family's future. They realized that to ensure their economic stability and future prospects, they needed to begin farming on their own land. The Robertsons were also fortunate that they could claim land using some of the 1830 treaty scrip they had obtained before Andrew's death. Records show that they claimed land with the scrip in the names of three of the children (Thomas, Sophie, and Martha), a total of 360 acres. The family moved onto the quarter section of land (forty acres) claimed in Sophie's name at the mouth of Beaver Creek. There they built a new home. That same year, Daybreak Woman agreed to allow Thomas Williamson to become Sophie's legal guardian, and Sophie, at eleven years old, moved back to live with the Williamsons at Yellow Medicine not long after the family moved to their new home at Beaver Creek.[2]

Beaver Creek

After the Treaty of 1858, former reservation lands on the north side of the river were opened to white settlement. Upriver from the Redwood Agency, a number of creeks flow into the Minnesota River from the north, and into these valleys settler-colonists came, built houses, and established farms. The valley closest to the Redwood Agency, less than one mile upstream, is Birch Coulee. Another four miles upriver is Beaver Creek. Along the south side of the river, between the Redwood Agency and Beaver Creek, ranged the villages of Mankato, Little Crow, and Big Eagle. The Robertsons' new home was located on Beaver Creek, close to its junction with the Minnesota River. The house sat up on the creek bluff, and it was the first in the creek valley coming up from the river. The rest of Beaver Creek's residents were settler-colonists—some European immigrants, others Euro-American migrants—strung farther up the valley along both sides of the creek. Daybreak Woman's stepbrother John Mooers, his wife, Rosalie, and their five children lived on the reservation, less than two miles from the Robertsons, near the mouth of the Redwood River.[3]

Dakota people who lived across the river were often in the Beaver Creek settlement visiting, trading, or borrowing tools, livestock, or guns from residents. Helen Carrothers, a young wife and mother and the Robertsons' nearest neighbor, had a particularly good relationship with some of these visitors. She spoke some Dakota and learned about Dakota traditions. She was also hospitable, often sharing food with Dakota neighbors who visited her frequently. One of the medicine men taught her some of what he knew about the healing properties of roots, herbs, and barks. Un-like Helen Carrothers, however, most of the Beaver Creek settler-colonists did not learn to speak Dakota. As a result, the Robertsons were interme-diaries between the white and Indigenous communities. For instance, in 1862, Little Crow asked Thomas to act as his translator for a negotiation with one settler for two cows. The leader traded for the cows on the prom-ise of the annuity money that was soon to come, providing two shotguns as collateral.[4]

From 1860 to August 1862, Daybreak Woman and her children worked together farming and raising livestock on their land at Beaver Creek. Thomas worked as an interpreter for the government, and Angus and Gustavus likely also found occasional work at the agency as interpret-ers, laborers, or clerks. By the summer of 1862, Frank was working as a government clerk. Daybreak Woman's two oldest children married in the first two years after they moved to Beaver Creek. Thomas and his wife, a Dakota woman named Niya Wašte Wiŋ, lived with the family at Beaver Creek. Marion wed Alexander Hunter in July 1862 at the Merchants Hotel in St. Paul, and the couple lived in Alexander's house at the agency, where he worked as an assistant carpenter.[5]

In 1860, the same year Daybreak Woman moved to Beaver Creek, Sam-uel Hinman, an Episcopal missionary, arrived at the Redwood Agency to establish a mission. Hinman was not yet fluent in Dakota, so he employed Thomas as his interpreter. Between 1860 and 1862, Hinman worked diligently to bring both the Dakota on the reservation and the nearby settler-colonists into his church. He was buttressed in his efforts by the regular visits of Henry Whipple, the new bishop for the Episcopal Diocese of Minnesota, established just a few years earlier in the town of Faribault. Bishop Whipple came to the Redwood Agency in the summer of 1860, when he visited a number of Dakota farmers in their homes on the reser-vation. He held a service for the Dakota in English, which was translated into the Dakota language for the audience, probably by Thomas Robert-son, whom Whipple hired as his official translator during this visit. At the end of the service, one of the "principal" men arose and said that those in attendance had held a council and agreed to ask the bishop and Hinman to establish a school for their children. Hinman returned to Faribault to get ordained and married, then returned with his new wife and a teacher to establish the Episcopal mission school. He also began plans for build-ing a church at the Redwood Agency.[6]

Mary Bury Hinman was eighteen years old and had just graduated from the Episcopal mission school in Faribault when she married Samuel Hinman and arrived in October 1860 to live and work at the Episcopal mission at the Redwood Agency. She soon learned enough of the Dakota language to converse with her Dakota neighbors and quickly made many friends among them. She was an active visitor of her neighbors, known for her service and generosity—she shared food and clothing, cared for the sick, organized a Dakota women's group and a children's choir. As a result, she acquired some influence among the Dakota women and persuaded many to send their children to her husband's new mission school and a few others to convert to the Episcopal brand of Christianity. By 1862, about fifty children were enrolled in the Episcopal mission school.[7]

Samuel Hinman's arrival set up a rivalry between Christian sects for the first time on the Dakota reservations. Heretofore the Presbyterians had worked without much competition as missionaries among the Santee Dakota, although until 1860 they had no established mission on the lower reservation. Thomas Williamson's son John, fresh out of the seminary, came to Redwood in October 1860, about the time Hinman arrived, to establish a new Presbyterian mission. The two missions, both run by dedicated and enthusiastic young men, sat not far from one another at the agency, competing for converts. Although John Williamson may have had an advantage in this competition, having grown up at Kap'oja and Yellow Medicine among Dakota people, the Episcopal missionaries, although newcomers, had a number of factors in their favor that led them to become influential at Redwood. First, Bishop Whipple had laid the groundwork for the Hinmans earlier that summer when he met with Dakota farmers, including leaders Wapaha Ṡa, Good Thunder, and Taopi, In addition, the Hinmans seem to have been charismatic, socially adept, kind, and generous people who made many friends among the Dakota. Another factor that likely aided the Episcopalians was that they tended to be more flexible in their approach to conversion; they were less insistent than the Presbyterians that converts give up all aspects of Dakota culture when they became Christians. Reservation physician Jared Daniels, who later became the Indian agent for the Lake Traverse Reservation in South Dakota, described the Presbyterians as the "most intolerant towards the Indians" among missionaries. Daniels himself was an Episcopalian who also served as Bishop Whipple's personal physician.[8]

Although she had been affiliated with the Williamsons' Presbyterian congregation since her Kap'oja days, Daybreak Woman quickly associated herself with the Episcopalians once they arrived at Redwood and became close friends with the Hinmans. She invited Samuel Hinman to hold services in her home at Beaver Creek, which he did regularly. In June 1861, when Bishop Whipple visited the Redwood Agency mission for the first time, he confirmed seven people, including Thomas Robertson, as members of the Episcopal Church. In his memoir of this visit, Bishop Whipple describes Thomas as "our interpreter" and lists Taopi, Good Thunder (Wakiŋyaŋ Waśte), Wabasha, Iron Shield, and Other Day as new Dakota church members.[9]

Later that year, Daybreak Woman shocked the Williamsons by leaving their church to join Hinman's. In a letter of October 1861, Thomas Williamson wrote that his son John needed help in his missionary efforts at Redwood because he was losing congregants because of Daybreak Woman: "Mrs. Robertson has left our church at the Lower Sioux Agency to be Episcopalian and has taken several women with her." Those women were probably her close friend Mary Prescott and Mary's two daughters, Julia and Sophia, all three of whom were confirmed by Bishop Whipple in 1861 and 1862. The Williamsons must have felt Daybreak Woman's defection keenly, as the two families had been so closely associated since Kap'oja days and Sophie Robertson was still under their guardianship in the household at Yellow Medicine. Marion, however, remained loyal to the Williamsons. She, with new husband Alexander Hunter, became members of John Williamson's Presbyterian congregation at the Redwood Agency shortly after they married in 1862. Daybreak Woman and the rest of her children became devoted Episcopalians for the rest of their lives. The family's close association with the Hinmans, Jared Daniels, Bishop Whipple, and the Episcopal mission at Redwood would prove deeply consequential in their lives after the 1862 war.[10]

On August 17, 1862, Daybreak Woman was settled in her Beaver Creek home. After several years of struggle to reestablish the family on a firmer financial footing after Andrew's death, their prospects had improved. They were living on and developing their own land. Her oldest sons— Thomas, Angus, Gustavus, and Frank—were farming, and Thomas and Frank had jobs at the agency. Marion, married and pregnant with her first child, was living at the Redwood Agency with her new husband. Several of Daybreak Woman's children were not with her at Beaver Creek: Sophie (fourteen) remained with the Williamsons at Yellow Medicine, Frank

Dakota congregants with Thomas Williamson (third from left, in hat) and women of the mission at the Williamsons' home, the Pajutazee mission, near Yellow Medicine, after a service on August 17, 1862. *Photograph by Adrian John Ebell, Minnesota Historical Society collections*

(sixteen) was living with the Prescotts at the Redwood Agency, and Gustavus (eighteen) was with John Mooers in Shakopee's village a few miles away. At home with her were the other children: Thomas (23) and his wife, Niya Waśte Wiŋ, Angus (twenty), Will (ten), and Martha (seven).

Like many of the people living on or near the Minnesota River reservations in the summer of 1862, Daybreak Woman did not anticipate the coming disaster that would destroy her home, undermine her family's newly reestablished economic security, and forever alter the society in which she had lived since returning to Mni Sota Makoce.

Heralds of Calamity

Not long after Daybreak Woman moved to Beaver Creek, Joseph R. Brown also left Redwood, replaced as Indian agent by an appointee of the new Republican administration after Abraham Lincoln's election in 1860. Brown began to build his stone mansion near the Sacred Heart Creek settlement, located about thirteen miles above Beaver Creek. Brown's replacement was Thomas Galbraith, who had no experience with or knowledge of the Dakota people (or any other Indigenous people). He was not up to the challenge. According to a friend who knew him well at the time of his appointment, Galbraith was a hard drinker whose "excessive use of liquor had brought about a serious impairment of his mental faculties" and "was really unfit to hold any official position"; he was "out of his head" much of the time. Inept at diplomacy, Galbraith treated the Dakota people with arrogance and was "wholly unfit" for the agent position. According to Big Eagle, many Dakota deeply disliked Galbraith and the other new Republican appointees on the reservation, and this animosity was a significant factor in causing the 1862 Dakota War.[11]

The farmer acculturation program Brown had initiated on the Lower Sioux Reservation accelerated in 1861 under Galbraith. Dakota hunters' resentment deepened as Galbraith continued favoring the farmers; he gave more supplies to the farmers on the reservation, which precipitated intensified harassment and violence against them. In addition, many Dakota continued to be rightly incensed about the incompetent and corrupt employees appointed to positions on the reservations under Galbraith, including A. Pierson, the new school superintendent, who planned to line his own pockets with as much money as he could from the education fund. This corruption, as well as the traders' greed, became evident at the 1861 annuity distribution, when the Dakota annuity was pilfered for inflated debt claims by traders and rewards that traders paid to cooperating government officials, leaving the people with very little. In the months prior to the 1861 payment, some Dakota men formed a soldiers' lodge to organize resistance and declared that they would take up arms if the US soldiers present tried to force them to give money to the traders. Hearing rumors of this plan, Galbraith sent for a larger than usual contingent of troops to be present at both 1861 payments. That year, most Dakota men resentfully paid their debts to the traders, but were heard to say it would be the last time they did so. Their deep dissatisfaction with the 1861 annuity distribution was a clear signal that Dakota people's forbearance was not limitless.[12]

Soon after Galbraith and the other new government appointees took office in 1861, many Dakota, Euro-Dakota, reservation missionaries, and others sent complaints to Washington alleging incompetence and corruption at the agencies. The complaints were numerous enough to prompt a government investigation, and a special agent was dispatched to look into operations at Redwood and Yellow Medicine. In 1862, the agent confirmed the corruption in his report to the commissioner of Indian Affairs, saying,

"I have seen proof enough to satisfy the nation and Congress, too, of the fraudulent transactions and robberies committed by the Indian officers." However, in the midst of the Civil War nothing was done.[13]

In 1861–62, in addition to people's increasing dissatisfaction with the Galbraith regime, relations between Dakota hunters and most of the traders at the two agencies became bitterly contentious. Many Dakota men were at odds with traders over the past payments for debts. The payments made to traders out of the 1851 treaty still rankled, and again traders greedily conspired to take the annuity payments from the Treaty of 1858. The problem was that the Dakota clients did not keep books themselves, so when confronted with account books showing that they owed traders money, they could not verify the amounts. The traders' claims, when combined with charges levied for depredations and kickbacks paid by traders to government officials, nearly equaled the amount of the annuity payment. The Dakota people knew or suspected they were being cheated by the traders, a suspicion verified by several white observers present at annuity distributions.[14]

As the 1862 annuity payment approached, many Dakota argued that all their debts to traders had been paid and nothing should be taken out of the anticipated funds. However, the traders insisted that there were still debts to be paid and demanded that the Dakota should all agree to give over money again at the next annuity payment. Wapaha Ṡa later drew a direct line from this conflict with traders to the outbreak of war that summer:

After we had been out [hunting] some time the traders, the most active of whom was Mr. Myrick, sent out for the chief to come in and sign papers for him in reference to selling the land on the north side of the Minnesota River. I refused to go in. The others, I am told, went home and signed some papers and received for doing so, horses, guns, blankets and other articles. I was told this after I came home. I always refused to sign papers for the traders, and therefore they hated me. By the result of this paper . . . the traders obtained possession of all the money coming from the sale of the land on the north side of the Minnesota River, and also half of our annuity for the year 1862. When this became known to the young men of the tribe, they felt very angry. The tribe then assembled a council of soldiers. . . . In that council it was determined that they would not submit to having half their annuity being taken from them, and it was ordered that all Indians should draw their annuity in full from the disbursing officer, and refuse to pay the credits to the traders for that year. I made a speech in council and told the Indians that I thought it was proper that they should obtain their whole annuities and refuse to pay the traders.... After this council I thought about this matter a great deal, but heard nothing about it further until early one morning, as I was making a fire, an Indian on horseback rode up to my house and said the Indians were fighting the traders.[15]

Good Star Woman (Wicaŋhpi Waśte Wiŋ), whose family lived near the Redwood Agency, also remembered the war as being a direct outcome of the traders' insistence that the Dakota people sign over most of their annuities in 1862. The traders insisted that all the Dakota must sign papers agreeing to allow them to collect payment for the debt directly from the government. She recalled that one trader "also told the Indians that if they didn't sign the paper they could get nothing at his store, saying, 'If you have to eat grass, go ahead and eat grass but don't come around here asking for food.'"[16]

The winter of 1861–62 was a cruel one for the Dakota families who continued to rely primarily on hunting and gathering for subsistence. Hunters had to compete with settler-colonists for increasingly scarce game, and cutworms had destroyed much of the 1861 corn crop, so there was not enough to sustain people through the winter. Many were hungry, and some starving, but most traders refused to extend further credit because they feared the government might fail to pay annuities in 1862 due to the Civil War.[17]

By the spring of 1862, traders on the reservation also thought that Galbraith intended to refuse license renewals to most of them when they expired the following year, which was another reason for them to cut off credit—they anticipated that they would not be able to collect payments for the debts already on the books. Since they thought they would be evicted in a year, they schemed to get their hands on the 1862 annuity payment. Two traders who did not cut off credit were Louis Robert and David Faribault. Robert had been assured that Galbraith would give him exclusive trading rights at Redwood, so he extended credit liberally on the assumption that he would be around long enough to get paid for his debts. Faribault also continued to extend credit as an independent (unlicensed) trader, although his stores were rapidly diminished by the summer. His liberal credit, including giving away fourteen head of cattle for food during this starving time, would be remembered.[18]

In June 1862, warriors from Shakopee's and Red Middle Voice's Bdewakaŋtuŋwaŋ bands on the Lower Sioux Reservation formed a soldiers' lodge of about a hundred men to organize and respond to the increasingly dire situation created by the delayed annuities and the traders' refusal to extend credit to obtain food. As they discussed the situation and what should be done, they also noted that many whites were off fighting for the Union in the Civil War. They began to wonder whether the time might be right to take action.[19]

Incapable or unwilling to deal with the hunger situation at Redwood, Agent Galbraith absented himself from the reservation for most of the spring. Conditions were so desperate that some people walked to New Ulm, the city at the southernmost edge of the reservation, seeking sustenance. Others asked the settler-colonists living adjacent to the reservation to share their food. Some killed the settler-colonists' livestock for food as they struggled to hang on until the annuity was paid. Urania White, one of Daybreak Woman's Beaver Creek neighbors, recalled that Dakota women were "compelled to ward off starvation by digging roots for food." That summer, women searched the prairie beyond the river bluffs to find the wild turnip they called tipsiŋa, which they dug up with sharpened poles. Daybreak Woman's home was the closest to the Minnesota River of all the settler-colonists in Beaver Creek, and the Robertsons' relatives and friends on the reservation visited often. Daybreak Woman shared what food she could with the visitors who came to her door; Thomas noted in his memoir that one Dakota family who lived directly across the river visited daily. The Robertsons also shared labor and food with Daybreak Woman's stepbrother's family, the Mooers.[20]

At Yellow Medicine, Sarah Wakefield, the wife of the agency physician, described many of the most desperately starving as sickened or dying from physical disorders that resulted from ingesting uncooked or inedible food: "I remember distinctly the agent giving them dry corn, and these poor creatures were so near starvation that they ate it raw like cattle. They could not wait to cook it, and it affected them in such a manner that they were obliged to remove their camp to a clean spot of earth." Wakefield concluded that "had the Indians been properly fed and otherwise treated like human beings," there would not have been a war.[21]

Although the annuity payment was supposed to come in June, by July it had still not arrived. As desperation increased, a rumor spread that there would be no annuity at all, creating even more anxiety. Also contributing to unease was Galbraith's attempt to convince the Dakota leaders at Redwood to accept greenbacks rather than gold for the payment, which they rejected. Galbraith issued some pork and flour at Redwood on July 7, but this food was soon gone. In mid-July, he arrived at Yellow Medicine to find large numbers of Sisituŋwaŋ and Waḣpetuŋwaŋ were there demanding their payment. Many were starving and desperate, and the bands' leaders insisted that Galbraith distribute the food in the warehouse. Galbraith resisted and only agreed to give out small portions of provisions—pork and flour, some clothing and some supplies. Again, the food lasted only a few days.[22]

By July 18, conditions were so abysmal at Yellow Medicine that Lieutenant Timothy J. Sheehan, in charge of the hundred soldiers there, feared an uprising was imminent. He sent to Fort Ridgely for more men and artillery. Sheehan was unable to persuade Galbraith of the danger he was creating by failing to feed the hundreds of hungry people, who were anxious, angry, and resentful as they waited day after day for the much-delayed payment. Galbraith arrogantly and obtusely claimed that there was no danger, saying the Dakota people gathering at the agency seemed quiet and calm. On July 21, Sheehan lost all patience with the agent and insisted that he give out the food in the warehouse or Sheehan could not be responsible for what happened. Galbraith agreed to distribute more provisions, but only after he took the annuity census. On July 26, he took the census, a process that took twelve and a half hours. But then, the census completed, Galbraith still failed to release the food. His unwillingness or inability to grasp the dire situation he was creating by not feeding the starving people may be partially explained by his drunkenness; he was said to have been intoxicated for much of the time during these tense days.[23]

By August 3, thousands of Sisituŋwaŋ and Waḣpetuŋwaŋ were camped at the Yellow Medicine Agency demanding their money and food. Some of the elderly and children were dying from starvation. The rest were barely surviving by eating the roots of marsh grasses and wild turnips. That night, a group of Dakota men held a council and agreed that they must take action. Arguing that since the food sitting in the agency warehouse was theirs, they decided to take it the next day and not wait for the agent to give it to them. Galbraith, although informed of the council's decision, did not take it seriously, again claiming there was no need to worry. His government clerk, James Gorman, later recalled that the agent "thought he knew as much about what was going on as we did, when he really didn't have the facilities."[24]

The next day, several hundred warriors gathered at the agency, broke down the door to the warehouse, and began to carry off sacks of flour. Sheehan ordered the cannon aimed at the warehouse door and shouted to the Dakota men that he would shoot them unless they desisted. The men fell back, forming a path to the warehouse door, down which Sheehan marched with a small detachment of soldiers into the agency building, where he found Galbraith, cowering in his office and drinking heavily. Sheehan demanded that the agent give out the provisions he had available in order to avoid a violent uprising and pressed him to hold a council immediately.[25]

Once Sheehan and his men had taken control, however, Galbraith still refused to give out the provisions, saying that if he conceded to Dakota demands now, it would set an undesirable precedent. Sheehan, now irate, insisted that Galbraith give out three days of food and hold a council with the leaders. Capitulating in the face of Sheehan's wrath, Galbraith held a council with Dakota leaders and told them to come back the next day for their provisions. Sheehan and Galbraith promised the Dakota leaders that food rations would be issued if they returned to their camps. The Dakota men agreed and dispersed.[26]

The next day, Galbraith insisted that Sheehan arrest two of the Dakota men who had taken flour. While Sheehan went about this task, Galbraith tried to sneak away from the agency with his family, but his flight was thwarted by several Dakota men, who escorted him back. Galbraith's craven attempt to flee the scene, his erratic, alcohol-fueled behavior, and his continued refusal to release the reminder of the food in the warehouse led Sheehan to appeal to his commanding officer, Captain John Marsh, at Fort Ridgely for reinforcements. Captain Marsh arrived three days later (August 7) with more troops, took command of the agency, and immediately ordered Galbraith to give out whatever was left in the warehouse. After the food was distributed, most of the Dakota families left the agency and returned to their villages to wait for the payment, and Captain Marsh took his men back to Fort Ridgely. The immediate crisis averted, despite his bungling, Agent Galbraith then set about recruiting Euro-Dakota men on the reservation for a volunteer militia to fight for the Union in the Civil War, a group he called the Renville Rangers.[27]

Meanwhile, at Redwood, the soldiers' lodge had worked to keep people from buying goods on credit because of the traders' plan to extract Dakota debts out of the annuity payment. At the end of July 1862, leaders of the soldiers' lodge went to Fort Ridgely to talk to Captain Marsh and to ask him whether he was planning on using his troops to force them to give up their annuity payments to the traders. Marsh said no, that his men would only be present to maintain order. When the Dakota men returned to Redwood and reported this news, trader Andrew Myrick shut off credit and insisted that the others do the same. Then, the soldiers' lodge went to Myrick and told him to stop cutting their reservation grass without paying them for it. Myrick replied that they would all have to eat grass before he would give them anything, saying he would not extend credit even after the annuity was paid. Myrick and some of the other traders repeated the "let them eat grass" rebuke over the ensuing weeks, some adding more slurs—including saying that the Dakota could eat their own "filth." The warriors responded by again threatening to cut off the traders' access to wood and hay on the reservation. The traders continued to warn the soldiers' lodge that unless they collected their debts at the annuity payment, Dakota people would be refused credit indefinitely.[28]

When Little Crow heard about the conflict over food at Yellow Medicine, he rode up quickly and attended the leaders' council with Galbraith. Little Crow extracted a promise from Galbraith to open the government warehouse at Redwood and provide food there as well. At the council Little Crow at first suggested that Galbraith arrange with the traders to give people food from their stores on the promise of the coming annuity payment, threatening that otherwise they "may take our own way to keep ourselves from starving." When Galbraith looked to Andrew Myrick for his response, Myrick repeated the phrase that by then had become familiar to the Redwood Dakota: "Let them eat grass." When the Dakota present became angry, Galbraith promised to release the government provisions at the Redwood Agency.[29]

However, he failed to keep his promise. He refused to hold a council with the Dakota leaders at Redwood and never released the government provisions. He stayed for several days at the agency to recruit for the Renville Rangers and then left with them on the evening of August 17. Galbraith assumed all was secure on the reservations once the crisis at Yellow Medicine was resolved; perhaps he saw that the crops planted by the Dakota on the lower reservation promised a bountiful harvest and

thought the bands at Redwood appeared less destitute than the upper reservation Dakota bands. For whatever reason, Galbraith decided to renege
on his promise and not distribute the food at Redwood, despite repeatedly
being told that people were hungry. This decision was a disastrous and
consequential one, for many people on the lower reservation were, in fact,
desperately hungry. As Robert Hawkewaste, a member of Little Crow's
band, recalled:

> There were several of us who went over to Yellow Medicine Agency
> because we had no food. We went over to see the agent. Our agent was
> up there at the time . . . and we heard we were going to receive some
> food, . . . and, as the agent promised us to receive some food down
> there [at the Redwood Agency], we came away. . . . When we came
> back they didn't give us any food as he promised—the agent did not
> give us food as he promised. . . . We were in a starving condition and
> a desperate state of mind.[30]

Galbraith spoke with Little Crow on August 15, later reporting the
leader was content and satisfied, having just built a cellar for his new
brick house. Two days later, he and the Renville Rangers left the Redwood
Agency, stopping in New Ulm en route to St. Paul. At New Ulm, Galbraith
reportedly became inebriated and talked as if he hoped to abandon his position as agent, make himself captain of the Rangers, and never return to
the reservation. His departure and his failure to authorize the distribution
of government provisions worsened an already bleak situation for those
who were desperate on the reservation, as they tried to hold on until the
annuity payment arrived.[31]

Galbraith's ineptitude as an Indian agent is evident in his ignorance of
what was clear to others who worked at the Redwood Agency—that there
was a strong and growing undercurrent of anger and resentment roil-
ing the Lower Dakota bands, fed by their increasing hunger. John Nairn,
the government carpenter, who had been working and living at Redwood
since 1854, was well aware of the increasingly tense situation, which had
been building since the reservations were established. Nairn later recalled,
"Among the Indians at the lower agency a feeling of discontent and dissatisfaction was observable soon after removal [after 1851] and was intensified
by the frequent change in superintendents and agents, who were generally men who were densely ignorant of the Indians and unqualified by

either training or knowledge for the responsibilities they assumed." Nairn spoke directly to Galbraith about his concerns on the evening of Sunday, August 17, when both men attended Samuel Hinman's Episcopal service. After the service, Nairn, Galbraith, Hinman, and Emily West, the Episcopal mission schoolteacher, gathered at the gate and talked for some time. West recalled, "Mr. Nairn said he feared there was trouble coming: he had been there a good many years and had never seen so much dissatisfaction among the Indians as at that time." Galbraith offered no response.[32]

Another white resident at the Redwood Agency, Jeannette DeCamp, whose husband operated the saw and flour mills, said that the dire want and the discontent of the Dakota on the lower reservation was evident throughout 1861 and 1862. Those who came to the mills to grind their corn or collect lumber talked frequently of their problems and their anger. According to DeCamp, "There were many things almost daily which showed that the Indians were very much dissatisfied with their conditions."[33]

In several Bdewakaŋtuŋwaŋ villages on the Lower Sioux reservation, resistance had been evident for some time, especially among the young men of the Shakopee and Red Middle Voice bands. Both villages were dominated by hunters; of all the bands, they were the two most resistant to farming and acculturation at Redwood. It was mainly the warriors from these bands who had formed the soldiers' lodge that was working against the traders. By August, they were holding nightly councils about the problems with the nearby settler-colonists, the traders, and the delay of the annuity payment.[34]

Little Crow cited Galbraith as well as the traders as responsible for pushing the Dakota men on the lower reservation to violence. A few weeks into the war, Little Crow wrote to Henry Sibley to explain why the Dakota had started the fighting: "For what reason we have commenced this war I will tell you. It is on account of Major Galbraith. We made a treaty with the government, and beg for what we do get, and then cannot get it until our children are dying with hunger. It is with [due to] the trader[s] that [the war] commence. Mr. AJ Myrick told the Indians that they would eat grass or there [sic] own dung. Then Mr. Forbes told the Lower Sioux that they were not men. Then Robert he was working with his friends to defraud our money."[35]

Other Dakota leaders corroborated Little Crow's assessment of the roles of the traders and Galbraith in bringing on the 1862 war. Paul Maza Kute Mani opposed the war and became a leader of the Dakota peace advocates. In a letter written to Governor Alexander Ramsey, Maza Kute Mani explained why some at Redwood were driven to war: "Payment was delayed and the traders would not trust them, but told them to leave their stores, and go eat grass like the oxen, that they were a lazy set and would have to starve if they did not . . . these things he said made them very angry, and after they had killed the trader named, they stamped his head in the dust till it was as fine as powder." Of Galbraith, Maza Kute Mani says, "his volunteering about that time [organizing the Rangers] caused them to believe that he did not intend making any payment, and it rather exasperated them." Galbraith's role as a catalyst for the conflict was shared by the editor of the *Mankato Independent*, who on August 23, 1862, called Galbraith's departure from the reservation "a fatal and very injudicious step."[36]

The War of the Hen's Nest

In his 1918 memoir, Thomas Robertson says of the US–Dakota War of 1862, "the Indians to this day call it the war of the hen's nest, or hen's eggs." The war was sparked by a confrontation that started with the theft of some eggs. On Sunday, August 17, four young Dakota men of the Red Middle Voice band from the Lower Sioux Reservation were on their way home from an unsuccessful hunting trip when they approached a farmhouse near the Acton settlement in Meeker County, north of the reservation.

The details of what happened next vary somewhat in accounts, but the gist of all the stories is the same: they were hungry and thirsty, they stopped to eat and drink, and they found a hen's nest with some eggs, which they took. According to Thomas, one man went to the farmhouse to ask for a kettle to cook their game and the eggs they had found, but the woman in the house, having discovered they had taken her eggs, refused. The man returned to the group, and his friends taunted him mercilessly for allowing himself to be rebuffed by the farmer's wife. Unable to endure the ridicule, the man picked up his gun and marched back to the farmhouse, daring his friends to come with him and show their bravery. When the woman's husband opened the door, the Dakota man shot him, and then the group killed the entire family. The perpetrators then rode swiftly to Shakopee's village on the Redwood River seeking support and protection.[37]

The Acton killings prompted a coalescence and explosion of the anger, resentment, and despair that had been building at Redwood for years

among the Dakota people who had been struggling to maintain their traditional way of life since the creation of the Minnesota River reservations.
Now, some claimed the Acton conflict as a pretext for going to war against
the whites. The timing seemed propitious, with the US government weakened by its war against the Confederacy. At Shakopee's village throughout the night of August 17–18, the soldiers' lodge met in council to plan
how to proceed. They debated all night, with arguments made both for
and against war. In the weeks after the war began, several men who were
present at the war council told Thomas Robertson what had transpired.
The consensus was war. In addition to exacting justice for their many
long-standing grievances against the government and the traders, their
more fundamental aim was to kill the settler-colonists and "drive them
out of the country, and regain the lands of which they had been robbed."[38]

As the council wore on through the night, the young warriors who
were the strongest advocates for war also pressured Little Crow to be their
leader. He refused them repeatedly, arguing that such a war would only
be disastrous; he argued that the Acton perpetrators should be turned
over to military authorities at Fort Ridgely. To those who stood before
him demanding war he said, "The white men are like the locusts when
they fly so thick the whole sky is a snow storm. You may kill one-two-ten;
yes, as many as the leaves in the forest yonder, and their brothers will not
miss them." After hours of debate, with the young warriors calling Little
Crow a coward for refusing to lead them, he capitulated. He told the young
soldiers that they would "die like the rabbits when hungry wolves hunt
them in the Hard Moon." But in the end, he agreed to lead them, saying,
"Taoyateduta is not a coward; he will die with you."[39]

6. Minnesota River,
August 18—August 26, 1862

Redwood Agency, Beaver Creek, Yellow Medicine Agency, Little Crow's Camp

Like a destructive storm, the war struck suddenly and spread rapidly. Everything was confusion. It was difficult to know who was friend and who was foe.

ESTHER WAKEMAN

That hazy, hot August morning, Daybreak Woman was up with the sunrise, preparing herself for the day. Still asleep in their beds were Thomas; his wife, Niya Wašte Wiŋ; and his siblings Angus, William, and Martha. As she looked down to the river flats, she could see a commotion—men were running around, but she could not tell why. She woke Thomas, asking him to investigate. The day would be like no other.[1]

Redwood Agency

Early on the morning of Monday, August 18, Dakota warriors attacked the Redwood Agency, initially targeting the traders, their clerks, and other employees, then expanding the killing to include agency employees and bystanders who resisted or were in their way as the Dakota fighters took the government horses and plundered the trader and agency stores. The warriors did not kill indiscriminately; consequently, many of those who lived at the agency were able to escape the initial attack and flee unharmed. In addition, certain agency employees were warned about the attack and either told to stay inside or directed how to flee safely, while others had their lives saved by Dakota friends who intervened to protect them. Of the more than eighty people who lived at the Redwood Agency, twenty-one were killed, ten were taken captive, and the rest escaped.[2]

The Dakota warriors first targeted the traders Andrew Myrick and

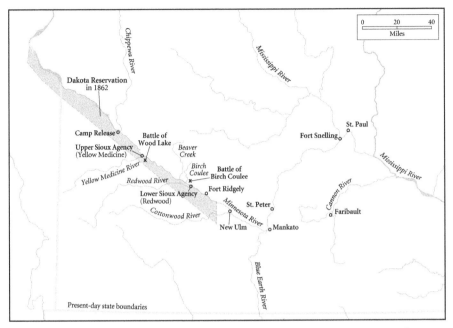

Places important to Daybreak Woman and her children during the US–Dakota War of 1862.
Map by Matt Kania, Map Hero, Inc.

Louis Robert. Early that morning, Joe Campbell and his brother went to Myrick's store, where Joe worked as a clerk, to get bill of lading for some goods they were going to pick up in New Ulm. Dakota men attacked while the Campbells were waiting outside for Myrick to appear. The warriors shot and killed two white men in the store. They then threatened to shoot the Campbell brothers, but several of their Dakota relatives stepped in and escorted them back to their house.[3]

Myrick was still upstairs above his store when the Dakota attacked, and he escaped the house through a door in the roof. The Dakota discovered him fleeing, however, and shot him, then stabbed him repeatedly with a scythe and, it was said, stuffed his mouth with grass. Three men were killed at Myrick's and five at Robert's post. The warriors then moved on to kill five at William Forbes's store and two more people at François LaBathe's. All the stores except LaBathe's were burned down after the attackers carried out the goods and furnishings. At the boardinghouse, four men and one woman were killed. Several men were killed at the stables as Dakota fighters were stealing the agency horses.[4]

The attack began early in the morning, and people at the agency who were not near the traders' stores, about a quarter mile northwest of the council square, initially did not know what to make of the gunshots and commotion. Some who were out just before 7:00 AM saw a file of Dakota warriors, painted and carrying guns, enter the agency grounds from the north and then break off into smaller groups and move toward the stores. The warriors were not perceived as a threat, as witnesses assumed the men were in war paint because they were skirmishing with Ojibwe raiders. The attack was so unexpected it was difficult for those in the midst of it to fathom. Even after noticing more frenzied activity—including warriors running around buildings, shouting, and gunshots—several survivors recount that it took them some time to realize that Dakota men were attacking and killing people and that they might be in danger. Thomas Robertson recalled that most people on the reservation were stunned by the outbreak of violence, saying, "this killing of whites was as much a surprise to the majority of Indians as it was to us."[5]

Frank Robertson was working as a government clerk at the agency and was living with the Prescotts on the council square. Philander Prescott was sixty-one years old and had been living among the Santee Dakota since the 1820s. Prescott's Dakota wife, Mary Keeiyah, or Naġi Owiŋna, was the niece of Bdewakaŋtuŋwaŋ leader Cloud Man and the daughter of Flying Man. Their daughter Julia (twenty-one) was the only child with them at the Redwood Agency. Daybreak Woman and Naġi Owiŋna were close friends.[6]

Early that morning, Frank was up, dressed for work, and having breakfast with the Prescotts when several Dakota emissaries, sent by Little Crow, came into the house and told them that there was trouble and they should stay inside to be safe. The men were cryptic in their warning and did not explain exactly what was happening. Frank's intuition told him to flee rather than stay, so he walked out the door with the Dakota men and headed home to Beaver Creek. He walked quickly past the Episcopal missionary, Samuel Hinman, who was out early preparing to go to Faribault. Hinman asked Frank what was happening. Frank said he didn't know, but relayed the message from Little Crow warning the Prescotts to stay in the house. Frank told Hinman he thought there was trouble, so he was going home to Beaver Creek.[7]

As Frank walked down to the river, White Dog, a Dakota farmer, ran by Hinman, saying there was "awful work" afoot and he was on his way to see Wapaha Ša about it. Then, hearing a commotion at the government stables, Hinman turned to see stable employees confronting Dakota men leading horses out. Suddenly, Little Crow appeared and stalked by with a fierce scowl on his face. When Hinman asked what was happening, Little Crow, who just the day before had attended the missionary's Sunday service, only glared at him silently and strode off toward the stables. A Dakota boy known as Neudah who was living with Hinman ran out of the stable and shouted to him to run—and run he did, as shots rang out. Hinman, along with other refugees, was able to make his way down to the ferry and get across the river, where they walked about thirteen miles to Fort Ridgely.[8]

Shortly after Frank Robertson left the house, Philander Prescott saw Little Crow walking past, so he went outside and asked what was happening. Little Crow told him to get back into the house and stay there. Prescott did so and heard the gunfire escalating. Not long after, Big Eagle came to the house to say widespread killing of whites was happening. He wanted Prescott to write a letter to the commander at Fort Ridgely making clear the leader was not involved in the violence. Prescott tried to write the letter for him but was shaking so hard from fear that he could hardly place the words on the page. Prescott asked what he should do with Naġi Owiŋna and Julia; he decided they would be safe because they were Dakota, but because he was white he should leave. Prescott fled and was killed on the road to Fort Ridgely. Thomas Robertson came upon Prescott's decapitated corpse about a week later, about seven miles from Fort Ridgley. He said it was the only mutilated body he saw during the war.[9]

Meanwhile, the Dakota farmers who lived nearest to the agency became aware of the attack. Taopi, one of their leaders and a Christian convert, had planned on meeting that morning with Hinman to discuss establishing a cemetery at the new Episcopal church under construction at the agency. Before Taopi left his house, another Dakota man came and reported that warriors were armed and coming to attack the agency. Taopi hurried toward the agency until someone shouted to him that Dakota attackers were killing the traders, so he turned back, climbed onto his rooftop, and surveyed the scene for himself. From his roof he could spot Dakota warriors burning and plundering the traders' stores and agency buildings. Soon the farmers gathered at Taopi's home to discuss what to do. Before they could take any action, warriors approached and ordered them to take off their white clothing and put on Dakota clothes. The Dakota soldiers threatened to kill them if they didn't join in the attacks. From that point, escape was not an option.[10]

Marion Robertson Hunter and her husband of one month, Alexander, were at the Redwood Agency when the attack began. They lived on the council square behind the carpenter shop, very close to the Prescotts' house and a few doors down from the Nairns. Alexander Hunter and John Nairn were friends who had known each other for over a decade—even before they had both come to Minnesota. They had worked together as carpenters at the Redwood Agency for some years. In his memoir, Nairn recalled that both he and Hunter were well liked by many Dakota people and that Hunter was "a favorite of many of them." He described Marion as "an educated and highly accomplished young lady of mixed Sioux blood." That Monday morning at 6:45, Nairn left his house and walked toward his shop to begin work. Suddenly he noticed men running between agency buildings and saw some commotion at the stables. When Nairn asked some of the Dakota running past him what was happening, none of them responded. Then he heard gunfire and watched as several Dakota men ran by him to the stables and began to take out the horses. At this point, Nairn recognized that something dangerous was afoot, so he ran back to his house, scooped up his wife, Magdelene, and their four young children, and ran for the ferry. When they found their path to the river crossing blocked by Dakota warriors, they scrambled up the river bluffs to hide in the trees.[11]

On the bluffs, the Nairns found Alexander and Marion. The two couples were discussing what to do when they were approached by a group of armed Dakota men. Fortunately, White Spider, Little Crow's brother, was among the group. Little Crow had instructed White Spider to try to save as many white women and children at the agency as possible, and the latter warned the two families to avoid the open prairie and roads, telling them to hide in the ravine that ran below the river bluffs as they fled. Magdelene Nairn offered White Spider her wedding ring as payment for his aid, but he refused it, telling her to remember his face instead. The Nairns and Hunters made their way down the bluffs into the ravine, where they began their flight from the Redwood Agency.[12]

They initially made only slow progress toward Fort Ridgely. They had to hide themselves periodically, and, having lost his toes to frostbite, Alexander could walk only "with great difficulty," according to Nairn. The Nairns' young children would also have slowed their pace. Just a few miles east of the agency, as they passed near a Dakota village (perhaps Wapaha Śa's), they were approached by a Dakota friend, who urged Marion and Alexander to wait in the village while he found them a horse and wagon to continue their journey. No doubt anxious to keep moving, the Nairns said their goodbyes to the Hunters and walked on. They eventually arrived at the fort safely.[13]

Marion and Alexander waited many tense hours at the village, unsure of their safety, but their friend never returned with the promised wagon. Afraid to stay any longer but unable to walk any farther that day, they went into the woods to hide for the night. In the morning, they set off on foot again for Fort Ridgely. They had walked only a short distance when a lone Dakota man approached them. He walked up to them without a word and shot Alexander through the heart. When the attacker took out his knife to cut her husband's throat, Marion begged him to stop, and he did. The man then took Marion prisoner and led her toward Little Crow's village. On the way there, a Dakota friend, Good Thunder, took Marion away from Alex's assailant and led her to Daybreak Woman, who by this time was also a captive.[14]

Beaver Creek

As a large contingent of Dakota warriors assaulted the Redwood Agency, others fanned out to attack settler-colonists in the nearby creek valleys—the settlements at Birch Coulee and Beaver Creek.[15]

The Robertsons' neighbors at Beaver Creek included the Earle family, who had arrived from New York that summer and whose newly built house sat near the top of the settlement up the creek valley. Ezmon Earle, who was seventeen years old in the summer of 1862, later wrote of his family's experiences at Beaver Creek and in the war.

> Beaver Creek, like all other water courses in Minnesota, runs in a valley much lower than the prairie land, the bottoms and sides of the bluffs being quite thickly timbered. The course is about north and south and the creek empties into the Minnesota River about two miles from our location. . . . [T]he Redwood Agency was distant about six miles and was in plain view from our house. . . . [T]he cattle and sheep ran at large during the day but were driven home and kept in yards enclosed by rail fence at night. The horses were always turned loose

when not at work and they with the others belonging to the other
settlers formed a herd of about twenty which always ran free day
and night unless at work.[16]

It was the settler-colonists' herd of livestock that the warriors first
sought when they came into the Beaver Creek Valley at dawn on the morning of August 18. When Daybreak Woman woke Thomas, he remembered,
she told him there "was something strange going on in the flat below our
house and she could not make out what it was." He immediately went to
the door and looked down at the plain below, where he saw Dakota men
driving cattle and catching horses. Like his mother, he "couldn't imagine
what it was all about."[17]

About half an hour later, a good friend of the family, an older Dakota
man named Katpaŋtpaŋ U (Comes Pulverizing), appeared at the door. He
lived just across the river from the Robertsons and visited their house almost every day. Katpaŋtpaŋ U reported that there was a party of Ojibwe up
the creek and some Dakota had followed to investigate. He asked to borrow
Thomas's gun to help them. This was not a strange request, as Thomas
had lent him the gun many times before. Thomas gave him the gun and
watched him start up the hill. Shortly thereafter, Gustavus arrived from
Shakopee's village to report to the family that a Dakota man had told him
the Sisituŋwaŋ were coming down to steal horses. Soon after, Katpaŋtpaŋ
U's wife and daughter arrived from their home across the river, just as Katpaŋtpaŋ U returned to the house. Thomas recalled that when his friend
came back, he "could tell by his countenance that there was something
wrong, something unusual happening." Katpaŋtpaŋ U told his wife, "you
take my niece [Daybreak Woman] and the children across the river and
keep them in the house and we will stay here and try and find out what is
being done." Daybreak Woman agreed to the plan, and she and the rest of
the family followed Katpaŋtpaŋ U's wife and daughter down to the river,
climbed into their canoe, and crossed to the reservation.[18]

Katpaŋtpaŋ U then turned to Thomas and told him what was really
going on. He reported that it was the "Lower Sioux who were taking the
horses and cattle and they were going to kill all the whites." He said that
"a party of hunters had already gone to kill people in the Big Woods and
that a large party had gone to kill all the people at the agency, that a party
of young Indians were now on the hill standing with some of our white
neighbors, ready to kill them." Katpaŋtpaŋ U asked Thomas to climb the

hill with him and warn the whites "to get out of the country as fast as they could." In the meantime, he would try "to hold back the young men." Thomas left with Katpaŋtpaŋ U, and as the two men walked up the hill, they heard gunfire from the direction of the Redwood Agency. Katpaŋt-paŋ U said, "I don't know what I can do for the whites."[19]

Up the hill, Thomas and Katpaŋtpaŋ U found several white men, including David Carrothers, the Robertsons' closest neighbor, surrounded by a group of young Dakota men with guns. As Katpaŋtpaŋ U talked to the Dakota group, asking them not to shoot the white men, Thomas edged David Carrothers aside and quietly asked him whether the Dakota had taken all the settler-colonists' horses. Carrothers told him they had two teams hitched to wagons and ready to leave farther up the creek valley at Stephen Henderson's barn, where the neighbors were gathering. Thomas told Carrothers and Henderson to get back there and leave as quickly as possible. Meanwhile, Katpaŋtpaŋ U bought the white men some time, as the younger Dakota men acquiesced to the older man's plea to not kill the settler-colonists and instead turned their attention to breaking into a nearby house (probably belonging to one of the Carrothers brothers) for plunder. Carrothers, Henderson, and the other white men ran back up the hill to collect their families and try to escape. Thomas and Katpaŋtpaŋ U quickly walked down the hill to the Robertson house, now empty.[20]

By the time they returned to the house, Thomas saw that all of the family's horses and other livestock were gone, so there was no prospect of riding out or reason to stay for the animals. Katpaŋtpaŋ U suggested they take his second canoe across to his home and decide what to do there. Just as they shoved off in the canoe, Thomas heard a rustling in the bushes on the riverbank. Looking back, he saw his brother Frank, and they paddled back to retrieve him. They found Daybreak Woman and the others safe at Katpaŋtpaŋ U's house, where they all stayed the rest of the day and that night.[21]

Meanwhile, back in Beaver Creek, the Robertsons' white neighbors were desperately trying to flee. A group of twenty-seven, about ten of them adults, left the Earles' home in several wagons and a buggy. They did not get far before being stopped by a war party. When the Dakota men told the settler-colonists that they were going to kill all of them, Stephen Henderson, the only settler other than Helen Carrothers who spoke fluent Dakota, negotiated with them, reaching an agreement to give up most of their horses in exchange for their lives. Once they turned over the horses, the settler-colonists walked on, but they did not get far before the Dakota

warriors changed their minds and began to shoot them. The attack on the
Beaver Creek settlement killed forty-nine people, including the Carroth-
erses' two young boys and Henderson's wife and two youngest children.
Carrothers, Henderson, Ezmon Earle, and Earle's father managed to run
and escape, along with a number of other teenage boys. The Dakota attackers took Urania White, Helen Carrothers and her sister-in-law Elizabeth Carrothers, Amanda Earle, and seven of their children as captives.[22]

On Tuesday, August 19, the day after the attacks on the Redwood Agency
and Beaver Creek, the Dakota soldiers' lodge ordered everyone in the area
to move to the Redwood River near Shakopee's village. There, the Robertsons took refuge in the house of Daybreak Woman's stepbrother, John
Mooers. Because he had lived with their mother in Red Wing's village
until he was fifteen, when he joined his father, Grey Cloud Woman II,
and the Robertsons on Grey Cloud Island, John had numerous strong
kinship relationships among the Bdewakaŋtuŋwaŋ Dakota. These relationships and John's solid standing in Dakota society proved significant
for Daybreak Woman and her children during the course of the war. John
and his French-Dakota wife, Rosalie, were able to protect their own six
young children, Daybreak Woman's half sister Jane Anne Mooers, and the
Robertsons. Thomas recalled, "he had many friends and relatives among
the Dakota," and therefore was able to keep them all safe. He also acted
quickly to warn his white and Euro-Dakota neighbors once he learned
that the Dakota were attacking, giving them time to escape.[23]

The same day the Robertsons took refuge with the Mooerses, Good
Thunder delivered Marion to her mother. It must have been a bittersweet
reunion as Marion shared the shocking story of Alexander's death with
the family. That first night with the Mooerses, another Euro-Dakota family was also brought by their captors after dark and hidden in the Mooers
house for a time. Susan Frenier Brown and her children (her husband
was in St. Paul) had been captured and brought downriver by warriors,
who asked Mooers to keep them in his house and protect them until they
could take them off again. In the chaos of the early days of the war, the
Dakota who took captives had to protect them from other Dakota people.
Sam Brown, who was sixteen at the time, recalled that although they
knew other people were also hiding at the Mooers house, they were not
informed and could not tell who they were: absolute darkness and silence
were imposed on them and others in the house. Neither were they told
who else was in the house, an indication of the precarious situation of

Euro-Dakota refugees, especially in the first days of the war. The other people Sam sensed were there in the dark on the upper floor of the house would have been the Robertsons, and the two families knew each other well. However, it was not safe to let it be known who was hiding or where.

In the first few days of the conflict, even Little Crow was not sure he could protect the captives whom he took in from his own angry warriors. When the Browns were brought to Little Crow's home by their captors for safety, the leader, fearful that he could not protect the one white man in the group (Susan Brown's son-in-law), devised a way for him to escape by dressing him up as a woman and sending him out in the dead of night to make a run for the fort. During this time, Little Crow also protected three white women and their children who were the Robertsons' Beaver Creek neighbors: Urania White, Helen Carrothers, and Amanda Earle. In doing so, he was putting himself at risk, for in the first days of the conflict, some angry warriors were threatening to take Little Crow's house and kill the captives sheltered there. Some were calling for the killing of all the Euro-Dakota, whom some hostile Dakota blamed for colluding with the white colonizers and undermining Dakota culture.[24]

On the same day that the Redwood Agency was attacked, Captain John Marsh, Fort Ridgely commander, led forty-six soldiers upriver to quash the revolt. Just as he and his men approached the Redwood Ferry crossing, Dakota warriors ambushed them near the mouth of Birch Coulee Creek, wiping out virtually the entire party, including Marsh himself. Dakota warriors attacked Fort Ridgely two days later, although they were unable to overrun it. Then, over four hundred Dakota attacked New Ulm and held it under siege. New Ulm's residents were able to defend the town, although twenty-six people were killed and most of the town was burned down. Thomas Robertson, like the other Euro-Dakota men in the camp, was pressed into fighting for the Dakota, first at the Battle of Fort Ridgely on August 22 and then several days later at the Battle of New Ulm.[25]

On Wednesday, August 20, Thomas and Niya Waśte Wiŋ had left Day-break Woman and the family with the Mooerses. They went to live in Little Crow's village, about three miles away, where most of the Dakotas were congregating. Thomas does not explain why he did this; perhaps it was because Niya Waśte Wiŋ desired it, but it was probably also be-cause he wanted to establish himself there and appear to be a supporter of the war. In various accounts of his role in the first few weeks of the war, Thomas repeatedly expressed his concern about protecting his mother and siblings. He thought the best way to protect them was to establish himself among the Dakota warriors in Little Crow's camp and appear to acquiesce to their cause. He was aided in this effort by living among them with his Dakota wife.[26]

The Dakota soldiers' lodge had about three hundred to four hundred men who announced and enforced Little Crow's orders. The soldiers' lodge ordered all men, including all Euro-Dakota men, to attack Fort Ridgely for a second time on August 22, having failed to take the fort in their first attack a few days earlier. Thomas, who since his father's death had seen himself as the family patriarch, decided to obey the command because he was afraid not doing so would draw suspicion to himself but more importantly threaten the family's safety. Although the order to fight was a general one that applied to "all able-bodied men, young and old, full bloods and mixed bloods," it is not clear based on Thomas's accounts of the war that his younger brothers Angus and Gustavus were pressed into fighting at Fort Ridgely or New Ulm. (There is evidence that Angus was present at a later battle, Birch Coulee.) Thomas's participation in the battles may have relieved his younger brothers from fighting while giving the family cover in the eyes of the soldiers' lodge. Of his decision to obey the order to fight, Thomas said, "I suppose I might have slunked out of going, but I wanted to go. I wanted to see what chance there was for getting away from the hostiles, not for myself but for the rest of the family, and the other prisoners in the hostile camp. If I had been alone in the hostile camp, knowing the country so well, I could have got away at night. But under the circumstances, if I had done so it would have been almost certain death for the rest of my family, and perhaps others."[27]

Daybreak Woman was dismayed with Thomas's decision, terrified of losing him. He recalled: "I went to my mother and told her I was going with them. She began crying and said that I ought not to go; but my idea was to do what I could to gain their goodwill, so as to protect my mother and my brothers and sisters as far as I could in that way, by letting them think that I would join and help them."[28]

A few weeks after the battles at Fort Ridgley and New Ulm, Thomas told a journalist that he had "for the sake of his family put himself at the front of the battle" and that he had taken aim "generally at random" to make it appear he was fighting. Although Thomas makes it sound easy, it must have been difficult to convincingly pretend to be fighting on the Dakota side when surrounded by enthusiastic soldiers who were likely watching him because his loyalty was suspect. His actions on the battle-field would come back to haunt him.[29]

Yellow Medicine Agency

By August 1862, fourteen-year-old Sophie Robertson had been living with the Williamsons at Pajutazee, about three miles west of the Yellow Medicine Agency, for almost two years. She was already a very accomplished girl, according to Jane Williamson, who reported in March 1862 that Sophie could read and write in both Dakota and English with great ease. She also said Sophie was "remarkably cheerful and kind-hearted" and that she "love to please and [was] very fond of music."[30]

Although various people who lived at or near Yellow Medicine had heard reports of an attack on Redwood throughout the day and evening of Monday, August 18, initially few credited them as real, so most did not flee until Tuesday. Just after sunrise on August 19, a Dakota man, John Other Day, led away about sixty-two people, mostly agency employees and their families. At about the same time, Thomas Williamson sent off his entire household except for his wife and sister in a wagon driven by his son-in-law Andrew Hunter (no relation to Alexander Hunter). This included the younger Williamsons and Sophie Robertson as well as a visiting photographer, Adrian Ebell, who had spent the previous days taking photographs of the people at the mission and the Dakota in the vicinity. Guided by several Christian Dakotas and friends of the missionaries, including Robert Chaska and Paul Maza Kute Mani, the group made their way down to the Minnesota River to a place where they could ford it safely. Maza Kute Mani carried Sophie across the river on his back.[31]

Along the way, the Williamson party met another group of refugees, who were from the Riggs mission. They joined forces, and the group of about forty people, including several agency employees, moved on together in two wagons and a buggy and on one horse, taking turns riding and walking. They crossed to the north side of the Minnesota River and headed toward Fort Ridgely. Deluged almost incessantly by rain in the first few days of their flight, the refugees were miserably wet almost continually until Thursday afternoon, when the rain stopped and they paused on the prairie to rest and eat. There, Ebell took out his camera and photographed the party. This photograph became one of the most well-known images of the US–Dakota War, widely circulated as a postcard. Foremost

The group of people fleeing the missions at Yellow Medicine Agency paused on August 21 to make bread (right midground). Stephen Riggs is seated in front of the woman who stands by the wagon wheel; Sophie Robertson is closest to the camera. *Photograph by Adrian John Ebell, Minnesota Historical Society collections*

in the group sits Sophie Robertson, reclining on one elbow in the tall prairie grass in her gingham dress. Diminutive for her age, her forehead smudged with dirt, she frowns into the camera, looking miserable. She must have been very frightened, not only for herself but for her mother and siblings. She had no way of knowing what had happened to them.[32]

On Friday, August 22, the caravan of refugees headed southeast for Fort Ridgely, passing the Robertsons' house at Beaver Creek along the way. Andrew Hunter and his wife, Elizabeth Williamson Hunter, were neighbors of the Robertsons at Beaver Creek—their house also sat on the bluff near the river, less than a mile away. They were good friends with Marion and Alexander Hunter (although, as noted, the two men were not related). Just the month before, both couples had joined the Zoar Presbyterian Church, founded by Elizabeth's brother John Williamson at Redwood. When Andrew took the buggy down the creek to check on his house, he encountered a Dakota man who told him all the whites at Beaver Creek either had been killed or had fled, which was not reassuring news for Sophie to hear. As she and the Hunters moved out from Beaver Creek and continued their journey to the fort, the refugees saw corpses—perhaps including those of their Beaver Creek neighbors—as well as abandoned plunder and burned-out cabins.[33]

At dark, they stopped about seven miles from the fort, which they could see as a red glow on the horizon—its buildings were on fire, having been under Dakota assault all day. Andrew Hunter took the buggy as close as he could, then left it to crawl into the fort. There he found the commanding officer, Lieutenant Sheehan, who told him it was not safe for the refugees to try to make it inside and suggested they drive on. They continued through the night, stopping once at dawn several miles northeast of the fort, then all day Saturday and Sunday until they thought it was safe to separate. The Williamsons, with Sophie, went on to St. Peter. By this time, her mother, siblings, and the Mooers had all moved to live in Little Crow's camp.[34]

Little Crow's Camp

In the first week of the US–Dakota War, small parties of Dakota fighters went off into the surrounding countryside and attacked settler-colonists along the Minnesota River. These raids caused a massive exodus of refugees. Most of the frightened settler-colonists fled to Fort Ridgely, New Ulm, St. Peter, and other towns, while others didn't stop until they made it to St. Paul. Within a week, the countryside was almost entirely depopulated of settler-colonists. The first three days of the war were the bloodiest and most dangerous for whites at the Redwood Agency and in the creek valley settlements on the north side of the Minnesota River, where more than 300 people were killed between August 18 and August 20. Although estimates of the total number of casualties in the US–Dakota War vary, most historians agree that at least 450 white civilians died in the war, and some have suggested as many as 800 perished. Relatively few Dakota fighters were killed; by Thomas Robertson's estimate, only 32 Dakota men died. The greatest Dakota loss of life occurred in the months and years after the war.[35]

During the first week of the conflict, Little Crow's camp increased in population by several thousand Dakota and hundreds of white and Euro-Dakota captives, with all their horses, wagons, and livestock. By the end of the week it had become extremely crowded, with as many as one thousand tipis. For the first time since she was a young child, Daybreak Woman was living in a tipi rather than a house or cabin.[36]

Held with the Robertsons were other Euro-Dakota families that they had known for years, including the Browns, Campbells, Faribaults, and Prescotts. Susan Brown and her family were in Little Crow's camp only a short time before her relatives, led by Akipa, came to take them back up-river to be among her family at Yellow Medicine. Also in the camp was a cousin of Mary Prescott, Mary Woodbury, who had come up to the agency from St. Paul to collect her annuities. Mary Woodbury's grandfather was Cloud Man, her mother was the Day Sets (Aŋpetu Inajiŋ Wiŋ), and her father was former Indian agent Lawrence Taliaferro. Her husband, Warren Woodbury, was in the Union Army. Mary Woodbury was visiting relatives near the Redwood Agency with her four young children when the war began. She later told her father that Little Crow intervened to save her and her children when warriors threatened to kill them, saying he did so out of respect for the former agent. Mary credited another Dakota man, Maḣpiya Wakoŋze, with protecting her family as well.[37]

Once in camp, many Euro-Dakota captives donned full Dakota clothing in place of their white clothes as a form of protection or at the insistence of their captors. Celia Campbell remembers her mother complaining about having to live in a tipi and everyone in her family being forced to put on Dakota clothing. During the first few days of their captivity, the Campbells were convinced, because of what they had heard or been told by some of their captors, that they would be killed. The Dakota woman Snana, who was married to Good Thunder and had become a member of Hinman's church in 1861, protected a young captive girl, Mary Schwandt, to replace the daughter she had just lost to death weeks earlier. Snana remembered that she hid Mary whenever she thought the captives were in danger of being killed and dressed the girl in Dakota clothing, "thinking that the Indians would not touch her when dressed in Indian costume."[38]

Nancy McClure Faribault's life in Little Crow's camp in the first week of captivity was characterized by almost constant fear that she and the other captives would be killed. When the Dakota soldiers returned to the camp after attacking Fort Ridgely, they were especially angry at the Euro-Dakota among them, for they had encountered stiff resistance from the Renville Rangers defending the fort. Faribault remembered, "they reported that there were many half-breeds at the fort who had fought against them.... [T]his made them very bitter towards us for they said we were worse than the whites and that they were going to kill all of us." Later that same day, she heard someone shout that they were beginning to kill the "half-breeds." Faribault grabbed her young daughter and ran with another woman to Shakopee's village seven miles away, where she had friends and relatives who would protect her. As she ran, she saw her husband, David, running into Little Crow's cornfield. The next morning, after leaving her daughter with relatives, she returned to the camp to find her husband, fearing he was dead. To her relief, she found that none of the captives had been killed; David was still alive.[39]

Helen Carrothers and Urania White, the Robertsons' Beaver Creek neighbors, were taken to Little Crow's camp with their surviving children and given to different Dakota families. When they first arrived, Little Crow ordered them to dress in the Dakota style and to braid their hair like Dakota women. They were given calico and broadcloth, instructed in how to make a dress in the correct manner, and given moccasins to replace their shoes. The captives lived in the tipis of their Dakota families and worked hauling water, collecting wood, gathering corn, feeding livestock, and otherwise contributing to subsistence. The tipis were twelve feet in diameter with dirt floors that were periodically covered with long river grass or rushes as a barrier to the damp conditions. For sanitary reasons and for access to resources, Little Crow's camp moved first to Shakopee's village and then again to Rice Creek. White describes the caravan to Rice Creek as being three miles long, including oxen, horses, dogs, cattle, mules, wagons, and people.[40]

Helen Carrothers was one of only a few captives who successfully escaped. After only a short time in Little Crow's camp, she took her two little children with her into a cornfield, successfully eluding her captors by hiding in the vicinity of the agency and in the Minnesota River bottoms for weeks until she eventually found a way to ford the river and begin her journey to Fort Ridgley. She eventually made it to the fort, crawling with her children on her back, almost naked, covered in sores and scratches and starving, but they were all three still alive.[41]

Jeannette DeCamp, the wife of the Redwood Agency miller, was taken captive with her two children and held in Little Crow's camp. After the camp moved to Shakopee's village, where Daybreak Woman and her family were living with the Mooerses, DeCamp met the two families. According to DeCamp, John Mooers and some of the other Euro-Dakota men were planning on helping her and some of the other white captive women to escape, although nothing came of the discussion right away. That same day, a female prisoner was shot and killed for trying to escape, undoubtedly stoking the fear of many of the captives. At the Rice Creek camp, DeCamp encountered Daybreak Woman and Marion for the first time. Their tipis were not far apart, and DeCamp frequently visited Marion in particular. The two women often read the Litany together, as Marion was the only person who had a copy of the prayer book. At Rice Creek, the Dakota soldiers held a council to discuss the white captives, and John Mooers said he thought the warriors might let them go to Fort Ridgely. However, after the council, Mooers warned DeCamp not to leave, even if the Dakota told her to do so, because he knew some who planned to ambush anyone allowed to leave the camp.[42]

Governor Alexander Ramsey appointed Henry Sibley, former fur trader and territorial politician, to lead an army of volunteers against the Dakota. On August 28, ten days after the attack on the Redwood Agency, Sibley and his men arrived at Fort Ridgely. Soon after, Sibley sent out a burial detachment, which included Joseph R. Brown and Thomas Galbraith. Seeing Shakopee's and Little Crow's villages abandoned, the burial detachment erroneously assumed that the Dakota had already moved farther upriver and it was safe to proceed. In fact, the Dakota were camped not far away at Rice Creek. They ambushed the burial party and pinned them down near the mouth of Birch Coulee Creek for thirty-six hours, killing thirteen soldiers and wounding four others, including Brown and Galbraith. More than eighty horses were slaughtered in the battle. At the same time, Little Crow led another contingent of warriors into central Minnesota, where they attacked and burned down the towns of Forest City and Hutchinson.[43]

Nothing was clear or predictable in the first weeks of the war, and the situation, especially for Euro-Dakota people caught up in the conflict, remained ambiguous and uncertain. Although Little Crow blamed them for contributing to undermining Dakota traditions and society, was suspicious of them, and threatened to have them killed at various points in the conflict, he also protected many Euro-Dakota friends and relatives (as well as some whites) and would rely heavily on the assistance of a number of Euro-Dakota men during the war. The conflict, especially in its first few days, was confusing for many Dakota people as well. As Esther Wakeman, White Spider's wife and Little Crow's sister-in-law, said, "Everything was confusion. It was difficult to know who was friend and who was foe." Similarly, Big Eagle recalled that when the Redwood Agency was first attacked, he went along not to kill people but to protect some "particular friends."

He said, "I think others went for the same reason, for nearly every Indian had a friend that he did not want killed; of course he didn't care about anyone else's friend."[44]

Euro-Dakota people like the Robertsons found themselves in a perilous and precarious situation. On the one hand, they were Dakota, and usually the Dakota did not kill their own. On the other hand, if they were perceived as having violated Dakota values of generosity and hospitality or other norms, their Dakota blood and kinship might not protect them. Moreover, while most Euro-Dakota had at least some family and friends who would protect them, they could not be sure that those friends and family members would be present at the right place and time. And although most of the ire of attacking warriors was directed at whites, many of the prowar Dakota saw Euro-Dakota people as complicit, either directly or indirectly, in the loss of the traditional Dakota way of life, and perhaps also as implicated in the corruption and chicanery of the government and traders given that many Euro-Dakota men were government employees or worked for traders.

Daybreak Woman and her children, as they experienced the upheaval and violence, could not have been sure of their own fates in this conflict. The capricious and ambivalent nature of Euro-Dakota people's status during the war is illustrated in one account of the Dakota raid at Beaver Creek. As Dakota warriors led their two wagons filled with plunder and captives down the creek valley toward the river, they came upon Daybreak Woman's house. When one warrior drove a hatchet into the door as an act of hostility, another man scolded him for doing so, saying, "This is an Indian's house."[45]

Only one Euro-Dakota civilian is known to have been killed in the war: François LaBathe, who was shot at his store in the initial attack at the Redwood Agency. One French-Dakota woman, the wife of Louis Brisbois, was nearly killed because she had not been kind or generous to other Dakota people, but she managed to escape with help from Nancy Faribault. A number of whites, such as Helen Carrothers, were spared death because of their kindness and generosity to the Dakota or because they also were protected by Dakota friends. While almost all the Euro-Dakota captives survived the six weeks of the war, they were frequently threatened with extermination by Dakota warriors. Little Crow himself warned the Euro-Dakota people in his camp that they would all be killed if any one of them tried to escape. Thomas Robertson thought the Dakota warriors would kill all the captives, including those who were Euro-Dakota, once it became evident they could not win the war.[46]

Thomas's account of the events at Beaver Creek shows that he did not see himself or his family as being in the same position as their white neighbors in the context of the unfolding conflict. It is telling that Katpaŋtpaŋ U, the Dakota man who came to report to the family what was happening, did not view Daybreak Woman and her children in the same way he did the settler-colonists at Beaver Creek. Katpaŋtpaŋ U asked Thomas to help him save the Robertsons' neighbors from the Dakota war party threatening them because Thomas was Dakota but also white—and therefore could act as a negotiator between the two sides. He told Thomas, "I don't know what I can do for the whites," indicating that he viewed the settler-colonists as definite targets, a group distinct from the Robertsons. It is also telling that Thomas warned his Beaver Creek neighbors to run for their lives to Fort Ridgely, while he and his family sought refuge on the reservation. Rather than seeing the fort as sanctuary, they sought protection among their Dakota friends and family across the river.[47]

In the US–Dakota War, while it was clear that settler-colonists and the US government were the enemy of the Dakota, neither Dakota nor Euro-Dakota could be sure, among themselves, who was friend or enemy. As the war evolved, the situation of the Robertsons, the Mooerses, and many other Euro-Dakota people became less that of relatives taking shelter and more that of captives of Little Crow and his warriors. What this captivity meant for them, no one, including their Dakota captors, knew.

7. Minnesota River, August 26–October 5, 1862

Yellow Medicine, Camp Release

Suppose the same number of whites were living in sight of food, purchased with their own money, and their children dying of starvation, how long think you would they remain quiet?

SARAH WAKEFIELD

Shortly after the Battle of Birch Coulee, Little Crow learned that Colonel Henry Sibley was marching up the Minnesota River with a large force. He decided to move his entire camp—all the Dakota and all the captives—up to Yellow Medicine, out of the easy reach of Fort Ridgely. On August 26, 1862, Daybreak Woman and her children, along with the Mooers family, packed tipis and whatever household belongings and clothes they had acquired over the previous ten days and moved with everyone else. The five-mile-long train of Dakota people, captives, and livestock arrived at the Yellow Medicine Agency two days later. Thomas recalled: "On this move to Yellow Medicine, John Mooers, who was a step-brother to Mother, took charge of her and the rest of the family and as he had many friends and relatives among the Indians, I felt that they were comparatively safe for the time being; so when some young men of old Red Iron's band wanted me to go with them, I consented and went with them to their village about twelve or fifteen miles up the Minnesota from Yellow Medicine."[1]

The Euro-Dakota captives and others in Little Crow's camp who did not support the war had little choice but to go along with the order. Missionary Gideon Pond, who later interviewed some of the captives, explained that "they believed that the lives of their friends and their own lives depended" on it. "If they had remained behind the leader of the hostile party had declared that he would take vengeance on such evidence of alienation from him; and on the other side, the exasperated whites whose friends had already been butchered by the hundred, would avenge themselves on the first Indians they should overtake."[2]

Stephen Riggs, the Presbyterian minister, said that Thomas Robertson told him he thought he could get away from the camp but was afraid to do so, fearing how the rest of the family would be treated. Henry Sibley later reported that Thomas had said, "the mixed bloods, with their families, are not permitted to leave the camp. And are virtually prisoners, as most of them are believed to sympathize with the whites."[3]

Yellow Medicine

At Yellow Medicine, Little Crow and his men met immediate resistance from the Dakota bands at the Upper Sioux Reservation. A volatile debate erupted between the Upper and Lower Dakota over the war as well as over the fate of the captives. A peace faction quickly emerged, comprising mostly Dakota farmers associated with the Hazelwood mission, including Gabriel and John Renville, Akipa, Solomon Two Stars, Paul Maza Kute Mani, Lorenzo Lawrence, and Joe LaFramboise. They elected Maza Kute Mani as their speaker. Some Dakota from the Lower Sioux Reservation joined the peace faction as well, having opposed the war from the beginning or having come to oppose it. Many of them, like the Euro-Dakota men who were captives, had been compelled to fight in battles for fear of reprisal. In addition, Waȟpetuŋwaŋ and Sisituŋwaŋ leaders, whose bands had been away on the western prairies when the conflict began, made clear to Little Crow that they were angrily opposed to his war. In a council of Sisituŋwaŋ and Waȟpetuŋwaŋ leaders, Standing Buffalo declared that the Bdewakaŋtuŋwaŋ had "cut our people's throats." Red Iron told Little Crow and the Lower Dakota that they had started the war, now they had to fight it without his band's help.[4]

Dakota values hold that *we are all related*—and relatives must support each other. Dakota decision-making required consensus, reached after much debate. But the war split the community in terrible ways, including an almost continuous argument over the fate of the captives. Many times, the disagreements came close to erupting into bloodshed. Almost immediately after Little Crow's men arrived at Yellow Medicine, the peace faction confronted them. Paul Maza Kute Mani insisted that the Bdewakaŋtuŋwaŋ hand over the prisoners. They refused, saying, "If we are to die, the captives will die with us."[5]

In an effort to persuade the warriors to give up the captives, the peace faction prepared for a council, cooking a large quantity of beef for a feast.

Although two hundred of Little Crow's men came, ate, and listened while Little Paul attempted to persuade them to free the captives, they remained adamantly opposed. The warriors announced that they would return the next day to force members of the peace faction to fight with them. That night, the peace faction formed its own soldiers' lodge to defend themselves against Little Crow's men, appointing Gabriel Renville chief soldier. Meanwhile, Little Crow avoided the confrontations and debates over the fate of the captives, probably because he was conflicted: he was related to a number of the peace faction leaders and also had friends and relatives among the Euro-Dakota captives.[6]

The next morning, as promised, Little Crow's men rode into the upper reservation Dakota camp and inflicted some damage. Then, Gabriel Renville led his soldiers into the lower reservation Dakota camp and demanded all the property taken from the Euro-Dakota captives be turned over to them. Renville and his men rode through the camp, shooting their guns and threatening violence, a display that prompted another council between the two sides. At this council, Paul Maza Kute Mani denounced the war and informed the Lower Dakota that they had formed their own soldiers' lodge to work against it. He shamed Little Crow's men for holding the Euro-Dakota as prisoners and for taking their property and declared that several Euro-Dakota families intended to recover their property. Gabriel Renville described this confrontation:

> We again painted our faces, took our guns, and went to the Mdewakanton camp; and when we arrived at their soldiers' lodge, Little Paul said what he was told to say. Then the public crier of the Mdewakantons arose and said, "the mixed-bloods ought not to be alive, they should have been killed. But now you say their property should be returned to them. We will never do so." . . . So the hostile Indians would not consent to have the property of the mixed-bloods returned; but Joseph Campbell's wagon, Mrs. J. R. Brown's wagon and horse, and Mrs. Andrew Robertson's wagon, were taken by us and returned to them.[7]

While his mother and siblings were in Little Crow's camp at Yellow Medicine, Thomas Robertson was living with his Sisituŋwaŋ friends upriver at Red Iron's village. One day, his brother Frank appeared and told Thomas that Little Crow wanted to see him. When Thomas and Frank arrived at Yellow Medicine, they found a council being held to discuss a note left by Sibley for Little Crow on the Birch Coulee battleground. Several Euro-Dakota men, including David Faribault and Joe Campbell, had read the note to Little Crow. However, Little Crow seemed to be reluctant to accept their translations. Thomas recalled:

> When I got to the council grounds, Little Crow beckoned me to sit beside him, which I did; then he handed me the note, which was only a few lines, and said, "I have had this letter read and interpreted by several, but I want to be sure what is in the letter, so I sent for you. Now read it and tell me what it says," so I read the note and interpreted it to him, after which he said, "Now I know because I know I can depend upon you to tell the truth. You can go now where you please."[8]

After this meeting with Little Crow, Thomas looked around the camp and found his mother and siblings with his uncle John Mooers. Thomas stayed with the family for the remainder of their captivity.

The note from Sibley asked why the Dakota had started the war and told Little Crow to send two Euro-Dakota men with his answer, saying they would not be harmed. Little Crow, with the help of his secretary Joe Campbell, wrote a detailed reply. When the letter was ready to be delivered to Sibley at Fort Ridgely, no one volunteered to go with Tom Robinson, the designated Euro-Dakota messenger, because they were too afraid. Thomas told Robinson to ask Little Crow whether he could go with him, but Little Crow said no. Thomas decided to convince the leader himself, explaining:

> I had known Little Crow since I could remember and knew he was friendly towards me and our family so after thinking the matter over a few minutes I concluded that perhaps he, Little Crow, did not want me to take the chance, so I said to Tom, let's you and I go and see him again. So we went and found him alone in his tent. When we went in and he saw me he said "Tunskuyolu" [nephew] and told me to sit down beside him. Then Tom told him that he had been to every one of the mixed bloods, but none of them would consent to go except me; that this note of Sibley's should be answered but that he did not like to try to make the trip alone. Then Little Crow, laughing, said "Are you not afraid?" I said that I was not afraid to go anywhere he told me to. Then

he [Little Crow] said, "You two can go then," and handed Tom the answer to Sibley's note.[9]

The two Toms, as they came to be known, were provided a buggy and mule by Little Crow to speed their journey. They successfully delivered the message to Sibley at Fort Ridgely, where they were interrogated. They stayed overnight at the fort and returned to Little Crow's camp carrying Sibley's response. In the letter, Sibley insisted the captives be released immediately, before any further discussions about peace would be held.[10]

The trip to the fort was an especially anxious journey for the Toms, because they knew they might be attacked by Dakota warriors or by the soldiers defending the fort. Sarah Wakefield, one of the captives, describes the deep anxiety surrounding this first trip: "One morning Tom Robertson and another man, a half breed, went with the letters; soon after the Indian soldiers left, crossed the river, and all in our neighborhood believed they had gone to intercept and murder them. There was great alarm, for the Indians said if they killed them they would return and kill all the rest of the half-breeds and prisoners."[11]

The Toms made a second trip to the fort to deliver another message from Little Crow to Sibley. This time Robertson secretly carried an additional letter sent by men from the Lower Sioux Reservation, friends and relatives of Daybreak Woman, who were in the growing peace faction. Robertson recalled:

That night Good Thunder came to me and told me some of the friendlies wanted to send a letter to Colonel Sibley, and wanted me to write it for them. I had in my pocket a short piece of pencil and an old memorandum book, but we had no light so Good Thunder went out and found somewhere a short piece of candle. He split a stick and sticking the candle in the split end and covering this and myself with blanket he lit the candle and I, in as few words as possible, wrote what he told me they wanted to say. I then asked him who was sending the letter, and he said, "put Wabashaw and Taopi's names to it," and this I delivered to Colonel Sibley on our second trip. The reason for my hiding the light when I wrote this was that some of the hostiles were becoming suspicious of us two messengers, especially myself, and I had to be very careful about what I did.[12]

On this second trip to Fort Ridgely, Angus Robertson and John Mooers accompanied the two Toms part of the way so they could retrieve a wagon. They found it and returned to Beaver Creek to wait for the Toms' return. This time, the Toms did not stay at the fort overnight but left it in the late afternoon and met Angus and Mooers at Beaver Creek, where they camped hidden in the ravine below the Robertsons' house. The next day, they headed back to Little Crow's camp, stopping to kill three sheep they found along the way, which they loaded in the wagon and brought back to camp. Halfway to Yellow Medicine, they met a group of their friends, peace faction Dakota, followed shortly after by a small group of Little Crow's men led by White Spider. The appearance of White Spider and his men appeared "suspicious" to Thomas, Angus, and Mooers, but they were not much alarmed, as they had an equal number of friendly Dakota now with them. Soon after, the White Spider party peeled off, followed by three of the "friendly" party. Thomas suspected his friends went to keep tabs on White Spider's group, "to make sure they did us no harm."[13]

The message Thomas carried from Sibley to the peace faction Dakota told them to get the prisoners and form a separate camp to hold them safely until Sibley could get to them. When Thomas, Angus, and Mooers returned to Yellow Medicine, they found that Little Crow's camp had moved north to Red Iron's village. Little Crow had intended to move west toward the Red River of the North, but Red Iron had refused to allow him to pass through Sisituŋwaŋ territory. Red Iron's village became the final locus of the Dakota camps. Those Dakota who had been in Little Crow's camp but now wanted peace pitched their tipis as near as possible to the peace faction Dakota, declaring their association with the peace faction by proximity.[14]

Captivity

The white captives lived in tipis or tents with or near their Dakota captors, while most of the Euro-Dakota held in the camp lived together as families and in close association with one another. The treatment and experiences of white captives varied widely. Some were closely monitored and forced to work, while others were given more autonomy and left to fend for themselves. A few were strategic in their response to the situation, choosing to cooperate and be as friendly as possible with their Dakota captors in order to survive, in a few cases even appearing to acculturate. One such captive, Sarah Wakefield, was criticized by other white captives for appearing to be too friendly with her captors and too ready to adopt Dakota ways, specifically her new role as her captor's wife. Some white captives were treated very well, including Mary Schwandt, the German immigrant teenager who later praised the Dakota woman Snana, who had purchased her from her captor, for caring for her like a mother. Maza Kute Mani recalled two Dakota men who treated their child captives well; one even sold his horse so he could clothe the white boy. Although a few captives eventually died of wounds sustained in the initial attacks, most survived the six weeks of the war.[15]

As the war came to an end and the captives were released, reports that most, if not all, of the white female prisoners had been raped by Dakota men became widespread. The claim that these women had been "ravished," "violated," or "outraged" (all nineteenth-century euphemisms for rape) by Dakota men, in addition to the killings of settler-colonists, fueled calls by whites for swift, violent retribution, including demands for the immediate mass execution of Dakota men and genocide of all Dakota people. Wakefield disputed the exaggerated claims in her own account of captivity, saying she knew of only two women who had been raped, and she thought some women had fabricated stories about being violated.[16]

While claims by whites about the rape of white female captives by Dakota men were indeed grossly exaggerated and sensationalized, there is evidence that some women were sexually violated. In his memoir, Thomas Robertson said of the captives that "the white women and children fared the same as the Dakota women and children in the camp." He only knew of one case of a young woman being treated badly by her captor "beyond the limit usually accorded to captives by Dakota." However, he also confirmed that "many of the women were outraged, but not in any other way abused." In an earlier account he gave of the situation for women captives, reported during the war, he said that he had not seen any instances of cruelty toward the captives "and scarcely any of violation, and those by rowdy, unsanctioned and unapproved by the chief." In his final assessment of the situation, near the end of his life, Robertson told a historian that "the violation of women prisoners was done to some extent, but not as much as has been represented by some."[17]

Two Dakota men were charged and convicted of rape in the postwar military commission trials, but the evidence shows that the sexual abuse of white captive women was somewhat more extensive. However, it is impossible to ascertain exactly how many women endured abuse because most were very reticent to make their experiences public. In nineteenth-century white society, most women who were raped did not reveal the crime or formally charge their abusers out of fear for their own reputations and the knowledge that they were more likely to be shamed and hurt by the revelation than were the men they accused. A young woman who had been raped was viewed as socially damaged by white society and would have had trouble marrying because she had lost her virginity, an attribute considered paramount for proper womanhood and marriage, and a woman of any age would have been deeply ashamed by the public revelation of sexual violation. Racism against Indigenous people would have also played a significant role in a white woman's decision to reveal that she had been raped; she would have been even more stigmatized in white society had her assaulter been an Indigenous man.[18]

At the end of the war, at Camp Release, an unknown number of the approximately forty white females between the ages of fourteen and forty held by Dakota men shared their stories privately with missionary Stephen Riggs. Some of these women told him they had been held as the wives of Dakota men and sexually violated. Two of the young women revealed that they had been raped repeatedly by multiple men in the first few days of the conflict, and their stories were corroborated by Jeanette DeCamp, who was held with them in the same house but not similarly abused. Only two women were willing to charge their captors with rape before the military commission. One other captive, Mary Schwandt, provided an account of her ordeal of rape during the first days of her captivity in a court deposition.[19]

Julia White, one of the Robertsons' Beaver Creek neighbors, is one example of a captive who was unwilling to accuse her captor of rape. Julia was taken away by Tate Hdidaŋ (Wind Comes Back), one of the party of Dakota men who attacked Beaver Creek, and held for a week in his tent before she was reunited with her mother in the camp. Her mother, Urania White, in her memoir, recalled her deep anxiety about her young daughter's fate during that week and her relief at their reunion. At his trial, Tate Hdidaŋ was accused of killing whites at Beaver Creek, taking a number of prisoners, and holding Julia as a captive. Although he was not specifically charged with rape, the presumption was that Julia had been sexually violated during the week he held her alone. John Mooers testified at his trial that he saw Tate Hdidaŋ with the girl, and Thomas Robertson testified that he saw Julia in his tent. David Carrothers identified him as one of the men who surrounded and killed the whites trying to flee at Beaver Creek. Tate Hdidaŋ was found guilty and was one of the thirty-eight Dakota men hanged at Mankato on December 26, 1862.[20]

While white female prisoners were vulnerable to sexual abuse, most Euro-Dakota women were protected from such abuse by the men in their families, with whom they lived in the camps. In addition to their husbands or brothers, Euro-Dakota women had other Dakota relatives and friends who protected them, as Good Thunder protected Marion Robertson from her husband's assailant. Indeed, the comparative safety of the Euro-Dakota women in the camps prompted some of the white women to seek shelter in their households.[21]

The experiences of captive children in the camps without their parents also varied. Some were treated very well, some were abused, and others were neglected and left to fend for themselves, while most fared no better or worse than everyone else in the camps. One illustration of what probably was a typical experience of captivity was related by the two young daughters of Joseph Coursolle (Hiŋhaŋkaġa), a French-Dakota man, and Jane Killcool, a white woman. The two girls were separated from their parents during their flight from the Redwood Agency attack but were hidden and protected by a Dakota warrior who found them hiding in the bushes. When reunited with their father after the war, Coursolle's six-year-old daughter, Elizabeth, reported: "The Indians didn't hurt us. But we didn't have good things to eat like mama makes. Sometimes we got awful cold. We slept on the ground! We didn't even have a blanket. And, oh, we were so lonesome!"[22]

Coursolle and his wife had agonized for weeks over the fate of their daughters. In late August, he had left Fort Ridgely with the burial party, and as they stopped to bury the corpses they found along the way, he had watched for his daughters' bodies. He noticed that most of the corpses were men or boys and hoped this meant his girls had been spared. Then, Dakota warriors attacked the burial party at Birch Coulee Creek. During the siege, Coursolle killed a Dakota sniper, earning the warriors' wrath. One of them shouted in Dakota, "Hear me, Hinhankaga [Hiŋhaŋkaġa]. We saw you shoot. You killed the son of Chief Travelling Hail. Now we kill your little girls!" Simultaneously deeply relieved to hear his daughters were alive and now seized with dread that they would be killed, Coursolle would have to wait another four weeks to learn whether killing the leader's son had cost him his children.[23]

The poor treatment of some of the white captives held during the war was inconsistent with traditional Dakota practice, which had normally seen captives treated well and adopted into families, often to replace lost children, eventually becoming culturally Dakota themselves. Thomas Robertson makes this point in his memoir, describing how Ojibwe captives were well clothed and fed and were seen as welcome additions to families and communities. While some white captives were treated this way, many others were not, including many of the children; they were treated more like temporary hostages than permanent additions to the community. This deviation from traditional treatment of captives also became a source of conflict among Dakota leaders. Also unprecedented was the total number of women and children taken captive, about 140, most of them in the first two weeks of the war. So many captives taken at once could not be well provided for or assimilated into Dakota society. One Dakota leader who supported the war, Big Eagle, opposed holding such large numbers of captives because they could not be properly cared for.[24]

Traditionally, the Dakota did not take their own people captive, so holding Euro-Dakota people captive was also controversial. Maza Kute Mani and others of the peace faction criticized Little Crow's men for holding Euro-Dakota captives, many of whom were their relatives. However, the Euro-Dakota people being held, such as the Robertson, Mooers, Brown, and Campbell families, were in a better position vis-à-vis their captors than the white captives. These families were held by people they knew, some of whom were friends or relatives, with whom they shared a culture and language, and so they had social and cultural advantages unavailable to non-Dakota captives. The Euro-Dakota stuck together, living with their extended families and staying close to other Euro-Dakota families, frequently cooperating and operating as a distinct social unit within the camps. They appear to have moved freely within the camp without close supervision, and some were allowed beyond the camp at times, although not necessarily without risk.[25]

It is clear that white prisoners often looked to some of the Euro-Dakota captives for aid or advice. Many approached John Mooers for information, protection, or help. Nancy Faribault describes one woman, an Irish immigrant, complaining about the frequency of camp moves and saying she was going "to see John Mooers about it." Mooers was "gratefully" remembered by many white survivors, in particular for sharing the provisions he had with the women and children and the ways he worked to improve conditions for all the captives. He was said to have "had much influence over the Indians" and was respected by both whites and Dakota people.[26]

The distinct status of the Euro-Dakota prisoners was also evident in the conflicts over the property taken from them in the war. Wagons and horses belonging to the Robertsons, Mooerses, Browns, and Campbells were disputed precisely because they were Euro-Dakota and thus should not have had their property confiscated, as Maza Kute Mani argued. As Gabrielle Renville explained, "Though they were white, [they] were children of the Indians. It was thought to be wrong that their property should be taken from them, and that therefore their horses and wagons should be returned to them." No such argument could be made on behalf of the whites, who were unambiguously enemies.[27]

By mid-September, two distinct Dakota camps had developed, one for peace and the other for war. Conflicts over the captives escalated between the two groups as Sibley and his troops moved closer, including a few physical clashes and raids that destroyed tipis, tents, and other property. On September 18, the Upper Dakota peace faction, which was most concerned about the fate of the prisoners, held a council to discuss the captives and how to proceed. The next day, they went into Little Crow's camp and tried to quietly remove some of the prisoners, but this led to more confrontations, arguments, and threats. That night, a rumor spread that Little Crow had ordered all of the captives killed, causing widespread fear.

Sam Brown recalled September 19 and 20 as days of great anxiety and gloom and nights of sleeplessness for the Euro-Dakota captives and the peace faction after the "hostiles" and "friendlies" quarreled once again and almost came to blows. According to Brown, "the quarrel got very hot—threats were made and guns fired. Tomahawks were shook at us and our situation was critical indeed." His said his mother, Susan Frenier Brown, cried all day, couldn't eat, and tried to hide her despair from her children, to no avail. A Dakota friend of the Browns stood sentinel at the family's lodge, vowing to protect them. Sam Brown claimed that Little Crow had given an order to his warriors to execute all the prisoners in the night, "but no one dared to execute his order—no not one."[28]

Celia Campbell, fourteen years old at the time, remembered her family living in almost constant fear of being killed. In the days before the final battle at Wood Lake, her father was away a few nights, trying to communicate with Sibley, who was by that time camped only a couple miles away. Her father's absence made the family more vulnerable to attack, and a

Dakota woman from Little Crow's camp ran up to warn them that there were plans to kill them in retaliation for Joe's efforts to contact Sibley. The next day, they were warned by another friend that there were plans to take Celia and her sister captive, so her mother sent the girls off to stay the night in the tipi of Blue Eyes, another Dakota friend, who hid them until their father returned the next morning.[29]

In the last weeks of the war, increasing numbers of captives moved into the Upper Dakota camp, many brought by captors who had decided to associate themselves with the peace faction. Others, with help, managed to escape from Little Crow's camp. By September 22, the majority of captives were in the Upper Dakota camp. In these last few weeks, both camps shifted their locations several times for sanitary reasons and to allow livestock fresh grazing. By the time Sibley arrived on September 26, the camps were located ten miles northwest of the Yellow Medicine Agency, across the Minnesota River from what today is the city of Montevideo.[30]

Camp Release

The last battle of the US–Dakota War was fought at Wood Lake. On September 21, the news came that Sibley and his forces were camped just below the Yellow Medicine River, only a few miles away from the Dakota camps. Little Crow's forces immediately began planning a large-scale surprise attack on Sibley's camp.

As they had been at the earlier battles of Fort Ridgely and New Ulm, Euro-Dakota men were pressed into fighting for the Dakota at Wood Lake. Thomas recalled:

> Soon after this, runners came reporting that Sibley was on his way. In fact, runners were coming in every few hours. The hostiles at once made preparations to meet him, and as runners again came in with word that Sibley was making his camp at Wood Lake or Lone Tree Lake, as the Indians called it, they decided to attack the camp that night, or early in the morning, and everyone was ordered to go that night.... This battle ground of Wood Lake is about twelve or fifteen miles from where we were then camped. As soon as it got dark, nearly all the men, both hostile and friendly, started, but on the way and in the dark most of the friendlies dropped out and came back to camp.[31]

The planned attack was upended when some soldiers who were harvesting potatoes from the Dakota farmers' fields at the Yellow Medicine Agency nearly ran over Dakota warriors preparing to attack. This precipitated the battle. While the Dakota soldiers had the initial advantage, once Sibley's army regrouped, the warriors could not rout them.[32]

During the battle, the peace faction recovered most of the captives still held in Little Crow's camp and moved them to their own (soon to be known as Camp Release), digging trenches and holes inside their dwellings to protect them. They feared the warriors, victorious or not, would return from the battle and try to kill the captives. The fighting was about fifteen miles away, but the captives could hear the gunfire and the reports of cannons in the Dakota camp. They listened closely for the battle's end.[33]

When the defeated Dakota warriors returned, they found that most of the captives, except for about sixty, were now protected by the peace faction in the Upper Dakota camp. Joe Campbell, who acted as Little Crow's assistant throughout the war, also had been actively working with the peace faction. After the defeat at Wood Lake, he asked Little Crow to turn over the remaining captives. The leader acquiesced, allowing Campbell to take forty-six captives over to the peace camp. The warriors were more focused on saving themselves and their families than on the fate of the captives.[34]

However, four long days ensued before Sibley finally arrived to liberate the captives, during which both Euro-Dakota and white captives were assailed with death threats. Time crawled by as the captives, gripped by profound anxiety, feared they would all be killed before Sibley arrived. Mary Renville, a white woman married to a Dakota man, John Renville, who was a member of the peace faction, recalled the precarious situation for the Euro-Dakota captives and an attempt on the life of either Thomas Robertson or Tom Robinson:

> They are constantly threatening the half-breed captives, and we are
> afraid they will put their threats into execution, for they made an
> attempt to kill one of them whom they had employed to carry letters
> to General Sibley, mistrusting his loyalty to the rebels. The friends
> and relatives of the half-breeds keep a strong guard about the tents
> whenever the sky looks dark in regard to them. One day just at night
> Mr. R. [John Renville] came in, took his gun and said "make haste and

get the dishes washed." "Why?" we asked. "Oh, nothing," he replied, "only they say that the half-breeds are going to be killed very soon now." We told him if that were the case we should not stop to wash the dishes. He continued, "it may only be a story. You may as well finish your work." No doubt they would have killed them long before this had they not feared a war among themselves.[35]

According to Nancy Faribault, some of the warriors who returned from the Battle of Wood Lake cursed the Euro-Dakota who had fought against them under Sibley (i.e., the Renville Rangers) and threatened to take vengeance on them. Faribault and other Euro-Dakota captives were told that Little Crow had declared that if any of them ran away during the Battle of Wood Lake, all those who remained would be killed. Nevertheless, a few decided to try to escape, including Mary and Julia Prescott, who safely made their way to Fort Ridgely. Faribault mused, "they seemed to know Little Crow's threat was a bluff."[36]

Faribault's account makes clear the ambiguous status of the Euro-Dakota captives. They feared for their lives. But on more than one occasion, white women who were seeking protection from their Dakota captors asked Faribault whether she would allow them to stay in her tipi. Although she considered these women her friends, she refused them, saying she "thought it best." Faribault did not view it in her own or her husband's interest to be seen protecting white prisoners. On the one hand, Euro-Dakota captives were in a position to offer whites protection; on the other hand, to do so meant putting themselves at risk by appearing too friendly or sympathetic to white captives.[37]

On September 24, Little Crow and about two hundred warriors—some still holding captives—headed toward Devils Lake in North Dakota, on their way to Canada. Many others, mostly Sisituŋwaŋ and Waȟpetuŋwaŋ who had not participated in the war, also fled west, fearing retribution. Those who stayed did so because General Sibley had promised that those who had not killed civilians would be considered friendly and would not be harmed.[38]

In addition, the Bdewakaŋtuŋwaŋ were not used to wintering out on the prairie; staying was a matter of survival. In the weeks leading up to the Battle of Wood Lake, increasing numbers of the Lower Sioux Reservation leaders and warriors who earlier had supported the war defected to the Upper Dakota camp. They thought, based on Sibley's promise, that they would be treated as prisoners of war, and only those who had killed civilians would be punished. Big Eagle explained in his memoir:

> I and others understood from the half-breeds that General Sibley would treat with all of us who had only been soldiers and would surrender as prisoners of war, and that those who had murdered people in cold blood, the settlers and others, would be punished in any way. There was great dissatisfaction among us at our condition. Many wanted to surrender; others left for the West. . . . Soon after the battle [Wood Lake] I, with many others who had taken part in the war, surrendered to General Sibley. Robertson and the other half-breeds assured us that if we would do this we would only be held prisoners of war a short time, but as soon as I surrendered I was thrown in prison.[39]

When Sibley arrived on September 26, six weeks after the war started, there were between 700 and 1,000 people at Camp Release. Historian Carrie Zeman estimates that the Dakota took a total of 344 Euro-Dakota and whites captive during the course of the 1862 war. According to the official list of captives liberated at Camp Release, 107 whites and 162 Euro-Dakota (269 total) were present at Sibley's arrival. On the list were Daybreak Woman and all of her children except Sophie; John Mooers, his wife, Rosalie, and their six children; and Jane Ann Mooers, Daybreak Woman's half sister.[40]

Thomas Robertson recalled what happened when Sibley arrived:

> The next day [September 28] Colonel Sibley and his command came into sight. So a few of us went out and met him and reported to him the situation as it was and conducted him to what has ever since been called Camp Release. . . . [A]ll, including friendlies, were disarmed, and excepting a few cases, the whole camp put under guard. No one could leave this camp without a special permit from Colonel Sibley. Any Indian could come into this camp but none ever got out. We were near the timber on the Minnesota River. So in a few days log pens were put up and as fast as they were apprehended, the men were put into these log pens and strongly guarded. . . . The women, children and a few trusted men were then sent under armed guard to the Yellow Medicine Agency, there to await further orders.[41]

After Sibley's arrival, the white captives were allowed to move to Sibley's camp until they could be transported to white settlements downriver. Sibley immediately ordered the creation of a military commission to try the Dakota men accused of crimes against settler-colonists, but he arrested only a few, allowing others to expect leniency. The released captives were interviewed to determine whether they were needed as witnesses at the trials, and a few of them stayed to give testimony. The majority of the white captives left Camp Release on October 4. On that same day, Sibley ordered all of the Dakota and Euro-Dakota down to the Yellow Medicine Agency, where the prisoners were put to work digging potatoes and gathering corn from the Dakota farmers' fields near the agency. The Dakota prisoners remained at Yellow Medicine Agency camp until October 12, when everyone moved back downriver to the Redwood Agency, arriving on October 15. The Dakota, the Euro-Dakota, and their military guards remained at Redwood for another three weeks.[42]

While all of the white captives were immediately removed from the Dakota camp upon Sibley's arrival, most of the Euro-Dakota captives were not. In the eyes of Sibley and his soldiers, they were Dakota, and therefore enemies, unless proven otherwise; their fates were yet to be determined. It took time for Sibley to sort out which of them could be deemed victims rather than perpetrators. The position of the Euro-Dakota captives remained fraught—for weeks they had feared the Dakota soldiers might kill them, and now they faced the possibility that the whites would punish them for being Dakota. Nancy Faribault revealed how precarious their situation was after Sibley and his troops first arrived:

> They came into the camp and took away the white captives first. General Sibley knew me, and told me to take my child and go with them. I asked him if all the half-bloods were going and he said they were not. I did not understand it all then, and I said I would stay awhile. Major Fowler, who was married to my husband's sister, then came and told me I had better go, as the soldiers were greatly enraged at some of the half-bloods, and their officers were afraid they could not "hold them." I told him I had a half-brother and half-sister there, and I would stay to protect them.[43]

Persuaded that the white captives had suffered greatly at the hands of their Dakota captors and angered after they observed Dakota people in possession of plunder taken from white victims of the war, a number of soldiers decided to take revenge and plotted a massacre of all the prisoners. This plot involved so many of the soldiers that Sibley and his officers, including Lieutenant Colonel William Marshall, quickly learned of it. Thomas Watts, a soldier at Camp Release, recalled the massacre plot as well as Sibley's and Marshall's efforts to prevent it:

> That afternoon [after the white prisoners were released from their Dakota captors] a scheme was incubated among our men that if carried out would have left a great stain on our escutcheon that time would not erase. It was intended to kill every living soul in that Indian village. Of course the horrible tales told by the released prisoners added fuel to the flames. Our two gun battery was planted on a knoll commanding the Indian Camp, and we still had a few horsemen with us. The plan was that at a given signal the guard surrounding the camp was to retire, then the battery was to shell the camp and the infantry was to do its work, and what was left, if any, the cavalry was to finish.
>
> Before the plan was complete, the news of it reached General Sibley's ears, he caused a wagon to be placed in the middle of our camp, mounted it and made a speech which was rather in the nature of a threat. The men retired to their camp fires to talk it over. The general response was "to hell with Sibley." . . . [W]hen reminded that there were some good Indians in the lot, the reply came that there were no good Indians but dead ones; and when pleadings were made [illegible] children, the answer to that was, "Nits make lice."
>
> After supper, speeches were made against the plot. Among the speakers were Lieutenant Colonel William Marshall and Lieutenant Averill, both very popular men in the command. . . . [T]hey caused many to be ashamed of themselves. It was promised that the Indians should be court marshaled [sic] immediately and that we should have the privilege of hanging the guilty ones. Finally the men, feeling a little sheepish, crawled into their tents to sleep it over. As time wore on more mature minds overcame the radical.[44]

Sibley and his officers were able to persuade their soldiers to stand down, but they could not prevent the violent acts of individual soldiers against Dakota prisoners. Another soldier recalled that while Sibley's orders were very strict about the safety of the Dakota prisoners, "on the sly many acts of cruelty were indulged in by the soldiers."[45]

When Sibley ordered the Dakota prisoners down to Yellow Medicine on October 4, he kept most of the Dakota men at Camp Release to await prosecution, leaving the Dakota women in the camp without the protection of the men in their families. Subsequently, the soldiers sexually exploited and assaulted Dakota women. In a letter to his wife, Sibley described his efforts to keep his men away from the women, yet he blames the women for not reporting the sexual abuse: "I find the greatest difficulty in keeping the men from the Indian women when the camps are close together. I have a strong line of sentinels entirely around my camp to keep every officer and soldier from going out without my permission; but some way or other, a few of the soldiers manage to get among *gals*,—and the latter, I notice, take care not to give any alarm."[46]

It is hard to understand how Sibley could expect imprisoned women to seek justice from their rapists.

In the first week after Sibley's arrival, it became clear that some Euro-Dakota captives would be favored over others and would be released, but exactly how that determination was made is not clear. Some were allowed to leave with the released white captives in early October. These included Daybreak Woman and her children Marion, Frank, William, and Martha. Thomas says his mother and siblings left just as the Dakota camp was moved down to the Yellow Medicine Agency: "About this time the surrendered camp, mostly women and children, was moved to Yellow Medicine. Mother and the family had been taken away with the other released prisoners. Mother and family through the kindness of Dr. J. W. Daniels, were sent to Faribault, Minnesota, where they were taken care of by kind friends." Thomas suggests that Daniels transported the family himself to his hometown. They left on October 6, just a few days after the main group of released captives, who left for St. Peter and other white settlements to the east.[47]

Nancy Faribault describes the departure of the captives and their journey to St. Peter:

At last a lot of us released captives were started off for the settlements below. There were seven wagon loads of us in the party, whites and mixed-bloods, all women. At St. Peter's a store building was cleared out, cooking stoves put up, and bedding given us. An officer whose name I am sorry I cannot recall, was in charge of us. Joe Coursalle, a noted half-blood scout, was with us. In the evening the German whose life I saved the first day of the outbreak, came into the room. He was intoxicated, had a knife in his hand, and said he was looking for an Indian to kill. The officer had gone out, but Coursalle was in and said to the reckless fellow, pointing to me, "here is the woman that saved your life." This seemed to quiet him, and he thanked me very kindly. Then the officer came in and said to him: "Get out you rascal. If you want to kill an Indian so bad, go West, out to the front."[48]

Not all of Daybreak Woman's children left Camp Release with her. Thomas, Angus, and Gustavus remained with the rest of the Dakota prisoners, as did John and Rosalie Mooers, their six children, and Jane Ann Mooers. Before leaving with her mother for Faribault, Marion testified against a Dakota man named Hiŋhaŋ Śuŋkoyag Mani, who was charged with the murder of her husband, Alexander Hunter. The other witness at the trial was Good Thunder, the man who had taken Marion from the accused and "carried her" to her mother. Thomas Robertson, Angus Robertson, and John Mooers all served as witnesses at the military commission trials that commenced at Camp Release on September 28 and ended at the Redwood Agency on November 3, 1862. On the last day of trials held at Camp Release, Thomas was arrested and put on trial, charged with fighting for the Dakota and killing a white man at the battle of Fort Ridgely. By the time her oldest son was standing trial, Daybreak Woman had arrived in Faribault.[49]

8. Minnesota River, October 6– November 4, 1862

Camp Release, Redwood Agency

I have no doubt but that a large number were condemned on general principles, which was more in harmony with the prejudices of the whites, than justice.

JARED DANIELS

B ecause Euro-Dakota men fought on both sides of the US–Dakota War, they were involved in the military commission trials after the war in a variety of ways—some as defendants, some as witnesses, and some, like Thomas Robertson, as both defendants and witnesses. Over the full course of the 395 trials, a total of nineteen Euro-Dakota men (including Joseph Godfrey, an African, European, and Dakota man) were tried for their participation in the war. Of these, four men were found not guilty, four were sentenced to prison, and eleven were sentenced to death. Three Euro-Dakota men were among those executed at Mankato on December 26, 1862. Most of the Euro-Dakota defendants who were acquitted remained imprisoned at Mankato until May 1863, when most of the Dakota were deported from the state.[1]

Euro-Dakota men who fought against the Dakota included the Renville Rangers, recruited by Agent Galbraith just before the war, who arrived at Fort Ridgely barely in time to defend it from the first Dakota attack. Another example is Joseph Coursolle, who escaped the Redwood Agency as it was attacked with his wife and infant son and enlisted in the mounted militia to fight the Dakota as soon as he arrived at Fort Ridgely. On the other side, Euro-Dakota men joined Dakota warriors at the battles of Fort Ridgely, New Ulm, Birch Coulee, and Wood Lake. Some also attacked and killed settler-colonists, while others fled from Dakota attackers or were taken captive. Although there were Euro-Dakota men who fought willingly on both sides of the conflict, some who were held as captives, including Thomas and Angus Robertson, were at battle sites because they were compelled to be there by the Dakota soldiers' lodge, and they complied out of fear for their own safety and that of their families.

Camp Release

On September 27, 1862, Henry Sibley ordered the formation of a military commission to try Dakota and Euro-Dakota men for perpetrating alleged crimes against whites. The prosecutions of these men as criminals for fighting in the US–Dakota War were unprecedented in the history of warfare between the United States and Native peoples, contrary to established norms for the treatment of prisoners of war, and of dubious constitutional and legal foundation. As they took place, many whites called for the immediate extermination of all Dakota people in Minnesota. These calls for genocide were declared in the state's newspapers and advocated by some of its most prominent leaders, including the state's governor, Alexander Ramsey. Sibley was also pressured by his commanding officer, Major General John Pope, to treat the Dakota people "as maniacs or wild beasts, and by no means as people with whom treaties or compromises can be made." Pope told Sibley, "It is my purpose to exterminate the Sioux if I have the power to do so." Although the military commission had no legal jurisdiction, and Sibley had no authority to create it, he saw that the military court "offered a practical alternative to preemptory executions." In essence, the trials would provide a legal guise to justify the executions of the Dakota men who had gone to war against the whites.[2]

Sibley's commission was composed of five military officers who had just fought in the war against the Dakota men on trial, ensuring that the panel of judges was prejudiced. There was one official interpreter and one official recorder. The first trials, starting September 28, focused on those who were accused of committing "outrages" against whites—namely, murder and rape. After the first week of trials, when it appeared that only those accused of specific crimes would be prosecuted, Sibley expanded the prosecution and had hundreds more Dakota men surrender their arms at Yellow Medicine through a ruse; he then put them under armed guard to await trials. After that point, the trials significantly accelerated in pace.[3]

At first, the military commission focused on those accused of murder and rape, including the murder of Alexander Hunter. In the first two days of the military commission, sixteen men were arrested based on these charges and detained for trial. Evidence given as the trials proceeded led to the arrests of more Dakota men, and by October 11, there were about one hundred being held for trial at Camp Release. Up to this time, everyone charged had been specifically accused of crimes by one or more witnesses. Then, Major General Pope ordered Sibley to arrest all the Dakota men in the Yellow Medicine camp under the assumption that they all were guilty of "complicity in the late outrages." Shortly after this mass arrest, forty-six of the men were deemed above suspicion and released from custody, including Gabriel Renville, David Faribault, three Robertson brothers, and John Mooers.[4]

After the mass arrest at Yellow Medicine, the military commission accelerated its proceedings to deal with the hundreds of men now being held for trials. It held twenty-nine trials in its first two weeks; it would conduct several hundred trials in the next three. Sibley directed the commission to streamline the process and move as quickly as possible to obtain verdicts, directing the judges that the only evidence needed to prove guilt was that a man had voluntarily participated in the war. According to historian Walt Bachman, "with these orders Sibley authorized his court to pursue a legally unjustifiable course: to convict and give the death penalty to regular Dakota soldiers." Although Sibley initially announced that those found guilty by the military commission would be executed immediately once convicted, this did not happen because he began to have doubts about his authority to do so. Major General Pope was also pushing for a large mass execution of Dakota men after the trials ended. President Abraham Lincoln squelched these plans with a telegram on October 17 informing Pope that no executions could occur without his sanction.[5]

Although the military commission rapidly condemned hundreds of Dakota men to death for simply being present on battlefields with a gun, it was much more careful in its prosecution of Euro-Dakota defendants. The transcripts of those trials are much more detailed than those for the trials of Dakota men, and they include many more witnesses and more evidence. The commission took more time to determine which Euro-Dakota had been willing, active participants in the war, as opposed to reluctant, inactive players on the battlefield. The court had to decide to what extent a Euro-Dakota man was coerced and what his actual role in the battles had been—was he a bystander or an observer, had he only pretended to shoot, or had he been an eager participant in the fighting? What constituted participation—having a gun, firing a gun, or actually shooting a white person?[6]

As the trials progressed, witness testimony revealed that some of the Euro-Dakota men who earlier had been deemed above suspicion appeared to have been active participants on the Dakota side. Consequently, after the first several weeks of trials, a number of these Euro-Dakota men were arrested and prosecuted for their activities during the war. Thomas Robertson was one of them. The charges: "the said Thomas Robertson a half breed did between the 18th day of August 1862 and the 28th day of September 1862 join with and participate in the various Murders Robberies and outrages committed by the Sioux Tribe of Indians on the Minnesota Frontier and particularly in the battles at the Fort, New Ulm, Birch Coolie, and with having said that he killed one of the Gunners at the Fort."[7]

In his memoir, Thomas says that Taju (Red Otter or Tazoo) was the Dakota man who accused him of killing a white man at Fort Ridgely and of "fighting against the whites." Taju had been convicted of murder and rape and condemned to death several weeks earlier. Upon his complaint, Thomas was arrested, put under guard, and put on trial the next day. Thomas testified in his own defense about his roles in the battles at Fort Ridgely and New Ulm:

After the stable [at the fort] was burned the Indians said they wanted to set fire to the Fort—and they could not get anybody to do it—and thought they wanted me to do it. I told them that I would rather not. I did not like to do it. A punk arrow is what they wanted me to do it with. The position, which it was necessary to take, exposed the person to certain death. When they had it fixed they wanted me to get through a window in the stable. When I went to the window to get out, I saw a man passing along the piazza at the Fort. An Indian was looking out at the same time. His name was Yankton. The Indian said: "Fire, and I will say that you killed the man." I did fire—but so as not to hurt the man. I had a smooth bore rifle. After the smoke cleared away, the Indian said: "I guess he killed him, because we didn't see anything of him." The piazza was a high piazza—second story of the barracks. The man had citizen's clothes. Immediately after there was a cannon shot fired into the stable. As soon as the shot was fired, I went through a back window and through a door into a little kind of shed. When we got out the Indian said: "the shot must have killed the man, as the whites got mad and fired into the barn." Immediately after that, the Indians all left—before sundown—some stayed, but the main body went off. I fired at New Ulm—some blank shots. At the Fort I threw away all of my bullets. I asked the Indians to let me go back, and told them I had no bullets. They would not let me, and said they could furnish me balls, and gave me some. I was not at Birch Coulee, or in the last fight or in any war party."

In a deposition given forty years later, Thomas added more details about his role at New Ulm, saying, "We went with the rest of the Indians to attack New Ulm. I tried to get away from them, but they would not let me go."[8]

In his memoir, Thomas provided more information about the event at Fort Ridgely for which he was put on trial, including the fact that he was directly ordered by a member of the soldiers' lodge to shoot the arrow and start the fire. This later account reveals that Yankton, the Dakota friend who suggested the shooting ruse, did so to save Thomas from having to shoot the arrow and start the fire as well as to provide Thomas cover in the eyes of the other Dakota men gathered in the barn by convincing them he was truly engaged in the fighting. It suggests that Yankton understood and sympathized with Thomas's dilemma. Thomas says the man "was a particular friend of mine who had stayed right with me ever since we left camp," indicating that Yankton probably stuck close so that he could help him.

Thomas also explains that he was in the barn with only a few others, one of whom was a member of the soldiers' lodge, and that it was this man who ordered him to shoot the arrow and start the fire. These additional details in the story make clear that it would have been impossible for Thomas to escape complying with the order given to him, for to do so would mark him as disloyal and put his life in danger. He recalled, "this member of the Soldier's Lodge stepped up to me and handing me the bow and arrow said, 'You will have to shoot this.' I realized at once that this was the same as an order from hostile headquarters, and trusting in providence to guide, I unhesitatingly took them. At this juncture, my friend nudged me and pointing out the window said 'there goes a man shoot and I will say you killed him.' I saw no reason for not doing what he said, and it flashed across my mind that he had some reason and putting my gun through the window I fired. My friend at once turned to the other members of the party and said, 'he shot him down, he shot him down.'"[9]

As in many of the Dakota trials, the full testimony given at Thomas's trial was not recorded in the transcript. We know this because in his memoir Thomas says that he was acquitted due to "good witnesses, one of whom was Lieutenant James Gorman, the officer of the day at the Fort, and others" who verified that no one was killed that day inside the fort. Gorman is not listed as a witness in the trial transcript, nor are any of the other witnesses Thomas remembers as important to his case. The only witness who is listed and whose testimony is in the transcript is that of Joseph Godfrey, who admitted that he had not himself seen Thomas shoot the man but only had heard the story from other Dakota men. At the end of his testimony, Godfrey said: "I don't think Tom is a bad man. I believe he was forced to fight." The commission accepted Thomas's explanations for his presence at the battles as exculpatory, and he was "immediately re-leased" once the court was convinced that he had not killed a white man, as charged. The judges afforded Thomas the benefit of the doubt, unlike the vast majority of Dakota defendants, who were condemned to death for simply being present at a battle.[10]

Angus Robertson's participation in the war, on the other hand, remains obscure. The trial transcripts show that he, like Thomas, was compelled to fight for the Dakota and that he was present at the battle of Birch Coulee. Thomas confirmed Angus's presence at the battle in his testimony in one of the trials, when he corrected the defendant's claim that Tom Robin-son's brother was seen riding a white horse at Birch Coulee. Thomas said, "Tashakaymuzza, my brother, was the Indian who rode the white horse at Birch Coulee." Angus himself confirmed his presence at Birch Coulee as a witness in another trial. Both brothers were also at the war's last battle at Wood Lake. At the trial of Zuya Sa, Thomas said of the defendant, "this old man came to my brother and myself and others of the half breeds be-fore the last battle [Wood Lake] and said we must go, or they would come around again." Thomas describes Angus as outfitted as a warrior before proceeding to the battlefield. Other than this evidence, Angus's roles at Birch Coulee, Wood Lake, and other battles of the war remain largely unknown. Unlike Thomas, he never came under the scrutiny of the mili-tary commission.[11]

Thomas Robertson was one of the most frequent witnesses in the mili-tary commission trials. He was listed as a witness in eighty-five cases, although his testimony was recorded in only forty-nine of the trials. He gave testimony in twenty-one cases before he himself was tried, and after his acquittal he was a witness in fifteen more cases. One of the trials in which Thomas provided lengthy testimony on behalf of a defendant was that of Katpaŋtpaŋ U, the family friend who came across the river to warn the Robertsons about the imminent attack on Beaver Creek and then took them to his own home to hide them. Although Thomas testified that Katpaŋtpaŋ U had protected his family and had stepped in to protect his white neighbors, the old man was convicted and sentenced to death for his participation in the war. He avoided execution when President Lincoln reduced the execution list. He went to prison in Davenport, Iowa, and was released in 1864.[12]

In the other cases, Thomas testified based on his knowledge of what happened in the attack on Beaver Creek. In addition to the testimony he gave against Julia White's captor, Tate Hdidaŋ, Thomas identified Nape Śni ("Napashue" in the transcript) as one of the first attackers: "I heard the prisoner say the morning after the first massacre that [his gun] was an old gun, but that he had killed 19 with it. This was in front of John Mooer[s]'s house. His wife and children were the first ones over at the Beaver Creek massacre." In another case, Thomas and his former neighbor David Carrothers, whose two boys were killed at Beaver Creek, identified Cetaŋ Huŋka as one of the Dakota attackers.[13]

Thomas was also a witness at the trial of the French-Dakota man Henry Milord. As with the trials of other Euro-Dakota defendants, it was lengthier and included more witnesses than those of Dakota defendants. In Milord's case, which included seven Dakota and Euro-Dakota witnesses, the testimony that he had killed whites and was active at a number of battles sealed his condemnation. The trials, like the war, divided the Dakota people, for whom being a good relative was the most important value: Milord's uncle, David Faribault, testified against him. Despite Milord being given a fuller trial than most, and despite his well-known association with Henry Sibley, he could not escape conviction and execution.[14]

Unlike his older brother, Angus Robertson acted as a witness in only a few trials. He gave his most extensive testimony in the third trial before the military court on behalf of Wicaŋhpi Waśtedaŋpi (also known as Caske, the name used for firstborn sons), in which he said the defendant had protected Sarah Wakefield and her children from death and treated her well in captivity. Despite this testimony, Wicaŋhpi Waśtedaŋpi was found guilty for the murder of a white man and "other sundry hostile acts towards whites" and sentenced to death. Although he was reprieved when President Lincoln reduced the execution list, he was mistakenly hanged at Mankato when the name Caske was called and he stepped forward, taking the place of another man who went by the same name.[15]

Not everyone accepted the claims of Thomas Robertson and other Euro-Dakota men that they had been unwilling participants on the Dakota side of the war. On December 12, 1862, Antoine Frenier, the French-Dakota man who was the official interpreter at the Dakota trials, published a letter in a St. Paul newspaper in which he blamed the Euro-Dakota for instigating the war: "None have been more guilty of exciting the Indians against the whites than the Half-Breeds, who have constantly [been] poisoning their minds with accounts of frauds against them." Frenier angrily claimed that two-thirds of all mixed-ancestry people had participated on the side of the Dakota; they had not been forced to fight, and yet many were now free. He specifically named Thomas Robertson as one of the Euro-Dakota men complicit in the war, saying he "took a prominent part in all the fights and yet he is free."[16]

Frenier's accusations highlight how the roles of some Euro-Dakota men in the 1862 war, especially their presence on the battlefields, were often ambiguous, reflecting their ambivalent status as people of mixed ancestry caught up in a violent conflict between Dakota people and whites. On the one hand, they were relatives, and kinship was the fundamental organizing principle of Dakota society; honoring the rules of kinship was essential to being a good person in Dakota culture. On the other hand, they were seen by some Dakota people, especially by those who supported the war, as active participants in the ruin of the Dakota way of life.

Redwood Agency

In mid-October, Sibley moved everyone downriver to the Redwood Agency. There the trials continued at François LaBathe's trading post, the one building not destroyed in the war. These cases were conducted very rapidly: 172 trials were held between October 25 and November 5. In these cases, the charges against the accused were very general; anyone who had participated in battles or attacks on whites was prosecuted. As the Dakota considered themselves prisoners of war who had surrendered, they saw no need to deny their participation in battles at the trials. Moreover, Sibley had assured them more than once that only those who had killed white civilians would be in trouble. But Sibley broke his promise, and the military commission decided that simple participation in battles warranted a death sentence. In almost every case, the specified charge was that the accused had joined and participated in various murders and outrages during the war, but for many the only basis for their conviction was their presence at a battle.[17]

In the end, almost four hundred Dakota men were tried during the five weeks at Camp Release and Redwood. Of the 323 convicted, 303 were sentenced to death and 20 to prison; 69 were acquitted (8 of these were released during early days of trials, while the rest were kept prisoners with the others) and 5 were proven not guilty. All the defendants who were found to have participated in any fighting, whether at battles or against civilians, were convicted and sentenced to death. President Lincoln later reduced the number of men sentenced to death from 303 to the 38, and these men were executed on December 26, 1862, at Mankato in the largest mass execution in US history. Between 354 and 357 men were held at the Mankato prison over the winter of 1862–63, where 59 of them died. Of the prisoners who survived to be sent to prison in Davenport, Iowa, 26 later received pardons from President Lincoln and 177 were pardoned by President Andrew Johnson three years later.[18]

The Dakota trials put prisoners of war on trial as criminals. As legal historian Carol Chomsky notes, "in no other instance in U.S. history did the U.S. government respond to war in this manner." In addition, the trials were procedurally illegal and unfair in myriad ways. They were conducted too quickly; the nature of the evidence accepted was inadequate and deficient; no counsel was provided to the accused; many were convicted simply for being present at battles, while others were convicted because they were present in a group with others who committed killings. In the majority of cases, testimony from witnesses was perfunctory and often only hearsay. Much of the evidence came from witnesses who themselves were on trial, which meant they had a self-interest in testifying. Because confessions could be used as evidence at military trials, numerous defendants who confessed were unaware that by doing so they were pleading guilty to the charges (in addition to having been assured by Sibley that only those guilty of crimes against white civilians would be punished). The defendants were not put under oath, which was a requirement for testimony in a military court.[19]

The roles and status of Euro-Dakota people before and during the War of 1862 defies simple categorization or definition. Whites called them "half-breeds," but in fact they comprised an array of ancestral and cultural combinations as well as a range of social and economic relationships with both whites and Dakota people. The experiences of Daybreak Woman and her children during the war reflect the complexity of their relationships and status in both societies. Their experiences and treatment during and after the war were distinct in important ways compared to most Dakota people, as well as many other Euro-Dakota. Because they were Dakota, when the war broke out they were warned, taken to safety across the river, and protected by Dakota friends, while many of their white Beaver Creek neighbors were killed. Marion's white husband was shot at close range as she stood next to him, but she was then rescued from the assailant by Good Thunder, a friend and relative. As captives, the Robertsons were better off than the white prisoners but also were frequently threatened with death. Because of his long relationship with the Robertson family, Little Crow trusted Thomas as a translator and as his letter carrier. But as the leader's emissary, Thomas secretly carried letters from the peace faction to General Sibley. Similarly, Thomas's Dakota friend Yankton protected him at Fort Ridgley and helped him convince the other Dakota of his loyalty. Thomas, Angus, and Gustavus Robertson were among the group of Dakota and Euro-Dakota men deemed "above suspicion" after the mass arrests at Yellow Medicine, but Thomas was subsequently put on trial, then acquitted upon the same kind of evidence that was used to condemn hundreds of Dakota men. Once found not guilty, he was released and re-armed, unlike the other Euro-Dakota men who were acquitted. Daybreak Woman and some of her children were allowed to leave the camp with the released white captives, but her half sibling Jane Anne Mooers, her stepbrother John Mooers, and John's family were not.[20]

It is not entirely clear why the three Robertson brothers stayed in the camp after Daybreak Woman left for Faribault. Having been deemed above suspicion, they should have been free to go with her, but they chose to stay. The three aligned themselves with Sibley and his officers at Camp Release and Yellow Medicine. Samuel Hinman, in a letter to Bishop Whipple dated October 17, 1862, reports that Daybreak Woman had safely arrived in Faribault with her younger children. He then says, "Angus and Gustavus are with Major Galbraith. Thomas is with Sibley." In his memoir, Thomas confirms Hinman's description of his postwar situation, saying that after Jared Daniels took his mother and the rest of his family away to Faribault, "I still remained at Camp Release with Colonel Sibley's command," indicating that it was his choice to remain. Thomas says nothing in his memoir about Angus and Gustavus, but the record shows that they remained with him through December 1862, when all three were listed on the census of the Fort Snelling prisoner camp.[21]

While the Euro-Dakota men designated "above suspicion" were at liberty to leave Sibley's camp, whether to leave and what to do were questions. Gabriel Renville, who, like the Robertson brothers, was deemed above suspicion of complicity in the war, faced this choice:

> As myself and Ah-kee-pah [Akipa, Gabriel's stepfather], and our families, had not been implicated in any of the outrages against the whites, we were given the privilege of being outside the Indian camp, coming and going as we pleased. This being the case, I went back to my old home across the Minnesota River. Soon after this, General Sibley with his command, bringing the Indians that were there with him, moved down to the Yellow Medicine Agency, and thence, taking all that were there, moved down to the Redwood Agency. Everything that I owned at my old home had been taken or destroyed by the hostile Indians. Having nothing to live on, and the outlook being very dreary, I moved my camp to Redwood Agency, and pitched my tent with the friendly Indians who were then camped on the north side of Sibley's command. The families of those who had been suspected of doing anything against the whites were camped on the south side of the troops.

In addition to losing their homes and livelihoods, no Dakota or Euro-Dakota person felt safe remaining in the Minnesota River Valley given the publicly expressed rage of whites and the widespread calls immediately after the war for the extermination of all Dakota people.[22]

By the time Thomas stood trial, Daybreak Woman had been in Faribault for less than two weeks, sheltering there with the assistance of her friends in the Episcopal church, Bishop Whipple and Samuel Hinman. Frank, Will, and Mattie were with her. Marion, by this time five months pregnant, was living with the Williamson family in St. Peter, as was Sophie. Daybreak Woman must have been shocked and frightened to learn that Thomas had been charged by the military commission. Jane Williamson, who was with Marion at the time she received the news, described her dismay, reporting that Marion felt "very sorry about Thomas" and immediately went upstairs to write him a letter. Daybreak Woman must have been profoundly relieved to hear that Thomas was acquitted a few days later.[23]

After his acquittal, Thomas was free to move around at will and even to arm himself. He asked General Sibley for permission to retrieve the gun he had lent to Katpaŋtpaŋ U on August 18, and he retrieved it from the stockpile of confiscated guns. When Sibley ordered everyone downriver to the Redwood Agency, Thomas asked for permission to deviate from the military caravan and visit his Beaver Creek home, where he found nothing but ruins. As it was a fine autumn day, he sat in a canoe on a sandbar for hours and shot ducks, which he brought back to share at the Redwood camp.[24]

When the trials ended, Thomas recalled what happened next: "As the military court had got through with their work, and nothing more to be done then, orders were issued to break camp, and some of the troops took charge of the, something over three hundred condemned men, who went by way of New Ulm to Mankato. Other troops took charge of the prisoners' camp, as it was called, consisting of women and children and a few men. With these last I went."[25]

9. Mississippi and Missouri Rivers, 1862–1866

Fort Snelling, Crow Creek

> As they look on their native hills for the last time, a dark cloud is crushing
> their hearts.
>
> JOHN WILLIAMSON

While Daybreak Woman and her younger children began a new life in Faribault, their relatives still at Redwood with the rest of the Dakota people lived the full consequences of the war. Major General Pope ordered General Sibley to bring all the Dakota who had not been sent to the Mankato prison to Fort Snelling, where they would be held by the military until the government decided their fates. A four-mile-long caravan of 1,658 Dakota people, including about 200 Euro-Dakota, along with their livestock, horses, and remaining household possessions, left the Redwood Agency on November 7, 1862. Thomas Robertson and his wife, Niya Waśte Wiŋ, his brothers Angus and Gustavus, and Daybreak Woman's Mooers siblings—Jane Ann Mooers and John and Rosalie Mooers and their six children—were all in this group. Women, children, and elderly men made up most of their number, but about 150 younger men who had been deemed "friendly," including the three Robertson brothers, were included. These men had all been determined not guilty of participation in the war and the killing of settler-colonists. Most had either helped whites escape, protected them in captivity, or worked actively against the war.[1]

Lieutenant Colonel William Marshall, commanding three companies of soldiers, led the caravan overland for the 110-mile trek to Fort Snelling. He did not understand or speak the Dakota language, so he conveyed his orders through the Dakota speakers in the caravan, including John Other Day, Taopi, Simon Anawaŋ Mani, Gabriel Renville, Sam Brown, the Robertson brothers, and John Mooers. Before starting the journey, Marshall, fearful that whites intended to assault the Dakota prisoners and try to kill them, contacted the local newspapers and asked the editors to tell their readers that they were innocent, mostly women and children, and that he would have three hundred troops to guard them. Marshall declared he would risk his life to protect the Dakota prisoners and would "feel everlastingly disgraced if any evil befell them while in my charge."[2]

The long train of Dakota exiles crossed to the north side of the Minnesota River at the Redwood Ferry on November 6 and began its overland journey the next day. They followed the road from the Redwood Agency to Fort Ridgely and then took the road to Henderson, where they picked up the stage route to Fort Snelling, passing through Chaska and Bloomington along the Lower Minnesota River. They arrived at Fort Snelling on November 13, a week after they had left Redwood.[3]

The march was organized by family groups and bands. Some of the women and children rode in wagons provided by the military; some, including the Mooerses and the Robertsons, had their own wagons. Some used a traditional Dakota method of conveyance, the travois, while many others walked much of the way. The Robertson brothers and Niya Waśte Wiŋ must have traveled along with the Mooers family, who had two teams of oxen and horses to pull their two wagons. In his memoir, Thomas says little of their experiences on the march to Fort Snelling except to report that they were attacked by whites as they passed through the town of Henderson.[4]

As Marshall feared such an attack from whites from the start, his plan was to keep the train out of sight and away from populated areas as much as possible. This plan worked until they reached Henderson, where on November 11 the train went through the town to pick up the road to St. Paul. As the caravan passed, enraged whites fell upon the Dakota prisoners, pulling them from their wagons, pelting them with stones and bricks, pummeling them with fists and bats, and throwing scalding water on a cart loaded with the elderly and children. One crazed attacker grabbed an infant from their mother, throwing it to the ground. Sam Brown describes the violence in his memoir:

> I went along with Colonel Marshall's detachment, the train measuring about four miles in length. At Henderson, which we reached on the 11th we found the streets crowded with an angry and excited population,—cursing, shouting, and crying. Men, women and children armed with guns, knives, clubs, and stones, rushed upon the Indians as the train was passing by and, before the soldiers could

interfere and stop them, succeeded in pulling many of the old men and women, and even children, from the wagons by the hair of the head and beating them, and otherwise inflicting injury upon the helpless and miserable creatures. . . . I saw an enraged white woman rush up to one of the wagons and snatch a nursing infant from its mother's breast and dash it violently to the ground. The soldiers instantly seized her and led, or rather dragged the woman away and restored the papoose to its mother, limp and almost dead. Although the child was not killed outright, it died a few hours after. The body was quietly laid away in the crotch of a tree a few miles below Henderson and not far from Faxton. Here, soldiers did what they could to protect these people.

The Robertsons and Mooerses did not suffer serious injuries from the attack, according to Thomas's account: "We encountered nothing of importance, until we got to Henderson where a large crowd had collected for the purpose, we were told, of massacring the whole outfit. We had a hot time getting through the town, but finally made it alright without anyone being killed, though a number of women and children were hurt with bricks and stones thrown but no shots were fired. We made camp several miles beyond the town. Without anything more of importance happening, we reached Fort Snelling."[5]

It has been well documented that many of the soldiers who accompanied both prisoner caravans and were tasked with protecting the Dakota were deeply hostile toward their charges. There were vicious attacks by whites on the Dakota men who had been convicted by the military commission when they passed by New Ulm, resulting in several deaths. There was also an attempted lynching of the Dakota prisoners held at Mankato that involved members of the state militia. Many of the individual accounts left by the soldiers themselves document their rage and hostility toward Dakota people and their desire for vengeance. Sibley, Marshall, and the other officers had to repeatedly remind their men of their duty to protect the prisoners, even threatening them, because many soldiers openly admitted their intentions either to stand aside while others attacked or to turn on the captives themselves. Although Marshall intentionally chose companies of soldiers who were not from the Minnesota Valley region because he wanted to assure the prisoners' safety, nevertheless it is likely that many of the soldiers guarding the marchers were in fact hostile toward them and some expressed that hostility in various ways.[6]

Dakota accounts of the march to Fort Snelling recall that the prisoners were frequently verbally abused by whites along the journey, and an unknown number were physically assaulted and perhaps killed in places other than Henderson. As the train was four miles long, assaults on individuals or families along its entire length would not necessarily have been witnessed by others. These women and children, separated from the men in their families and uncertain about what the government intended to do to them, were undoubtedly intensely fearful of the soldiers who guarded them, and those who were attacked would have been afraid to report it.

Good Star Woman was eight years old when her family marched to Fort Snelling. She recalled multiple instances of violence against the prisoners along the route:

> The soldiers brought wagons for the women and children, while
> the Indians who had horses took them, and put their belongings
> on travois. Good Star Woman's father had a horse and travois and
> she travelled that way, with her two younger sisters her father covered them with a buffalo hide with the hair on the outside, but she
> sometimes lifted the corner and peeked out. When they passed
> through towns the people brought poles, pitchforks and axes and hit
> some of the women and children in the wagons. Her father was struck
> once and almost knocked down. The soldiers rode on each side of the
> column of Indians and tried to protect them but could not always do
> so. A boy was driving an ox cart and the white people knocked him
> down. Some Indians died from the beatings they received. At night
> they camped close together and the soldiers camped in a circle
> around them. Once an Indian was struck and killed. They scraped
> the fire aside and buried him under it, so the whites would not find
> the body. They went on the next morning.[7]

Another child in the long caravan to Fort Snelling with her family was Maza Okiye Wiŋ (Woman Who Talks to Iron). Her father, Maza Mani (Walking Iron), died from wounds suffered at the Battle of Wood Lake. Maza Okiye Wiŋ witnessed a soldier kill her grandmother on the journey. Her account, passed down from grandmothers to granddaughters in one family, highlights the vulnerability of the women and children in the caravan and reveals why the Dakota prisoners were afraid to report such outrages at the time they occurred:

My grandmother, Maza Okiye Win, was ten years old at the time and she remembers everything that happened on this journey. The killing took place when they came to a bridge that had no guard rails. The horses or stock were getting restless and were very thirsty. So, when they saw the water they wanted to get down to the water right away, and they couldn't hold them still. So, the women and children all got out, including my grandmother, her mother and her grandmother. . . . [W]hen all this commotion started the soldiers came running to the scene and demanded to know what was wrong. But most of them [the Dakota] couldn't speak English and so couldn't talk. This irritated them and right away they wanted to get rough and tried to push my grandmother's mother and her grandmother off the bridge, but they only succeeded in pushing the older one off and she fell in the water. Her daughter ran down and got her out and she was all wet, so she shook her shawl off and put it around her. After this they both got back up on the bridge with the help of the others who were waiting there, including the small daughter, Maza Okiye Win.

She was going to put her mother in the wagon, but it was gone. They stood there not knowing what to do. She wanted to put her mother someplace where she could be warm, but before they could get away, the soldier came again and stabbed her mother with a saber. She screamed and hollered in pain, so she [her daughter] stooped down to help her. But her mother said, "Please daughter, go. Don't mind me. Take your daughter and go before they do the same to you. I'm done for anyway. If they kill you the children will have no one." The daughter left her mother there at the mercy of the soldiers, as she knew she had a responsibility as a mother to take care of her small daughter.

The account goes on to describe how the daughter went back that night to give her mother's body a decent burial, but she could not find it and never learned what the soldiers had done with the body.[8]

Maza Okiye Wiŋ's account, as related by her descendent, describes further aspects of the Dakota experience of the march to Fort Snelling that is not provided in other published sources. She documents how conditions on the march led many to become weakened and ill as they trudged overland in the November cold:

They would camp someplace at night. They would feed them, giving them meat, potatoes, or bread. But they brought the bread in on big lumber wagons with no wrapping on them. They had to eat food like that. So, they would just brush off the dust and eat it that way. The meat was the same way. They had to wash it and eat it. A lot of them got sick. They would get dysentery and diarrhea and some had cases of whooping cough and small pox. This went on for several days. A lot of them were complaining that they drank the water and got sick. It was like a nightmare going on this trip.[9]

After Henderson the caravan continued its journey seventy miles to Fort Snelling through several populated areas, including Faxon, Chaska, Eden Prairie, and Bloomington, without encountering any additional violence from white mobs, although the prisoners continued to be vilified and threatened along the way and may have been subject to individual acts of violence that were not recorded. The missionary John Williamson, who had accompanied the prisoners, reflected that, given the hatred and threats displayed by whites along the route, the Dakota on the march to Fort Snelling had been in serious danger of being massacred:

We were under the escort of three companies of soldiers in [the] charge of Lieut. Col. Marshall, who exerted himself to the utmost to assist and protect his helpless charges. Notwithstanding it was a camp composed almost wholly of women and children; the indignation of the people of Minnesota against all Indians is so great that had they been in [the] charge of any other of our officers, I do not doubt that they would have been mobbed and many of them killed. As it was they performed the march with much fear, and notwithstanding the guard of soldiers, they received sundry salutations in the form of stones and sticks, to say nothing of curses which were heaped upon them from the doorways and hillsides.[10]

The train of Dakota people reached Fort Snelling on November 13. When they began, there had been 1,658 people, according to Sam Brown's account. The census taken at Fort Snelling on December 2 counted only 1,601 people. Assuming Brown's initial number is accurate, 57 people died or otherwise disappeared (perhaps fled) in the three weeks after the caravan left the Redwood Agency. These losses were neither officially recorded nor remarked upon by those whose accounts of the march have been published. Undoubtedly the oral history of many Dakota families documents some of them.[11]

Fort Snelling

Major General Pope ordered General Sibley to bring all Dakota people from the Minnesota Valley to Fort Snelling, where they would be held in a concentration camp until their anticipated deportation from the state. The widespread assumption among politicians and government officials was that all the Dakota people, regardless of their complicity, would be exiled because their presence would no longer be tolerated by white Minnesotans. From the military's viewpoint, concentrating all the Dakota people at Fort Snelling made logistical and strategic sense: soldiers were there, food and supplies were readily available, and the primary means of transportation in and out of the region (the Mississippi River) would enable swift deportation the following spring, after the ice melted.[12]

Everyone living at the Fort Snelling concentration camp was there because they were Dakota. No one in the camp was considered guilty of crimes or of active participation in the war—they were women, children, or elderly, or they were men who had been exonerated of complicity in the war and the killing of whites. Many of the Dakota and Euro-Dakota men in the camp had risked their lives protecting or rescuing settler-colonists and captives. The camp included the Euro-Dakota who had been held as captives themselves, except for a few, including Daybreak Woman and Nancy Faribault, who had been released with the white captives. A few fortunate Fort Snelling prisoners were paroled from the camp to live with relatives or friends nearby, in Mendota or St. Paul. The vast majority of the camp's residents were women and children whose male relatives either had died in the war, had fled the country, or were imprisoned at Mankato awaiting execution or prison sentences. In addition, a number of men who had been acquitted by the military commission were still held at Mankato.[13]

Living in the camp with his Dakota parishioners from the St. John Episcopal mission at Redwood was Samuel Hinman. Bishop Whipple traveled from Faribault, the seat of the Episcopal Diocese of Minnesota, to visit the camp weekly. Presbyterian John Williamson was the only other missionary besides Hinman who could be found in the camp every day—

Dakota woman and child, Fort Snelling concentration camp, 1862. *Photograph by Joel Emmons Whitney, Minnesota Historical Society collections*

he boarded at what had once been the Indian agent's house up on the bluff near the fort. Fellow Presbyterian missionary Stephen Riggs split his time between Mankato and Fort Snelling, as did Father Augustin Ravoux, a Catholic priest who lived in Mendota. The missionaries competed mightily to convert the imprisoned Dakota to Christianity. They also spent much of their time teaching the Dakota prisoners to read and write in their own language, and soon the prisoners at Mankato were able to exchange letters with their families at Fort Snelling.[14]

Thomas Robertson was a confirmed Episcopalian and had been the interpreter for Hinman's Redwood mission, so it was not surprising that Hinman asked him to act as his assistant in his missionary work in the camp. In addition, Thomas was employed by the government as an aide in the camp. He recalls: "I stayed with them [the Dakota at Fort Snelling], as Lieutenant McKusick, an old acquaintance and in charge of the camp or bullpen, as it was called, asked me to stay with him and do the work of issuing rations, wood, etc., and also the Rev. Hinman, for whom I had interpreted before, wished me to do his interpreting in teaching and other missionary work among them through that winter."[15]

Thomas does not mention in this recollection that he had another reason for wanting to stay in the camp: his wife, Niya Waśte Wiŋ, was there, as were two of his brothers. All three brothers appear on the census of December 2, 1862. It is not clear from Thomas's memoir when Angus and Gustavus left the Fort Snelling camp to join Daybreak Woman in Faribault. While at the camp, they would have received government food rations, and perhaps, like Thomas, they found some employment.

The Fort Snelling camp was organized by bands, with each living in its own section of the penned area, between two and three acres in size. The Euro-Dakotas in the camp composed their own band. In addition to the four Robertsons and the nine Mooerses, there were about thirty Renvilles, thirteen Campbells, and several other families, as well as a few individuals, including Thomas Robinson. There were 112 Euro-Dakota people in the camp. Nine bands of Dakota made up a population of 1,489 people. The camp's commander, Lieutenant William McKusick, kept a daily roster of the camp population by band to determine amounts of food rations and supplies to issue. The Dakota prisoners received military food rations of beef, pork, and flour.[16]

From December 1862 until March 1863, the camp was located on the floodplain below Fort Snelling, where between 200 and 250 tipis and tents were erected, surrounded by a sixteen-foot wall of wood. Soldiers guarded the interior and exterior perimeters of the stockade's walls, both to contain the Dakota prisoners and to prevent hostile whites from St. Paul from entering the camp, attacking people, and stealing their property—especially their livestock and wagons.[17]

Prisoners were not allowed to leave the camp permanently unless paroled by permission of the military commander, which was only granted if the parolee had a home with friends or family in the vicinity. During the day, people were allowed to leave the camp and move around the surrounding environs with an authorized pass. People left to collect wood, to fish, swim, and wash clothes in the river, to gather wild foods, to visit Little Crow's former village at Kap'oja, and to trade or shop in St. Paul. Beginning in January 1863, a store operated in the camp where internees who had cash could purchase bread, tobacco, soap, tea, cakes, dried apples, and gingerbread. In the spring of 1863, some were employed to work for the government unloading grain, burying dead animals, and cutting wood.[18]

However, it was dangerous for the Dakota prisoners to leave the camp, especially in the first weeks after their arrival. After two weeks at the fort, John Williamson wrote his father that there "were repeated threats that the citizens of St. Paul and Minneapolis were preparing to make a raid and clean out the whole camp." Bishop Whipple said that the wall had been built to protect the Dakota, especially the women, from the white men who came into the camp to rape and commit other acts of violence. However, the wall and the guards who walked its perimeter did not necessarily ensure the safety of those in the camp. Bishop Whipple recalled that Samuel Hinman was beaten "insensible" and required stiches in his scalp after "white roughs" from St. Paul broke in one night and assaulted him. Local newspapers reported at least two Dakota men were murdered either just within or just outside the stockade. Other such violent assaults may have occurred and not been recorded.[19]

The women in the Fort Snelling camp, who with their children constituted the majority of the prisoners, faced the continuous threat of sexual assault not only from white invaders but from the soldiers garrisoned at the fort. The *St. Paul Daily Union* of November 22 describes the rape of a Dakota woman by a group of men: "*An Outrage.*—A day or two ago the newspapers announced that a s—— had been accidentally shot at the Fort, by some soldiers engaged in target practice. The truth of the matter appears to be, that the s——s have been in the habit of gathering wood for their campfires and one of them, thus engaged, having wandered some little distance from the encampment, was seized by a number of soldiers and brutally outraged."[20]

Most rapes and other assaults on the Dakota prisoners were not publicly reported. However, personal sources from this time, such as Bishop Whipple's letters, reveal that such attacks took place much more frequently than was apparent in the press. There were also widespread rumors of attacks on Dakota women, including claims that soldiers were regularly killing women, slitting their throats and burying them surreptitiously.[21]

Although no one was allowed to enter the Fort Snelling camp without permission of the military commander, passes were easy to obtain. Soon the Dakota prisoners in the camp found themselves subjected to the scrutiny and attention of white visitors and tourists who viewed them as a form of entertainment and curiosity, often showing no respect for their privacy and entering or peering into their homes uninvited. Visitors included military officers, legislators, government officials, photographers, and journalists. They moved through the camp at will, as though they were examining specimens in a zoo or museum. Professional photographers from St. Paul took photographs of the Dakota prisoners from which they could profit. A few photographers provided their subjects with portrait daguerreotypes, which they sent along with letters to their relatives imprisoned at Mankato.[22]

Overcrowding led to poor sanitary conditions and soon to illness. Measles was already prevalent in St. Paul, St. Peter, Mankato, Shakopee, and Faribault, where war refugees had fled and where soldiers were garrisoned; all reported outbreaks and deaths, mainly of children, from the disease. Conditions in the camp made the Dakota especially vulnerable to the rapid spread of its debilitating symptoms, including fever, cough, vomiting, diarrhea, and red and watery eyes. In April 1863, Dr. Thomas Williamson estimated that more than two hundred Dakota people, mostly children, had died at the Mankato prison and the Fort Snelling camp. Other diseases also sickened and killed people at Fort Snelling, including typhoid, diphtheria, and scarlet fever.[23]

Good Star Woman remembered the terrible toll the measles took on the camp and her own family: "They were provided with food. The soldiers drove a wagon among the tents and gave crackers to the children and bread to the older people. Measles broke out, and the Indians thought the disease was caused by the strange food. This was the first time they had ever had the disease. All the children had measles and one of her sisters died. Sometimes 20 to 50 died in a day and were buried in a long trench, the old, large people underneath and the children on top."[24]

Gabriel Renville described the fear and despair that gripped the prisoners at Fort Snelling by the end of December: "Then a fence was built on the south side of the fort and close to it. We all moved into this inclosure [*sic*], but we were so crowded and confined that an epidemic broke out among us and the children were dying day and night, among them being Two Stars' oldest child, a little girl."[25]

In January 1863, Bishop Whipple wrote to his wife, "You have no idea of the very wretched condition of those poor creatures at Fort Snelling. I suppose not less than 300 will die before spring. The measles and pneumonia are doing a fearful work of death." A week later, Stephen Riggs reported that the Fort Snelling camp "is a very sad place now. The crying hardly ever stops. From five to ten die daily." To compound the grief, whites were digging up and mutilating the buried dead. Riggs said the Dakota prisoners "are now keeping their dead and burying them in their teepees."[26]

As they grieved the deaths of family members and friends, the Fort Snelling prisoners, dispossessed and homeless, were also gripped by a constant, deep anxiety about what would become of them and their families. Many of the men in the camp hoped they would be allowed to return to their farms on the reservations or establish themselves just across the border in Dakota Territory. They thought that because they had protected whites, opposed the war, and been found innocent by the military commission they would be freed and not deported from the state. In a letter dated December 18, 1862, Wapaha Ša and other Dakota leaders held at Mankato and Fort Snelling wrote to President Lincoln asking to be allowed to return to their farms. In the letter the leaders of the Upper Dakota bands asked permission to go live on the Coteau des Prairies in eastern South Dakota, while those of the Bdewakaŋtuŋwaŋ wanted to return to their farms on the Minnesota River. Their requests were denied.[27]

Gabriel Renville described the dark mood of the prisoners after the mass execution at Mankato on December 26: "The news then came of the hanging at Mankato. Amid all this sickness and these great tribulations, it seemed doubtful at night whether a person would be alive [in] the morning. We had no land, no homes, no means of support and the outlook was most dreary and discouraging. How can we get back again? . . . were the questions which troubled many thinking minds, and were hard questions to answer." Renville, desperate like many others to get himself and his family out of the camp and to find a means of supporting them, went to General Sibley and proposed he employ a number of the Euro-Dakota and Dakota men as frontier scouts. Among the men on Renville's original proposed list were John Mooers and Tom Robinson. Sibley agreed with the plan.[28]

In the winter of 1862–63, about fifty Dakota and Euro-Dakota men were authorized to work for the government as scouts on the western frontier of Minnesota into Dakota Territory. These men and their families were allowed to stay in the state and were provided rations and some supplies by the government. The first group of scouts left in February 1863, moving up the Minnesota River to set up camp on the Redwood River. A few months later, their families, about 137 people, were allowed to leave the main prison camp and locate themselves apart from the rest of the Dakota prisoners on the prairie southwest of Fort Snelling. In May, some of these families traveled up to be near their men, camping close to Fort Ridgely, where they were under the protection of the military. They returned in August to Fort Snelling under military guard. Rosalie Mooers and her children were among these scout families. However, Jane Ann Mooers was deported from Mni Sota Makoce with the rest of the Dakota prisoners in May 1863.[29]

On April 23, the steamboat carrying the prisoners who were being shipped from Mankato to a federal military prison in Davenport, Iowa, arrived at Fort Snelling. The forty-eight men acquitted by military commission who had been held at Mankato were let off the boat and reunited with their families. Some of these men and their families would be allowed, along with some men held at Fort Snelling, to avoid deportation. Due to the efforts of Bishop Whipple and Henry Sibley, small groups of Dakota and Euro-Dakota people were given permission to stay in Minnesota. However, they could only inhabit certain places and were placed under the protection and supervision of prominent white men, including Bishop Whipple and Alexander Faribault at Faribault and Henry Sibley at Mendota. Taopi and his family were allowed to settle in Faribault, as were others, about forty people in all, while another thirty prisoners were released to live at Mendota. Although they were relieved to avoid deportation, staying in Mni Sota Makoce was dangerous; Dakota people could be legally hunted as if they were animals after the government of Minnesota placed a bounty on Dakota scalps and encouraged white citizens to shoot any Native person on sight.[30]

Early in May 1863, the Dakota prisoners who had survived the overcrowded, unsanitary conditions and the measles epidemic that ravaged the camp over the winter, about 1,300 people, were put on two steamboats and shipped down the Mississippi River and up the Missouri River to the Crow Creek Reservation, newly established at Fort Thompson on the Missouri River in what is now south-central South Dakota. The first boat left on May 4 with 771 people and the second boat on May 5 with 547 people.

The military marched the Dakota prisoners onto the boats in their bands; leading the way was Wapaha Ṡa. When one of the boats stopped to take on cargo at St. Paul, an angry mob pelted the Dakota on the boat with rocks and other objects, severely injuring a number of women, until the soldiers intervened. The deported Dakota were accompanied by missionaries John Williamson and Samuel Hinman. Williamson reported that at least twenty-eight people died en route to Crow Creek due to overcrowded, unsanitary conditions and bad food. Williamson described the Dakota deportees as being packed on the boats "like slaves." Many others died not long after arriving at Crow Creek, perhaps as many as 250 in the first few months after their arrival.[31]

Crow Creek

In May 1863, Thomas Robertson left on the second steamboat with the Dakota deportees for the trip to the Crow Creek Reservation. Angus and Gustavus had already left Fort Snelling to reunite with Daybreak Woman and the rest of the family at Faribault. In his memoir, Thomas recalls: "I was employed by the government as interpreter and went with the last lot that left Fort Snelling. We at once commenced the work of establishing what is still known as the Crow Creek Agency. During my stay at this agency, besides my duties as government employee, I assisted the Rev Mr. Hinman in his teaching and other missionary work. During the summer some Winnebago were brought to that agency, and a part of my work was to issue beef and other rations twice a week to both Sioux and Winnebago."[32]

At Crow Creek the Dakota deportees found drought and desolation. When they first arrived, there was as yet no infrastructure at the reservation; army tents had been set up to house them, there was only one two-story frame house erected, and the perimeter of the reservation was not yet completely staked out. The region was in the middle of a drought, and the soil was poor for farming anyway. The only suitable arable land was by the river, which tended to flood. With little timber and no lakes, it was a barren place—very unlike Mni Sota Makoce. The Dakota at Crow Creek also found themselves surrounded by unfriendly whites in the territory who, according to Hinman, tried "to rob the Indians any way they can." Near-starvation conditions existed from the beginning at Crow Creek; government food rations were inadequate and often spoiled. Reverend Hinman reported that weekly food rations lasted only one or two days.

There was also no physician or medicine provided to treat the ill. Hunger and exposure fostered disease, and many infants and children died in the first year.[33]

Thomas worked and lived at Crow Creek until February 1864, when he returned to reunite with his mother and siblings in Faribault. Since Thomas does not mention Niya Waśte Wiŋ in his memoir, it is not clear what happened to his wife. She was counted on the December 1862 census as an internee at Fort Snelling, but since individual names were not counted in subsequent camp records, these do not reveal whether she survived the camp and was deported. If Niya Waśte Wiŋ was at Crow Creek, the couple was only together for nine more months, until Thomas left. He would not return until December 1864. Thomas notes simply that "the trip was in the interests of some of Bishop Whipple and Mr. Hinman's missionary work among the Indians there at Crow Creek Agency." The timing of this trip, just before Christmas, suggests Bishop Whipple and Hinman had sent Christmas gifts—probably food and clothing, perhaps funds—collected from the parish in Faribault or in other parishes in the diocese for the Dakota at Crow Creek. Whether their marriage ended or whether Niya Waśte Wiŋ was one of the many who died at Crow Creek remains a mystery.[34]

The burden of survival at Crow Creek, both physical and cultural, fell almost entirely on women. In the wake of dispossession and exile, thrust into an extremely inhospitable environment, women exhibited tremendous strength and creativity in their efforts to keep themselves and their families alive, applying their traditional skills and knowledge but also taking on new economic roles. However, destitution also wrought degradation: John Williamson and Samuel Hinman both reported that it became common practice for women to scavenge the manure of horses and other animals for grains of corn. In a letter of protest to the US government about the forced exile of the Dakota people and the horrendous conditions at Crow Creek, Bishop Whipple said: "[The Dakota] were taken by no authority except that 'might makes right' and were sent to the Upper Missouri and landed at a place which General Warren who surveyed it certified to me was unacceptable for habitation. They died by hundreds of diseases and starvation. I have been told the soldiers saw women pick over the dung of cavalry horses to find half-digested grains to keep themselves and babes from death."[35]

Many people at Crow Creek lacked not only food but adequate clothing. Good Star Woman recalled in her memoir: "Their destination was Fort Thompson, where they were kept in a stockade for three years. Many starved to death there. The Indians were almost naked, they wound burlap around their legs to keep warm. Many of the women had to wear burlap gotten from the soldiers and nobody had any sleeves on their garments."[36]

Sexual exploitation and sexual assault were the other degrading and dehumanizing experiences of the women at Crow Creek. The struggle to survive, just to have the most basic food and clothing for themselves and their children, drove some women to sell their sexual services to the soldiers and other white men at Fort Thompson, and some women traveled to other forts in the region as a means of survival. The soldiers at the fort also routinely raped and sexually assaulted Dakota women—behavior that was either overlooked or condoned by their commanding officers.[37]

Despite widespread hunger at Crow Creek in 1863, the reservation superintendent, Clark Thompson, would not initially allow the Dakota deportees to have guns for hunting and treated them as prisoners. However, when buffalo were discovered not too far away, he relented and allowed them guns to hunt; the meat saved some from starving that first winter. In the spring of 1864, some Dakota attempted farming, but the drought continued, making it impossible. About three hundred people died at Crow Creek in the first two years due to starvation, disease, and exposure. People began to leave as early as 1864, walking back to Mni Sota Makoce to join scout camps on the Minnesota River or the Coteau des Prairies in eastern South Dakota, or to join the Dakota settlement at Faribault.[38]

In the fall of 1865, more than two years after their arrival, a US government peace commission, including Henry Sibley, arrived at Crow Creek to meet with the Dakota deportees. Wapaha Ṡa reported the abuses and corruption of the Indian agent as well as lack of food and clothing, explaining that the Dakota were starving to death. As a result, the commission recommended the removal of the Dakota people to a new reservation. In 1866, they were sent to the Santee Reservation on the Niobrara River in Nebraska, where they found environmental conditions more favorable for farming. There they were joined by the Dakota men who had at last been released from the Davenport prison after the end of the Civil War, Lincoln's assassination, and a pardon by Andrew Johnson.[39]

Although Daybreak Woman and her children escaped deportation to Crow Creek, her half sister and namesake, Jane Ann Mooers, did not.

Jane Ann was thirty-six years old when the Dakota War began and had lived with her half brother John's family on the reservation for almost ten years. It seems unlikely she would have voluntarily separated herself from the family and gone to Crow Creek, so she probably did not have a choice in the matter. While Rosalie and the Mooers children were allowed to stay in Mni Sota Makoce with other scout families, Jane Ann may not have been allowed by the authorities to stay because as John's half sister she was not considered part of his immediate family. Her nephew Thomas was on the journey with her to Crow Creek in May 1863, and he stayed there until February 1864. Presumably, Thomas would have looked after his aunt Jane Ann. Once Thomas left, however, she no longer had close family members at Crow Creek to support her.

Jane Ann Mooers was one of the hundreds of people who died at Crow Creek in 1863–64. In the summer of 1864, Daybreak Woman traveled there to tend to her sister in her final days and to help put her to rest. Bishop Whipple made the visit possible, paying a man to escort Daybreak Woman and one of the girls (probably Sophie or Mattie) to the Crow Creek Reservation. There, Daybreak Woman said goodbye to her younger sister, another daughter of Grey Cloud Woman.[40]

10. Cannon and Straight Rivers, 1862–1868

Faribault

I had to come here to work to support myself and some of my children

Daybreak Woman and her children Frank (sixteen), Willie (eleven), and Mattie (seven) traveled to Faribault in October 1862, escorted by Dr. Jared Daniels, the government physician from the reservation. Her good friends, all people connected to the Episcopal mission at the Redwood Agency and to Bishop Whipple, had invited her to take shelter among them in the town, the seat of the Episcopal Diocese of Minnesota. These included Samuel Hinman, Jared Daniels (who was Bishop Whipple's personal physician), and the bishop himself. Although she had known the Faribault family since she was a young girl in Prairie du Chien, she had no close personal connection to anyone in the town and would not otherwise have moved there. Daybreak Woman's ardent Episcopal faith and the active membership and leadership that she and her son Thomas provided to the Dakota mission determined the family's place of resettlement as well as their subsistence and eventual economic recovery after the war.

On the way to Faribault, the Robertsons stopped at St. Peter, where the Williamsons were now living. There Daybreak Woman saw Sophie, who had escaped with the Williamsons, for the first time since the war began. Marion, who by this time was about five months pregnant, stayed on to live with the Williamsons through most of her pregnancy. The Williamsons' ability to shelter two of Daybreak Woman's daughters in their family relieved her of some of the anxiety and burden she must have been feeling as a war refugee.[1]

Samuel Hinman, in a letter to Bishop Whipple of October 17, 1862, reported Daybreak Woman's arrival in Faribault: "I write to inform you of the safe arrival of Mrs. Robertson and Frank. Willie and Mattie are with them. Angus and Gustavus are with Major Galbraith. Thomas is with Sibley. Mrs. Robertson reports 'All Mr. Hinman's Indians have done nobly.' Good Thunder and Taopi planned and carried out the liberation of the 200 prisoners at the peril of their lives. . . . I have been to see Julia Prescott and her mother at Minnehaha and hope soon to go to the Agency to see the rest of my flock." In a postscript, Hinman added that a "box of clothing for Miss Prescott and her mother and for Mrs. Robertson and other female refugees" would be a worthy objective for fundraising in the diocese's parishes. Julia and her newly widowed mother, Naġi Owiŋna, were also members of the Episcopal church at Redwood. They had returned to the Prescott family homestead, located not far from Minnehaha Falls in what is now Minneapolis.[2]

Faribault

By 1862, Faribault was a rapidly growing and prosperous town, and it would continue to flourish during the almost nine years Daybreak Woman's family lived there. Located thirty-four miles directly east of the town of St. Peter and about seventy-five miles south of St. Paul, the town sits in a beautiful natural setting surrounded by river bluffs and extensive woods, at the junction of the Cannon and Straight Rivers. It was the site

Faribault, Minnesota, 1862. *Photograph by Benjamin Franklin Upton, Minnesota Historical Society collections*

of a Waĥpekute Dakota village for many years; Alexander Faribault, a French-Dakota man, built a fur post on the river near there in 1826. When the Treaty of 1851 took the land from the Dakota people, he was among the founders of the town of Faribault, where he built a flour mill.[3]

The waterpower supplied by the rivers made it a milling center, and the fertile surrounding region made it an agricultural depot. The town became the county seat for Rice County and a center of commerce for the surrounding country. By 1862, it had numerous stores and trades shops, churches, schools, hotels, restaurants, and places of entertainment, such as billiard rooms and bowling alleys. Its population boomed in the early 1860s, increasing from 1,500 in 1860 to 2,400 by 1865. There were also three nearby limestone quarries, wagon shops, livery stables, a broom factory, a barrel factory, a tannery, a foundry, and several steam-powered mills. A number of professionals lived in Faribault, including several physicians, two dentists, and attorneys. The town appears to have been socially organized as well, especially around music; Faribault had a brass band, a string band, a vocal club, and a singing school. In 1866, the *Faribault Republican* claimed the town was the largest grain depot in the state, with four grain elevators. By that time there were about three thousand residents, seven churches, six public schools, and several Episcopal church schools, and a state residential facility for deaf people was under construction.[4]

Other Dakota people also came to Faribault the next summer. Many were Daybreak Woman's friends, members of Redwood Agency Episcopal Church, including Good Thunder, Taopi, and their families. Taopi had asked Bishop Whipple to help the Dakota who had protected whites and opposed the war to avoid deportation and stay in Mni Sota Makoce. Whipple in turn asked Alexander Faribault, who had donated land for the Episcopal church and schools in Faribault already, for help. The Faribaults had been neighbors of Daybreak Woman's family in Prairie du Chien; John Baptiste Faribault and Daybreak Woman's grandfather, James Aird, were generational peers in the fur trade.[5]

The Dakota refugees settled on flatland adjacent to the Straight River, a site below Faribault's home on the bluffs about one mile south of the town. Threats against them by townspeople led Faribault to publish a letter in the town's newspaper: "Having been informed that a report is current that I am harboring guilty Indians, and that there are now at my place a large number, some of whom are known to have participated in the out-break, and that threats of violence to any Indians found there have been made, I deem it my duty to quiet the fears of persons who might believe such report to be true, though I hope my fellow citizens will examine for themselves."⁶

He went on to list the families living on his land, including the family of Good Thunder, who he pointed out was currently working as a scout for Sibley, and Taopi, whom he describes as having been important in saving white captives. The letter seemed to have the desired effect of reducing the fear and open hostility of the townspeople toward their new Dakota neighbors, at least for a time.

Hard Times

When she arrived in Faribault with her three youngest children, Daybreak Woman was destitute. Except for the land they owned at Beaver Creek, the family had no assets, wealth, or income. Their ability to subsist by farming on their land had been ruined—houses and farms destroyed, livestock lost—and it was not clear whether or when they might be able to return to Beaver Creek. Their jobs working for the government, the traders, and the Episcopal mission were gone. The Dakota War had caused the complete collapse of the economy and society in which Daybreak Woman and her children had lived and supported themselves.

An undated letter Daybreak Woman wrote shortly after arriving in Faribault indicates her economic desperation. In it, she appeals to the superintendent of Indian Affairs for funds she claims are owed to Andrew for money he spent as part of the 1858 treaty delegation.

> Dear Sir,
>
> If you have any human feelings to take notice of a poor woman's letter as a gentleman. I had to come here to work and support myself and some of my children. What I wish as a favor if you would be so kind and write and say my husband was entitled to [illegible] dollars for going with the Indians to Washington, as you said last winter when I saw you at the agency, will you be so obliging as to write.
>
> Respectfully, Jane A Robertson⁷

It is not clear whether she ever received the reimbursement she sought.

Without the land they had been farming, Daybreak Woman and her children once again faced the financial struggle and poverty common for widows in the mid-nineteenth century. Although as an educated woman she could teach, those positions generally went to men or young, single women. Faribault also had a few factories that may have hired women, but such jobs also usually went to younger women. Domestic work was Daybreak Woman's most likely option, either working in someone else's home or taking work into her own home. It would have been much easier for Frank to find employment, because he was an educated young man and he already had experience working as a government clerk on the reservation. He could work as a manual laborer, in a mill or factory, as a farm hand, or in a job that required education and particular skills, such as teaching, secretarial, and business positions. In the 1860s, retail establishments, stores, and restaurants were just beginning to hire women in larger numbers; these jobs generally still were mostly occupied by men.[8]

When Daybreak Woman and the children first arrived in Faribault, and perhaps for some time after, they lived with Reverend Hinman's family and in the homes of his friends and members of the Episcopal Church, as they had no means of paying rent or buying property. Marion rejoined them in the spring of 1863 and gave birth to her first child, Alexander Hunter. Gustavus and Angus also joined them in 1863. For some years, the family would continue to depend on the charity of the Episcopal church—through Bishop Whipple, Reverend Hinman, and parish donations—as well as employment from the church. Daybreak Woman's close association with the Episcopal mission at the Redwood Agency was key to her family's ability to survive and eventually recover from the financial ruin wrought by the war.

Bishop Whipple's account book shows that he paid Daybreak Woman $17.37 in April 1863 "out of the fund for sufferers" (funds raised for victims of the war) for "her daughter." In addition to charity, he employed Thomas to help sustain the family. Bishop Whipple paid Thomas for a variety of work, starting with his mission work assisting Reverend Hinman at Fort Snelling and Crow Creek and continuing after Thomas returned from Crow Creek and joined the family at Faribault in February 1864. For four months, Thomas remembered, he worked "in Bishop Whipple's studio translating a part of the prayer book and other work in that line." The result was a published Dakota translation of the Episcopal Church Prayer Service. After that project was complete, Whipple continued to employ Thomas in various ways, paying him for plowing in May 1864 and for buying potatoes in June. Later that same month, he paid Thomas again for undesignated work.

After June 1864, there are no entries in Whipple's account book related to Daybreak Woman or her children, which suggests that the family found other means of subsistence. According to June Robertson Lehman, a historian and descendant, the family farmed at Faribault, so they must have rented land or perhaps were given land by the church.[9]

In February 1865, Thomas and Gustavus enlisted in the 1st Minnesota Artillery to fight for the Union in the Civil War. They served most of their time at Chattanooga and mustered out in October 1865. Presumably, part of their military pay went to support their mother and siblings in Faribault. By the end of 1865, Daybreak Woman and her children, including Sophie, were together again at least for a short period. By this time, they were farming, and some of them may have been working for wages in or around Faribault. Angus and Frank may have found jobs as laborers or clerks. Daybreak Woman, Marion, and Sophie might have found jobs as domestic workers. Although there is no evidence of family members' employment during all of these years, the federal census of 1870 shows that Sophie was working as a domestic and Frank as a clerk at the post office.[10]

During these years after the US–Dakota War when anti-Dakota hatred was still prevalent throughout Minnesota, at least two of Daybreak Woman's children evidently were accepted by Faribault's white society despite their Dakota heritage. In July 1870, the city's newspaper announced that Frank Robertson had joined the other young men of the town to organize a new baseball club, the Athletic Club, and he was acting as the club's vice president. In 1870, Sophie married Henry Weatherstone, a white man from the nearby town of Warsaw, and the next year Frank married Clara Grafton, a white woman from Winona.[11]

The family's economic situation improved slowly in the years after the war. In late 1865, after mustering out of the Union Army, Thomas and Angus left Faribault and set out on their own, working as scouts in western Minnesota and eastern South Dakota. Since early 1863, numerous scout camps had been established in western Minnesota and in Dakota Territory. The government employed Dakota and Euro-Dakota men to report on the whereabouts of potentially hostile Dakota bands to the west and on Dakota incursions into Minnesota. Many of these camps were located on or near the border of Minnesota and Dakota Territory. John Mooers, Gabriel Renville, Tom Robinson, Paul Maza Kute Mani, and other Dakota and Euro-Dakota men also worked as scouts.

In 1866, when Thomas and Angus were scouts, Gustavus and Frank were still with Daybreak Woman in Faribault, as were Sophie (eighteen), Will (sixteen), and Mattie (eleven), as well as Marion and her son, Alexander. Daybreak Woman decided to sell part of Mattie's land at Beaver Creek, petitioning the probate judge for Renville County as the child's mother and legal guardian to sell her quarter section. Daybreak Woman declared in the petition that she was unable to clothe and educate Mattie without money from the property. Her petition was granted, and the land was sold for $475 in December 1866 at a public auction in Beaver Falls, a community platted in 1866 about 1.5 miles up Beaver Creek from their old home.[12]

Bishop Whipple was persistent and public in his criticism of the government's treatment of the Dakota people. He made demands for government support on behalf of the exiled Dakota at Crow Creek and called for support for the Dakota who were still in Mni Sota Makoce, being joined in his efforts by Henry Sibley and Samuel Hinman. Between 1863 and 1867, they petitioned the government repeatedly on behalf of the Dakota who had protected whites and been active in the peace faction during the 1862 war. On February 9, 1865, Congress finally responded to their call for compensation for these people, passing "An Act for the Relief of Certain Friendly Indians of the Sioux Nation in Minnesota." The act appropriated $7,500 to be divided as a reward to those who had rescued whites or had actively opposed the war. Whipple drew up a list of "friendly" Dakota and proposed a way to divide the reward money among them, which he sent in a letter to the commissioner of Indian Affairs. He suggested Thomas Robertson and Tom Robinson, among others, each be paid $100 for their efforts on behalf of the peace faction.[13]

Throughout these years, Whipple and Hinman also repeatedly asked the government to give the "friendly" Dakota land on the former Minnesota River reservation. In 1865, Congress appropriated twelve sections of land along the Upper Minnesota as allotments for them; Hinman was authorized to choose the land. However, as he was organizing people to leave Faribault and resettle on the Minnesota, whites in the river valley objected vociferously, and Major General Pope refused to allow any Dakota people to move back to the Minnesota River. Unable to leave Faribault, Hinman instead rented one hundred acres near the town and bought seed and farm equipment so the Dakota refugees could farm. Other Dakota refugees then came to Faribault upon hearing of this new situation, including those fleeing the desperation at Crow Creek. The new arrivals put more pressure on the area's natural resources, especially timber. This and their general presence caused increased hostility from whites in the town, who began to complain once again of the Dakota refugees.[14]

The Dakota refugees at Faribault struggled mightily to sustain themselves. They grew corn and other crops, and many left in autumn to hunt in the surrounding woods or to the west on the prairies. Nevertheless, many remained dependent on charity. Though they tried to seek employment, whites in Faribault refused to hire them. When the crops planted in 1865 were washed out by a flood, the Dakota dug ginseng on Faribault's land and sold it for income. In the 1880s, historian Edward Neill explained how Faribault became a source for this enterprise: "Early in the sixties, ginseng, an aromatic tonic root, exported to China, and used by the Orientals as a remedial or luxury preparation, began to be extensively gathered, as it is found indigenous in certain localities here. Ten dollars a day or more was often made by a single individual." A buyer in Faribault purchased ginseng for twenty-five cents per pound and shipped it to St. Paul, and then eventually to China.[15]

On April 1, 1866, Alexander Faribault was supporting fifteen Dakota families (about eighty-five people), providing goods, clothes, and funds. The ginseng on his land was completely depleted, and his generosity toward the Dakota refugees had brought him to financial ruin. He told them that he could no longer sustain this support and that they would have to leave. He sent a claim to the US government asking to be reimbursed for $3,871, which he claimed was only half of the amount he had actually spent to aid the Dakota in Faribault. In June 1866, a government special agent came to Faribault to investigate the situation and found twelve families (sixty-five people) living in tipis. The investigator concluded that the Dakota at Faribault were only barely subsisting and were almost completely dependent on the benevolence of not only Faribault but also Bishop Whipple, Samuel Hinman, and Jared Daniels.[16]

In 1867, the funds that had been appropriated pursuant to the 1865 Act for the Relief of Certain Friendly Indians finally arrived. Daniels distributed the money to the Dakota in Faribault's house on the bluffs. That same year, the government ordered the Faribault Dakota removed to the new Santee Reservation in Nebraska. In the summer of 1867, Hinman escorted many, although not all, of the Faribault Dakota refugees to Santee, where he established an Episcopal mission. Going with them were a number of other Dakota people who had been living at Mendota, Bloomington, and Wabasha. Taopi and a few other families did not go to Santee; some used their reward money to buy houses or farmland in Minnesota. In the 1870s and 1880s, a small group of Dakota families returned to take up land near the former Redwood Agency site. This community became the nucleus of a new Dakota population that eventually became the Lower Sioux Community at Morton, Minnesota.[17]

Alexander Faribault never recovered financially. His largesse toward the Dakota refugees, his support for his own large, extended family, and his failed investments left him destitute by the 1870s. As an elderly man, he was dependent on the charity of friends and the city of Faribault until his death.[18]

While in Faribault, Daybreak Woman's family's situation continued to change. In early 1866, Thomas married a Sisituŋwaŋ woman, Ida Shortfoot, and was living with her family in eastern Dakota Territory, where he was employed as a scout for the US government. Their first son was born in 1866 and their second son in 1867. That year, Daybreak Woman's first grandchild—Marion's three-year-old son, Alexander Hunter—died. The cause of his death is not documented. Alexander was buried in Daybreak Woman's parish cemetery, the Episcopal Church of the Good Shepherd.[19]

Marion must have been devastated by the loss of her only child. It may have been a catalyst to reset her life, or perhaps she already had plans to remarry when Alexander died. On May 29, 1867, Marion married Lawrence Prescott, the son of Daybreak Woman's good friend Mary Prescott. The couple married in Hennepin County, probably at the Prescott family home near Minnehaha Falls. They then moved to the new Santee Reservation in Nebraska and had their first child, Ephraim, in 1868.[20]

ΛVΛV

The US–Dakota War destroyed the society that Daybreak Woman had known her entire life, one in which Indigenous and Euro-Indigenous people constituted the majority of the population. When she moved to Faribault after the war, she found herself, for the first time in her life, in a place where the majority of the population was white—in a time when white Minnesotans vilified and despised all the Dakota people as "savages" and hunted them for the bounty on their scalps. The small groups of Dakota and Euro-Dakota people who were allowed to remain in the state because they had been deemed "friendly" avoided deportation to Crow Creek, but they were not free to go where they wanted to try to rebuild their lives, and most received no support from the federal government. Most of them lived in poverty, dependent on charity and the support of their white protectors, such as Bishop Whipple or Sibley at Mendota. In 1867, most of the Dakota people who had initially managed to obtain permission to stay in Minnesota after the war were forced to leave and settle on the new Santee Reservation in Nebraska. Other Dakota people whose families were not deported, such as Marion and Lawrence Prescott, decided to move to Santee for the opportunity of settling on the land and establishing new lives.

While Frank and Sophie stayed in Faribault, each soon to be married, the rest of Daybreak Woman's family also moved west. About the same time Marion and Lawrence moved to the Santee Reservation, Thomas and Angus found a new opportunity at Lake Traverse Station (later known as Browns Valley), located near the headwaters of the Minnesota River. Daybreak Woman, Will, and Mattie joined Thomas and Angus on the new Lake Traverse Reservation sometime in 1868 or 1869.

11. Minnesota River and Lake Traverse, 1868–1904

Lake Traverse Reservation and Beaver Falls

She well remembered the time when the land on which Brown's Valley now stands between the lakes was covered with a heavy growth of timber, and was a favorite rendezvous of the Indians.

SAM BROWN

Browns Valley is situated between Big Stone Lake and Lake Traverse on a continental divide: Lake Traverse flows north into the Red River, and Big Stone Lake flows south into the Little Minnesota River, then the Minnesota River. Traders had been active in the area since the early 1800s, including Daybreak Woman's grandfather, James Aird, as well as her mother, Grey Cloud Woman, who with Hazen Mooers kept their trading post on the east side of Lake Traverse in the 1820s and 1830s. The most westerly band of the Santee Dakota, the Sisituŋwaŋ, had established villages on Big Stone Lake and Lake Traverse and ranged well into Dakota Territory, west of the state of Minnesota, to hunt. In August 1862, they were hundreds of miles to the west of the Minnesota River reservation and remained there through the war. The Waḣpetuŋwaŋ, whose traditional territory was western Minnesota, had closer connections to the Minnesota River reservation, and many more of them were caught up in the war. Some of them had permanent homes on reservations, and many had intermarried with Bdewakaŋtuŋwaŋ; some younger Waḣpetuŋwaŋ men had fought for Little Crow, without the approval of their chiefs, most of whom opposed the war. Waḣpetuŋwaŋ farmers at the Yellow Medicine Agency, including Paul Maza Kute Mani and Gabriel Renville, were leaders of the peace faction that emerged during the war and were among those deemed above suspicion after the war. Many of them became scouts and, after 1867, leaders on the Lake Traverse Reservation.[1]

In 1865, Henry Sibley approved Joseph R. Brown's request to allow the

Brown family cabin, Browns Valley, Minnesota, 1972. *Minnesota Historical Society collections*

Sisituŋwaŋ and Waȟpetuŋwaŋ who had not been implicated in the war to settle on the shores of Lake Traverse, where they could fish as well as farm. Once again, Brown wanted to position himself and his family to trade with the Dakota people, so in 1866, at the age of sixty-one, he took his family to the south end of Lake Traverse. There he purchased land, erected a log cabin he had brought from Fort Wadsworth (Fort Sisseton), and founded the town of Browns Valley. The Browns used the cabin as trading post, stage-line stop, tavern, inn, post office, and mail station.[2]

Lake Traverse Reservation

The impetus for the creation of the Lake Traverse Reservation in 1867 was twofold: it sprang from the need of the Sisituŋwaŋ and Waȟpetuŋwaŋ to have a protected home and from the desire of the Dakota and Euro-Dakota scouts who had served the government since 1863 to settle permanently on the land. In 1867, Brown and a delegation of Dakota and Euro-Dakota men representing the two bands went to Washington to ask for a reservation as well as to request the restoration of annuities from the treaties of 1851 and 1858, monetary compensation for loss of the Minnesota

River reservation, and payments to certain persons who had provided service to the government or who had provided the Dakota people with food and provisions since 1863. The delegation argued that the vast majority of Sisituŋwaŋ and Waȟpetuŋwaŋ had neither instigated nor participated in the US–Dakota War but nevertheless had lost their annuities and reservation land. The resulting treaty, proclaimed in 1867, established two reservations (Lake Traverse and Devils Lake) but did not restore the treaty annuities. Each family was allotted 160 acres of land, but the treaty stipulated that significant improvements had to be made to the land within five years before a patent would be issued.[3]

The Lake Traverse Reservation's agency headquarters was located near Brown's post until 1870, when it was moved to the reservation. Dakota hunters traded furs (mostly muskrat pelts) at the Browns Valley post throughout the 1870s. The Browns also partnered with others and set up a general merchandise and farming supply store. The family had the government contract to supply Fort Wadsworth, located twenty-four miles to the west, and they operated the first stagecoaches to Redwood Falls and Fort Wadsworth—important transportation services since the railroad

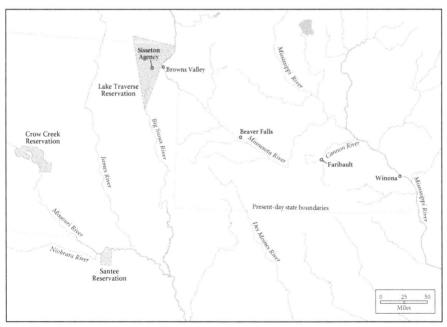

Places Daybreak Woman or her children lived after the US–Dakota War of 1862. *Map by Matt Kania, Map Hero, Inc.*

did not reach Browns Valley until 1880. The Sisseton Agency, located about fifteen miles west of Browns Valley, was a stagecoach stop on the way to Fort Wadsworth.[4]

Thomas Robertson was the first of Daybreak Woman's children to become associated with Browns Valley. He arrived in what was then Lake Traverse Station in September 1867 and enrolled as a member of the reservation. Angus was there as well, for both brothers had been serving as scouts in the region, and they seem to have been virtually inseparable for most of their lives.[5]

In 1866, when Thomas was working as a scout on the border between Minnesota and Dakota Territory, he married Lydia Shortfoot, the daughter of a Sisituŋwaŋ man, Maḣpiya Ho Taŋka, known to whites as Short Foot. The Shortfoot family lived on the Coteau des Prairies in what is now eastern South Dakota, which would become part of the Lake Traverse Reservation. Thomas and Lydia had two sons, born in 1866 and 1867. Later, in 1872 or 1873, Thomas married Lydia's sister, Ida, with whom he had an additional seven children. Angus Robertson also married two sisters in the Shortfoot family. Angus married Emma sometime in 1869, and they had four children; he married Nancy in the late 1880s, and they had three children. Maḣpiya Ho Taŋka took an allotment on the reservation and farmed there, not far from Angus. In 1918, Thomas wrote that his eighty-seven-year-old mother-in-law was still growing her corn and other produce on the Shortfoot farm.[6]

Thomas found another government position soon after moving to Browns Valley. In 1868, Congress appropriated funds pursuant to the Treaty of 1867 but stipulated—at the request of Gabriel Renville and others, who claimed that the Indian agent at Fort Wadsworth was corrupt—that Bishop Whipple take charge of the purchase of goods and their distribution to the Dakota on the new reservation. Bishop Whipple asked his friend Jared Daniels to assist him in this work; Daniels agreed, and then immediately employed Thomas Robertson as his assistant and interpreter. Daniels first visited the reservation in the fall of 1868, distributing provisions and clothing to the Dakota living near Fort Wadsworth, then returned to Faribault that winter, leaving the monthly issue of food rations to Thomas. Daniels returned in spring to encourage farming around Fort Wadsworth and persuaded about 160 Dakota families to settle on farms. In 1869, after Ulysses Grant succeeded Andrew Johnson as president, Daniels was appointed as the new Indian agent.[7]

From 1868 until late in 1871, Thomas worked as Daniels's assistant, distributing clothing, government rations, and other provisions to Dakota families as well as planning and building the infrastructure of the Sisseton Agency, as it came to be called. Daniels also asked him to take a census of all the Dakota people who would collect provisions under the new treaty. Thomas worked closely with Gabriel Renville, the leader of the new reservation, in this work. Daniels recalled in his memoir: "Mr. Robertson was retained for an interpreter as he had lived among these people since his own birth and was well acquainted with every one of them." In the spring and summer of 1869, Thomas, Renville, and Daniels collaborated to establish the new Sisseton Agency. Renville selected the agency site, and workers erected a warehouse, blacksmith shop, agent's house, and boardinghouse. Daniels moved his family to the Sisseton Agency soon after his house was finished, and in July, Bishop Whipple visited to see how things were progressing. The Dakota who chose to farm in 1868 and

Council house at Sisseton Agency, Lake Traverse Reservation, 1895. *Minnesota Historical Society collections*

1869 produced large harvests of potatoes, corn, and garden vegetables, and Daniels told them they could trade their surplus for supplies or for pork and flour. Daniels also asked Renville to select men for a police force to guard the reservation from liquor sellers, and he provided them with guns and ammunition from Fort Wadsworth.[8]

By the time Daniels left in December 1871, he had built a sawmill and forty-six houses, and reservation farmers were cultivating 720 acres. In the next few years, the agency expanded to include the residences of additional government employees, including the carpenter, millwright, teachers, head farmer, and physician. The agency office was a large, two-story brick building that included the physician's office, a council room, the agent's and clerk's office, and a large storeroom.[9]

When Daybreak Woman moved to the Lake Traverse Reservation with Will and Mattie in the late 1860s, Gustavus, Frank, and Sophie stayed behind in Faribault. Frank had a job working as a clerk in the post office, and Sophie was working as a live-in housekeeper for a farmer in Warsaw, a settlement not far from Faribault. Sophie was twenty years old and had formed an attachment to Henry Weatherstone, a young farmer whose family lived next door to her employer. His father, like hers, was a Scots immigrant. Sophie and Henry married in early June 1870, and she moved with him to Warsaw, where she resumed her work as a housekeeper for his neighbor.[10]

At the Santee Reservation in Nebraska, Marion and Lawrence Prescott had a second child, a daughter, in December 1869. Very shortly before or after his daughter was born, Lawrence, who was only thirty-one years old, died; the cause of his death is not documented. Marion must have felt cursed, losing her second husband, as she had her first, after only about two years of marriage. She and her children left the Santee Reservation and returned to Faribault to live with Frank. Perhaps the shock of losing Lawrence caused Marion to delay naming the baby, for in the federal census of August 1870, she lists her second child as eight months old, a female with no name.[11]

In 1871, all the rest of Daybreak Woman's children left Faribault. In March, Frank married Clara Grafton and moved to live with his wife's family in Winona, Minnesota. Marion moved with her children to the Lake Traverse Reservation to live with her mother, Will, and Mattie. Sophie and Henry Weatherstone moved onto land near Beaver Falls, close to where the Robertsons had lived before the 1862 war. Gustavus, still single at twenty-seven, joined them at nearby Beaver Falls to farm. Prior to leaving Faribault and getting married, Sophie had sold her section of land where the Robertsons had lived at Beaver Creek to a white man who re- membered her as an "Indian woman." She and Henry must have used the proceeds from that sale to establish their new farm.[12]

Daybreak Woman spent the 1870s and 1880s living on the Lake Tra- verse Reservation. For most of the 1890s, she lived in Beaver Falls with Sophie's family. The last few years of her life she was in Browns Valley, the gateway town to the Lake Traverse Reservation. She and her children all enrolled as members of the reservation, although not all of them lived there continuously. Thomas and Angus settled in 1868 and never left. In the 1880s, Gustavus moved there to farm, stayed for about ten years, then returned to Beaver Falls. Frank never lived on the reservation. Will lived on the reservation at the Sisseton Agency through the early 1880s, then left to live and work for years on the Pine Ridge Reservation, returning in summers to visit. In the early 1900s, late in her life, Sophie moved to Browns Valley and then to a home on the reservation. Daybreak Woman's oldest and youngest daughters, Marion and Mattie, spent the rest of their lives at Lake Traverse.[13]

The years between 1868 and 1873 were relatively propitious for Daybreak Woman and her family. All her children were thriving and had new oppor- tunities to settle on the land or find employment. By 1873, Gustavus, Frank, and Sophie had all married and started new lives in Beaver Falls or Winona. Thomas and Angus were settled with their families, farming on the reser- vation. At the Sisseton Agency, Daybreak Woman lived with Will, Mattie, Marion, and her Prescott grandchildren. In the early to mid-1870s, Will worked for the Brown family store and stagecoach station at the agency, then as a government clerk. After Joseph R. Brown died in 1870, his son Sam became the head of the family and the business. During these years, in addition to maintaining and managing her family's household, Daybreak Woman also found occasional employment as a nurse and midwife.[14]

As her older children established new lives for themselves, Daybreak Woman became focused on making sure her youngest child, Mattie, who turned eighteen in 1873, had some financial security as she moved into adulthood. In March 1873, she sought help from Sam Brown, who was in the business of acquiring unused land scrip for individuals and families, purchasing land with the scrip, and then selling it for a profit, which he shared with the scrip owners. Brown entered into such an agreement with

Will and Mattie Robertson, so the Robertsons must have retained some scrip that they had never used. Daybreak Woman wrote: "Will you be kind enough to sell some of Mattie's land as soon as you can she needs some money and if you could possibly sell it to get her something. . . . I am sorry to trouble you after you have been so kind to do what you have done."[15]

Over the next few months, Daybreak Woman's attention turned from Mattie's financial security to nursing her eldest daughter, Marion, through a serious illness, the nature of which is not documented. On May 24, Will wrote that his mother could not take time to visit Browns Valley because she was too busy nursing Marion and would not be able to leave until she recovered. That recovery never occurred. On June 4, 1873, Daybreak Woman suffered a devastating loss when Marion died at the young age of thirty-three, leaving five-year-old Ephraim and three-year-old Dessie orphans. Daybreak Woman, with Will's help, raised Marion's children, and they grew to adulthood in Will's household.[16]

As the 1870s progressed, Browns Valley and the Brown family became increasingly significant in the lives of Will, Mattie, and Daybreak Woman. The Brown family built several additional family homes at Browns Valley. Several of the Browns and their relations also lived and worked at the Sisseton Agency, about fifteen miles to the west, where there was a family home and business post. The youngest Brown son, Joe Jr., worked for the family business at the Sisseton Agency and became a close friend of Will Robertson. Joe's sister Augusta Brown (Gusy or Gusty), who lived at Browns Valley and helped run the family inn, became very close friends with Mattie.

The two families were in and out of one another's homes at the agency and visited frequently back and forth between the agency and Browns Valley. Daybreak Woman and Susan Brown also became close friends and, eventually, co-grandmothers, when their four youngest children married. By 1874, Joe Brown Jr. was openly courting Mattie, and they married in 1875 with the approval of both families. Daybreak Woman must have been happy and undoubtedly relieved when her youngest daughter married, knowing that Mattie would have greater economic security and a promising future with Joe, who was developing his own farm on the reservation and had the contract to carry the mail between Fort Wadsworth and the Sisseton Agency.[17]

Unlike their siblings' courtship and marriage, Will and Gusty's relationship was not readily embraced by all of the Browns, some of whom thought Gusty could do better for herself in marriage. Although by 1876 Will was steadily employed and was teaching himself advanced book-keeping, his modest income and uncertain economic prospects were im-pediments in the eyes of Gusty's older brothers, and the couple, realizing this, kept their feelings for each other a secret for some time. Gusty turned down Will's proposals of marriage three times because she knew her elder brother Sam, who acted as the family patriarch after their father died, and others in her family would disapprove of the match. Finally, in April 1876, Will could wait no longer, and he wrote to Sam, who was in St. Paul, seeking his sanction:

> Now that I have headed this, I don't know how to proceed, but, as I am going to write about something that, to me, is very important, I will dip into the facts and come to the point at once. You must forgive me for not telling you what you should have known long ago, that my feelings for Gusy is something more than friendship and that our attachment is mutual. You had a right to know this, but Gusy wanted me to wait, she did not want it in everybody's mouths like it was with Mattie and Joe. She was right, hence, I have never told you. Sam, I love Gusy, not with a mere passion of the moment—a school boy love—but with a love so strong that I am happy only when she is near me. I will not dwell on how much I love her—let it suffice that I love her, God knows—with all my heart. . . . Gusy and I will be very happy indeed if you approve of this; in your hands is our future happiness or misery. I hope you can trust your sister's future in the hands of one who loves her with his whole soul.[18]

Sam wrote back, in a rather terse but not unkind reply, saying that while he was not enthusiastic, he would not disapprove the match: "I cannot say that I 'really desire' you to marry Augusta. I have no choice—that matter rests entirely with you two, so far as I am concerned. If you are her choice 'for better or for worse,' I have nothing to say against it. . . . But if she will marry, I think she would be getting a good man by marrying you."[19]

Family drama ensued, as Gusty's brother Angus, adamantly opposed to their engagement, worked to undermine it, turning their mother against the match after she initially approved it by "his scandalous talk and groundless stories," which "caused her to change" toward Will. When Gusty remained undeterred by Angus's tactics, he resorted to trying to shake Will's attachment by fabricating tales of Gusty's sexual promiscuity during a recent trip. Angus also claimed that, despite his apparent sanction, Sam strongly disapproved of the match, sowing doubts in the family as to where he actually stood. Finally, Sam wrote and made clear to Gusty that he really did bless the union. Will thanked him, saying, "Gusty feels relieved, she feels that there is one at least in her family who is not going to fight her, and I am glad, too, heartily glad."[20]

For her part, Gusty wrote of Will that she did not think she could ever "find anyone better or who loves me more than he does." Moreover, she told her brother, "I have made up my own mind I would marry a man that was good and honest—if he did not have but one shirt on his back." During the fall of 1876, Gusty prepared to marry and leave Browns Valley to move up to the agency and live with the Robertsons. She sold her pony, sewed as many clothes for herself as she could, and planned her wedding. A few months later, at the end of January 1877, Will and Gusty, accompanied by several Brown siblings, traveled to Herman, Minnesota, where they were married by a Catholic priest. After the wedding, they all returned to Browns Valley to celebrate with a wedding dinner. Although Will and Gusty were Episcopalians, there was as yet no Episcopal church at Lake Traverse, and they preferred a marriage by a Catholic priest to one by the Presbyterian missionaries on the reservation.[21]

This preference reflected the religious-based factionalism that dominated Lake Traverse politics at the time. Dakota families on the reservation were politically and religiously divided from its inception. The Christian Dakota who had been associated with the Presbyterian missionaries at Yellow Medicine, the Williamsons and the Riggses, opposed the leadership and policies of Gabriel Renville. Renville embraced farming as an economic necessity but rejected conversion to Christianity and continued to live according to traditional Dakota spirituality, culture, and customs. The Presbyterian Dakota who had been active in the peace faction during the war and then had served as scouts, such as Paul Maza Kute Mani, were shut out of the 1867 treaty negotiations by Joseph R. Brown and Renville. Brown made sure that Renville was appointed the reservation's leader, ensuring that leadership on the reservation would favor Renville's approach and policies.[22]

The factionalism that developed on the Lake Traverse Reservation was not simply one of Christians versus non-Christian Dakota, for there were Episcopalians closely aligned with Renville, including the Robertsons. To be precise, the split was between the Presbyterian Dakota and Renville's faction, which was traditionalist Dakota but also pushed for economic "improvement." The Presbyterians objected to the treaty provision requiring people to work, which they considered uncharitable (and therefore un-Christian), and they also objected to those who continued to practice traditional Dakota customs that they perceived as particularly offensive, especially polygyny, which Renville and others who supported his leadership practiced.[23]

In contrast to the Presbyterians, the Episcopalians on the reservation, such as the Robertsons, embraced Renville's leadership and accepted his limited acculturation. They did not see the necessity or desirability of forcing assimilation on those who preferred to continue to live in traditional ways. Thomas said later: "Chief Renville was the most intelligent and far sighted uneducated Indian or mixed blood that I ever knew, and if his plans for his people, as incorporated in the Treaty of 1867, had been by the government carried out to the letter, these people would have been 100% better off now. But no! The whites wanted this little bit of land, too and the Government had to get it for them."[24]

Agent Jared Daniels also described the political division on the reservation: "About a third of the Waȟpetuŋwaŋ band, that belonged to the mission at Yellow Medicine before the outbreak, were not satisfied with the treaty because of its requiring them to work for the supplies they received, and they continually opposed the chief and his council in every innovation they made to better the condition of all. In their bigotry, from the missionary education they could not, or would not, see the great good that was being done by men that had more than one wife." Daniels says Presbyterians Thomas Williamson and Stephen Riggs asked to have him removed because at the Fourth of July celebration he allowed the people to engage in their traditional pastimes, including dances, sports, horse racing, and wearing Dakota dress.[25]

Renville and Daniels worked closely together in the early years of the reservation. Renville liked Daniels because he was honest, understood traditional Dakota ways, and supported his leadership. Their partnership came to an end in 1871 after the federal government adopted a new policy that handed over the administration on reservations to particular Christian denominations. In 1871, the government granted the Presbyterians control of the Lake Traverse Reservation, and they nominated Moses Adams as Indian agent to replace Jared Daniels, who they claimed was unacceptable because he was an Episcopalian closely affiliated with Bishop Whipple. Daniels left the agency in December 1871.

Renville was bitter about Daniels's ouster and blamed Stephen Riggs and the Presbyterian Dakota for his removal. He told Daniels he was very sorry to see him leave and feared what would happen under the new Presbyterian Indian agent. His fear turned out to be well founded: Adams imposed Presbyterianism on the reservation and made it illegal to practice traditional Dakota customs. One year after Daniels left, Adams confined Renville and his entire council to the reservation jail for each having more than one wife. Daniels said, "Among all the agencies I have visited, I have found the missionaries of the ABCFM [Presbyterians] the most intolerant towards the Indians. They seem to be living in the fifteenth century and do not comprehend the present."[26]

Adams's regime as Indian agent exacerbated political conflict on the reservation as he insisted on establishing new rules based on his own interpretation of Christianity. Sam Brown, who was Renville's nephew, became active in supporting Renville's leadership and asked both Bishop Whipple and Henry Sibley to help get Adams removed, but the Indian Office refused. Adams didn't leave until 1875, after a four-year power struggle between the Presbyterians and the Brown/Renville faction. Subsequent agents did not insist on imposing their own religious beliefs on the reservation, but in 1883, the federal government adopted religious repression as an official policy. The Indian Department issued a "religious crimes" code that made it illegal to practice Dakota dances, religious rituals, and polygyny, and government agents were authorized to enforce the code by searching households and seizing sacred objects such as medicine bundles and pipes.[27]

In 1883 a committee comprising Renville, Solomon Two Stars, Thomas Robertson, Joe Brown Jr., Good Boy, and the reservation's first Episcopal priest, Reverend Edward Ashley, wrote a constitution for the reservation modeled on the Cherokee constitution. The proposed constitution was controversial and further exacerbated factionalism for several years until its adoption in 1884. The Episcopalians dominated the committee (Robertson, Ashley, and Brown) and worked in concert with Renville (who did not convert to Christianity but became closely aligned with Ashley) in crafting the new government and its code of laws. As a result, the Presbyterian faction objected, seeing themselves as shut out of power and unhappy with the laws, which did not sufficiently reflect their own religious

St. Mary's Episcopal Church, built in 1882, at Old Sisseton Agency, South Dakota, July 2019. *Photograph by author*

values. In effect, during the years that the constitution was debated, the reservation was split into two church parties vying for political power, even though Renville and most of his supporters were not themselves Episcopalian. Thomas Robertson says nothing of this political conflict in his memoir, although he was in the center of it. He does say:

Securing a copy of the Cherokee code, in the Indian Territory, which was in English, we took that as a basis and translating much of it into the Sioux language and making some additions of ours, it was sent to Washington and at once approved and returned to us. Under this code was legislative body, a president, secretary, treasurer, sheriff, a supreme court composed of five members, township justices and constables. I was elected for two terms and served under this code as chief justice for four years and up to the time of passage of the Dawes Severalty bill, under which lands in severalty were allotted, and this code was done away with and we were told that we were now under the Federal and State laws.[28]

The Dawes Act, passed in 1887, allotted 160 acres per family on reservations and then sold off the remaining land to non-Indigenous settler-colonists. Implementation of the act eliminated communally held tribal lands on reservations across the United States, dramatically reducing the land base of many tribes. Renville adamantly refused to sell the tribal land at Lake Traverse, but, as Thomas Robertson says, the government commission "schemed" to convince people to sell off the land left over after the family allotments, offering a price below its value, arguing that they might get less if they didn't make the deal they were being offered. In the end, a narrow majority of Lake Traverse reservation voters approved the sale of the nonallotted land. Each member received a check for $214.62, and the government opened the reservation to whites beginning on April 15, 1892.[29]

Increases and Decreases

Daybreak Woman continued to live with William and her Prescott grandchildren at the Sisseton Agency until Will and Gusty married, at which point she moved to live with Mattie and Joe. In September 1876, Mattie gave birth to her first child, a daughter she and Joe named Augusta after her best friend and his sister. Gusty went up to be with Daybreak Woman and Mattie through the birth. The next year, Mattie had a second child, William Russell. The 1870s were a prolific decade for Daybreak Woman's other children, too; Thomas and Angus at Lake Traverse, Sophie and Gustavus at Beaver Falls, and Frank in Winona all had multiple children. By early 1879, she had twenty-one grandchildren, thirteen of whom were living on the reservation. In April 1879, Mattie gave birth to her third child, another boy. A few weeks later, Joe wrote his brother Samuel that "we are all well and manage to live—an increase—It's a big boy this time and looks so much like its Dad that everyone thinks he is good looking."[30]

In the months preceding the birth of Mattie's "big boy," through the winter and spring of 1879, diphtheria swept through the Lake Traverse Reservation. A highly contagious bacterial disease that attacks the respiratory system and covers it with a thick membrane that makes it difficult to breathe and swallow, diphtheria was often fatal for infants and young children. In January, Will Robertson reported that many little babies were dying on the reservation from the dreaded disease. The epidemic had raged through February and March, with as many as six dying per week. Everyone in Will's household was very sick, including his one-year-old son, but all had come through it. While the epidemic abated, the disease lingered.[31]

A week after Mattie's seemingly healthy son was born, however, he died. The most likely causes of death for newborn infants at the time were congenital anomalies, gestational immaturity, birth complications, and other unobservable physiological problems. But even if an infant lived a month beyond birth, the child was very likely to die in their first year. In fact, infant mortality reached its peak in the United States in 1880, with 22 percent of children dying in their first year of life.[32]

Just two months after their infant's death, Mattie and Joe's two-year-old son, William Russell, also died, perhaps from diphtheria. Then, tragedy was compounded when, shortly after her children's deaths, Mattie herself died. Whether the cause was the same disease as her little boy or another ailment is not clear. Will Robertson wrote of the family tragedy in a letter to Sam Brown:

> Joe handed me your letter of consolation last evening about twelve. Little did you think that your brotherly and loving letter was going to do double duty. Poor Joe, he is sorely stricken in his early life! To lose two dear little children was a sore trial for him and close upon the death of his little boy Russell comes the death of his wife. Oh, Sam, it was hard for him! He bears up well, but to see that hard, sad look upon the poor boy's face fairly grinds my heart and my sorrow was as great for the living as for the dead. The dead are happy, we hope! The living have to suffer. Of course, all of us feel the blow, but *my* heart aches for the bereaved husband. Mattie was conscious to the very last nearly and she died about half past eleven last night. She said she was happy and ready to die.[33]

Daybreak Woman, the primary nurse and midwife for her children, was at the center of this series of devastating events, enduring this continuous toil and sorrow. She helped bring an apparently healthy baby into the world only to lose him shortly thereafter, then nursed and lost her little grandson a few months later. Still grieving, she turned to nursing her daughter. She watched Mattie, a young woman whose life had been happy and promising just a few months earlier, wane. Daybreak Woman, Will, Joe, and Gusty gathered at her bedside as Mattie passed on. In subsequent months, her family's grief was further compounded when, over the course of November and December, Will and Gusty lost newborn twin boys. One of the infants died soon after birth; the other slowly wasted away and died a month later.[34]

In the wake of this devastation, Daybreak Woman continued to live for a time with Joe Brown and her granddaughter Augusta, as she had with Marion's children. By June 1880, she was living with little Augusta in Will and Gusty's home. In the ensuing years, Daybreak Woman and Susan Brown took turns caring for their motherless granddaughter. Eventually, Susan Brown moved in with Joe and lived with him for some years, while Daybreak Woman visited frequently. During these years, Daybreak Woman and Susan became closer; the two took turns living in their children's homes, helping to care for their mutual grandchildren.[35]

Beginning in the 1880s, Daybreak Woman spent some winters in Beaver Falls with Sophie, returning to the reservation in the spring, summer, and fall to live and earn some money. Some years, she may have taken one or both of her Prescott grandchildren with her. Other years, she stayed on the reservation through the winter. She remained in demand as a midwife and nurse, especially for friends and family. In February 1883, she was in Beaver Falls when she received a request from Sam Brown to come to Browns Valley and attend his wife in childbirth. Daybreak Woman, seventy-three years old, wrote back, explaining why such a journey would be difficult for her:

> I received yours the day before yesterday. You want me to come the middle of March. I understood your wife did not expect to be sick until April. I could start from here the last week of March as I have not much "wrapping" to keep me warm. I would be very glad if I could go but March is a very cold month and I don't know how to get to the agency from Wilmot as the train that I go on from here goes there besides I have no money to go with, if the winter is not very cold and I had the money I could come if someone would meet me at Wilmot. I have to go 20 miles before I get to the cars in a sleigh. Love to your wife and yourself from all here. Please let me know if you can send me the money.

The nearest train to Beaver Falls was twenty miles away at Olivia. In the end Daybreak Woman decided not to attempt the journey, probably at Will's advice, because traveling in the winter was too arduous and the chance the train would be snowed in was too great.[36]

Daybreak Woman continued to live with Will and Gusty until 1884, when they left to take positions as teachers in the day schools on the Pine Ridge Reservation, coming home to visit most summers. After they moved, Daybreak Woman lived with Thomas. In the 1880s, Gustavus and his family also moved to Lake Traverse, so she may have lived with him or with Angus during these years as well. Thomas and Angus established farms near what would become the town of Veblen, South Dakota, and Gustavus lived in the vicinity of what would become the town of Peever, about five miles east of the Sisseton Agency.[37]

In 1885, at the age of seventy-five, Daybreak Woman was still working for a living, doing what she had been doing her entire life: taking care of people. That summer, her charge was her friend Susan Brown, who was in poor health. In August, she wrote a letter to Sam Brown asking him to collect her wages from his siblings:

> Last April I was asked if I could take care of your mother, and each of the family was to give me ten dollars each for a month and I am sorry to say you and Gusty are the only ones has [who have] paid me, it's nearly four months since. If you would be kind enough to write to your sisters to see if they could let me have it. If I was able to work as I used to, I would not ask for it, but I have not been well this summer to earn what I need. I am sorry to trouble you. I have to buy her medicine. I am very thankful for what you gave me, and would be ever so much obliged if you could help me.[38]

Over the next year, Daybreak Woman's own health and ability to work declined. In 1886, she was with Joe, Augusta, and Susan Brown at the Sisseton Agency when she became gravely ill and appeared to be near death. Thomas came down to the agency to take her back to his farm. The doctor's assessment was that she "had just run out from age and she will not gain any strength to amount to anything." She did recover, but this illness was a harbinger of an eventual decline in her ability to work as hard as she had previously to support herself, as well as her ability to live independently.[39]

In her last five years on the Lake Traverse Reservation, Daybreak Woman was often with Thomas and with Will and Gusty when they returned home for summer visits. Ephraim and Dessie Prescott were with Will and Gusty at Pine Ridge for some years. By 1888, Dessie, then eighteen years old, was likely living with Daybreak Woman at Lake Traverse.

By the summer of 1890, Ephraim was married and living at Lake Traverse with his new wife. Sometime that same year Dessie died. As with her mother, there is no record of the cause of her death. There is nothing in the extant family correspondence about Dessie's death or the deaths of two of Angus Robertson's children that year. According to genealogical records, Angus's daughter Etta (twenty) and son Wilder (six) also died in 1890. So many deaths in the same family in one year suggests that there might have been an epidemic on the reservation. In 1890, there was an influenza pandemic that killed many in Russia and made its way to the midwestern United States. In addition, croup and scarlet fever were prevalent in the region that year. Tuberculosis was also a frequent scourge on the reservations in South Dakota at the time; Elaine Goodale Eastman reported that "whole families succumbed to the plague of tuberculosis" on the Pine Ridge Reservation, and measles continued to be a great killer as well. Losing Dessie must have been a great blow to both Will and Daybreak Woman, who were closest to Marion's children and had raised them to adulthood. When the year 1890 came to an end, Daybreak Woman, eighty years old, had outlived three children and eight grandchildren.[40]

Beaver Falls

Sometime after 1891, Daybreak Woman moved back to Minnesota to live permanently with Sophie's family at Beaver Falls. The town was economically dependent on its proximity to the Minnesota River, about a mile and a half away, which provided the primary means of transportation for the region prior to the arrival of the railroad. Its residents and businesses clustered close together, surrounded by nearby farms, including those of the Weatherstones and Robertsons. Steamboat traffic carried supplies from settlements downriver, and Beaver Falls residents sent their farm products and other goods back to those markets. In the late 1870s, Beaver Falls had a population of a few hundred and a bustling business and community center of the county. However, this river-centered activity, as well as the town's economic prosperity, quickly diminished when the railroad bypassed Beaver Falls in the late 1870s and was built through the northern part of Renville County. The town lost its designation as the county seat, lost businesses, and lost some of its population. Over the course of the 1880s and 1890s, the population continued to dwindle, and by the early 1900s, it had become a virtual ghost town.[41]

When Sophie and Gustavus arrived in Beaver Falls in the early 1870s, they found a growing and bustling community. They also found several of their former neighbors, including David Carrothers, James Carrothers, Stephen Henderson, and Andrew Hunter (Thomas Williamson's son-in-law), who all returned after the war to rebuild their homes. David Carrothers's house was the first built on the town's Main Street. By the time the Robertsons returned in 1871, the town had a store, hotel, sawmill, gristmill, wagon shop, blacksmith shop, shingle mill, brewery, hardware store, meat market, banker, physician, attorney, post office, school, and newspaper.[42]

Not far away, their friend Good Thunder and a number of other Dakota people returned to settle on farms. Good Thunder bought land in 1881 and began farming near his previous farm on the Lower Sioux Reservation. Five years later, Bishop Whipple finally convinced the government to purchase land for some of the Dakota refugees in Minnesota. Samuel Hinman moved back from the Santee Reservation with his wife, Mary Myrick (the daughter of trader Andrew Myrick, who was killed at the Redwood Agency), and their infant daughter to establish a new Episcopal mission, St. Cornelia's. In December 1886, Hinman reported to the bishop that he was getting settled, with the help of Sophie's husband, Henry Weatherstone, who lent him a large box stove for his new home.[43]

The congregation of St. Cornelia's Episcopal Church near Lower Sioux Agency, 1885. *Photograph by N. B. Andersen, Minnesota Historical Society collections*

In 1889, the Episcopalians at Beaver Falls established Christ Church, and the Weatherstones and Robertsons were among its founders and leaders. Both Sophie and Daybreak Woman were active in the Ladies Guild, as were Gustavus's wife, Christina Blume (whom he married in 1874), and his mother-in-law. The guild women made and sold quilts and held fairs, suppers, and pie, basket, ice cream, necktie, and strawberry socials to raise money for the church. Sophie, as a leader in the guild, fostered close connections with Good Thunder's community and their new church. In 1893, she entertained the women from St. Cornelia's in her home, "where they worked on a quilt for their hostess." That same year, the Christ Church Ladies Guild attended a service at Good Thunder's village. Urania White, the Robertsons' Beaver Creek neighbor before the war, came back to visit and joined the group. White "had the pleasure of seeing her Indian mother, Mrs. Crooks, to whose watchfulness [as a captive during the war] she owed her life."

In 1891, the Ladies Guild of Christ Church made a quilt to honor all the women who had been important in the church's history, reaching back to the St. John mission that Hinman established at the Redwood Agency in 1860. There are 350 names on the quilt, and one of its blocks is devoted to Mrs. Jane Robertson. Also honored on the quilt are Sophie Weatherstone and Christina Blume Robertson.[44]

By 1891, Dakota families owned about 623 acres of land near Redwood. Good Thunder's settlement drew people from Faribault and Mendota who had never left the state as well as returnees from exile. Samuel Hinman died only two years after his return, before the new church was completed. At his funeral on March 27, 1889, held in the mission school, Episcopal Bishop Mahlon N. Gilbert presided over the service and addressed the many Dakota people in attendance. Sophie Robertson Weatherstone interpreted his address into Dakota for the audience.[45]

The Last Decade

In August 1894 Daybreak Woman celebrated her eighty-fourth birthday with Sophie, Gustavus, Will, and their families in Beaver Falls. Will and Gusty and their four children traveled from the Pine Ridge Reservation for the ten-day reunion. Will wrote to Sam Brown describing the gathering and his mother's condition—and his own fears: "We find mother in her usual health—very good for one of her age. She is getting very childish but not cross though. Gus and Sophie bought her a nice rocker, and when she went to bed she took it with her to her room for fear that the children might mar it, it was very funny, but we did not let her know that we thought it so. Poor old mother, how she clung to me when I told her 'good bye,' it was hard to part with her. I many never see her alive again, you know."[46]

As she had been on the Lake Traverse Reservation, Daybreak Woman was surrounded by grandchildren: six Weatherstones, with whom she lived, and five Robertsons, who lived close by. Four years after losing her two adult granddaughters, Dessie Prescott and Etta Robertson, Daybreak Woman lost yet another granddaughter when Gustavus's oldest, Berthe, only twenty-one, died in childbirth along with her baby. Two years later, Sophie's twenty-year-old daughter Marion died. As with her aunts Marion and Mattie and her cousin Dessie, the cause of Marion Weatherstone's death is not documented.[47]

As the 1890s progressed, Daybreak Woman became increasingly frail; she lost her eyesight as well as her physical mobility, eventually requiring a wheelchair. She became very reliant on Sophie's youngest son, Robert, who was a small boy, only five years old in 1895, to help her. Robert was steadfast in his devotion to his grandmother. Thomas Robertson said later of Robert, "during the years of her helplessness he was a little boy and she was blind and he stayed right with her all of the time and led her around."[48]

In 1902, Sophie and Henry Weatherstone retired from farming in Beaver Falls, bought land on the Lake Traverse Reservation, which they left to their son to farm, and bought a house in Browns Valley. It was there that Daybreak Woman lived until she died in 1904. Her body was taken to St. Mary's Episcopal Church at the Sisseton Agency for the funeral service and burial in the church cemetery.[49]

Daybreak Woman rewarded Robert's devotion in her will, dated May 17, 1899, by leaving him her entire estate, which consisted of her 160 acres of allotted land on the Lake Traverse Reservation. Robert was only fourteen years old, and other members of the family contested the will. The estate languished in probate for many years, but eventually the court divided it among Daybreak Woman's surviving children—Thomas, Angus, Frank, William, and Sophie—in 1918. Thomas gave his share of the estate to Sophie, because she took care of their mother for over a decade.[50]

Daybreak Woman's grave is marked by a large and handsome marble memorial. Her obituary in the Browns Valley newspaper, mainly written by Sam Brown, said, "She was an intelligent woman and when in a reminiscent mood could relate a fund of interesting history concerning the real

Headstone marking the grave of Jane A. Robertson, Daybreak Woman, July 2019. *Photograph by author*

pioneer days of this section of the country." None of Daybreak Woman's children are buried with her in the Episcopal cemetery at the old Sisseton Agency, but many people from families she knew well, some since her early childhood in Prairie du Chien, surround her there, including numerous Campbells, Renvilles, and her close friend and co-grandmother Susan Brown, who also died in 1904.[51]

Epilogue

Speaking of history, owing to my personal knowledge of events occurring during my life and especially during this time I am writing of, my faith in history has been somewhat shaken.

THOMAS ROBERTSON

In 1918, Thomas Robertson, age seventy-eight, as one of the claimants to his mother's estate, provided testimony about his family to the probate court. After Thomas signed his deposition, the court examiner wrote at the bottom of the page: "Testimony of this witness was taken in English language, as he speaks English as well as he speaks Dakota. As far as appearance is concerned he is a white man." The notation reflects how white society's racism, which insisted on a binary definition of cultural identity—one must be either white or nonwhite—has rendered Euro-Dakota people invisible in white society today as well as in the heretofore dominant historical narrative of Minnesota's past. It also reflects the broader failure to incorporate the Dakota story into the region's history, especially before and after the US–Dakota War.[1]

Although her maternal grandfather and her father were white men, Daybreak Woman's Dakota identity was remarkably robust and resilient, as were her bonds with her Dakota kin, especially her mother and grandmother, who raised her until the age of twelve. After fourteen years with her Anglo father in Canada and a mission-school education, she chose to return to Mni Sota Makoce and brought her Scots immigrant husband with her. They established their new life and family among the Dakota, living in multicultural communities comprising Dakota, Euro-Dakota, and non-Dakota people. This society was temporarily shattered by the 1862 war and the forced exile of the Dakota, but Dakota and Euro-Dakota people reconstituted these communities in new places—in South and North Dakota, in Nebraska, and in Canada—and it was not long after the war that exiles began returning to Mni Sota Makoce as well. Moreover, some people who had lived on the reservations, including Daybreak Woman and her children, stayed in Minnesota after the war. There were also other Euro-Dakota people who had never lived on the reservations, the progeny of generations of intermarriage between European and Dakota people who had established lives elsewhere in the state and who were never expected to leave, including the Faribaults, McLeods, and Prescotts.

Because Daybreak Woman chose to return to the Dakota homeland, her children also developed strong Euro-Dakota bicultural identities. Like their mother, they were all bilingual and literate in both Dakota and English, and they all had Dakota names. They, like their mother, moved easily in both Euro-American and Dakota societies. Until 1862, the Robertsons lived in communities that accepted Euro-Dakota people as the norm; they could be both Anglo and Dakota. After 1862, however, there was no longer social space to be Anglo-Dakota. People had to choose Dakota society or Anglo society; to be accepted into white society, it was necessary to hide one's Dakota identity. Most of Daybreak Woman's children chose to live in Dakota society, settling on the Lake Traverse Reservation. Sophie and Gustavus both returned to the family's previous home, the white settlement at Beaver Falls, but they reestablished connections with Good Thunder's community at Redwood, often visited the Lake Traverse Reservation, and eventually lived there for periods of time. Frank was the only one of Daybreak Woman's children to choose Euro-American society and settle apart from the family and the Dakota community: he became an insurance salesman in Winona, Minnesota. Thomas and Angus married Dakota women and became successful farmers on the reservation. William had a long career as a teacher in the day schools on the Pine Ridge Reservation (as did his wife, Augusta Brown Robertson). After they left teaching in 1910, they operated a trading post there for some years before retiring.

Family and community were the primary determinants of the course of Daybreak Woman's life; she always was with one of her parents until she married, she rejoined her mother soon after getting married, and after she had her own children there was never a time she didn't live with or near at least one of them. As a young woman, she was unusual in having a choice between assimilating into Anglo-American society with her husband, disassociating with her Dakota heritage, or living as an Anglo-Dakota woman in a society that was still dominated by Dakota and Euro-Dakota people. Matrilineal bonds were particularly significant in Daybreak Woman's life—her grandmother and mother raised her, she lived side by side with them as she became a mother herself, and her own daughters and their daughters were core relationships in her life.

Another significant influence in Daybreak Woman's life was her Christian faith, especially her close association with the Episcopal Church, which became very influential in the lives of her children as well. Her membership and leadership in the Episcopal mission at the Redwood Agency and the family's friendship with Samuel Hinman and Bishop Henry Whipple proved key to their ability to find shelter in Faribault after the war and begin to rebuild their lives. At Faribault, Lake Traverse, and Beaver Falls, Daybreak Woman and her children were devoted Episcopalians.

Daybreak Woman never lived a life of leisure or economic affluence by the standards of nineteenth-century middle-class white American society, although she did enjoy a minimum threshold of economic security provided by her father and her husband until Andrew's death in 1859. She always worked, both at home to contribute to the family's subsistence and for wages. As a young, single woman, she worked as a teacher; as a wife and mother, she took in boarders, cooked for government laborers, and taught in the reservation schools; after 1862, she did any kind of work she could find, mostly domestic service. Even as an elderly woman, she worked for wages and did not expect her children to support her, although she made her home with her various children once they were adults and had livelihoods. Much of her labor was physically demanding; in this respect she was like the vast majority of nineteenth-century American women, whose work, whether paid or not, was arduous, time-consuming, undervalued, and often unacknowledged by society as vital to their families' economic well-being.

Daybreak Woman's grandmother and mother were part of the last two generations of Santee Dakota women living in eastern and central Mni Sota Makoce to engage in the fur trade. By the time Daybreak Woman returned in 1837, the fur trade along the Mississippi and Lower Minnesota Rivers was in decline, and the lucrative trade had shifted west to the Upper Minnesota River and beyond. Daybreak Woman and Andrew, with Grey Cloud Woman and Hazen Mooers, turned to farming instead. Eventually, both families lived in Dakota communities and earned their livelihoods by teaching their Dakota kin and friends how to farm, as European-Americans took the land and made it impossible to subsist as they always had. The Robertsons and the Mooerses were two of the most prominent Anglo-Dakota families who worked as government interpreters, farmers, teachers, and clerks among the Dakota people, first in their villages on the Mississippi and Minnesota Rivers and then, after 1851, on the Upper and Lower Sioux Reservations. With many other Euro-Dakota people—including the Campbells, Faribaults, Prescotts, and Browns—their lives comprised both Anglo and Dakota societies for generations before and after the US–Dakota War of 1862.

Daybreak Woman's life spanned most of the nineteenth century and provides a window into the rich and complex multicultural history of North America. Her story brings to the foreground people—Dakotas, Euro-Dakotas, and women—whose experiences and contributions have been vastly underrepresented in the historical literature. Daybreak Woman was also Jane Anderson Robertson; she was Scots, English, and Dakota; she was American; and her story is fundamental to an inclusive regional and national history.

Appendix 1:
Daybreak Woman's Family

The Children of Grey Cloud Woman (Maḣpiya Ḣota Wiŋ) (c.1775–1844)
and James Aird (1757–1819)
    Margaret Aird (Maḣpiya Ḣota Wiŋ, Grey Cloud Woman II)
        (1893–1850)

The Children of Grey Cloud Woman II (Margaret Aird Anderson) and
Thomas Anderson (1779–1875)
    Angus Malcom Anderson (1808–1840)
    Jane Anderson (Aŋpao Hiyaye Wiŋ, Daybreak Woman) (1810–1904)
    A third child, a girl, died in infancy or early childhood

The Children of Grey Cloud Woman II (Margaret Aird Anderson Mooers)
and Hazen Mooers
    Mary Mooers (1825–?)
    Jane Ann Mooers (1826–1863)
    Madeline Mooers (1829–c.1852)

The Children of Daybreak Woman (Jane Anderson Robertson) and
Andrew Robertson (1790–1859)
    James Wabasha (1837–1840)
    Thomas Anderson (1839–1924), married Niya Waśte Wiŋ,
        Lydia Shortfoot, Ida Shortfoot
    Marion Wallace (Minnie) (1840–1873), married Alexander Hunter,
        Lawrence Prescott
    Angus Malcolm (1842–1935), married Emma Shortfoot,
        Nancy Shortfoot
    Gustavus Alexander (1844–1915), married Christina Blum
    Francis Anderson (Frank) (1846–1919), married Clara Grafton
    Mary Sophia (Sophie) (1848–1935), married Henry Weatherstone
    William Marshall (1852–1943), married Augusta Brown
    Martha Catherine (Mattie) (1855–1879), married Joseph Brown Jr.

Appendix 2:
The Santee Dakota and the Fur Trade; Women in Nineteenth-Century Dakota Culture

The woman who is the mistress of the tent, always occupies the place next to the door at the right hand side as you enter.

THE DAKOTA FRIEND

The Santee Dakota hunted, fished, gathered wild foods, and during the summers planted corn and other vegetables in villages located on rivers and lakes in Mni Sota Makoce. They lived season to season, traveling to the places that were resource rich at a particular time of the year. They lived in community, working together and sharing the products of their labor. Their way of life was physically demanding and required every adult's work and cooperation. Women's labor was as essential as men's, and in Dakota society women were highly respected for their significant contributions to both the subsistence and the well-being of their families and their communities.[1]

Women's economic roles were extensive and included responsibility for the entire household, including fabricating the structures in which they lived and the interior furnishings of their homes. They processed animal hides from which they manufactured clothing, moccasins, and blankets; vessels for storing, carrying, and cooking food; and other functional items. They cultivated, tended, and harvested corn and other vegetables, and they processed, preserved, and cooked all the plant foods that they gathered as well as the meat and fish that the men provided. They tapped maple trees for sap and processed it into maple sugar; they harvested wild rice from the lakes; they dug roots for medicines and food, picked and dried herbs and flowers for tea, and collected medicinal plants and barks. Women also brought beauty to the things they made, creating intricate decorations of quills and beads and feathers for clothing, moccasins, and other items. Grandmothers and mothers taught girls how to do all of this work.[2]

Dakota women also were essential keepers of Dakota culture, particularly grandmothers. Women generally were responsible for teaching their children and grandchildren Dakota values. Grandmothers were especially revered as storytellers and historians, and they played a matriarchal role in Dakota households, which were organized and run by the women of the family. Men married into women-centered households composed of generations of women and their children living with their husbands. Polygyny was common, and it was not unusual for a Dakota man to marry a woman as well as her sisters. Grandmothers acted as the household gatekeepers, sleeping by the door to monitor the comings and goings of family members and making sure no one unwanted entered. As Sarah Penman explains, Dakota grandmothers "were respected for their knowledge, wisdom, and power as life-givers, healers, dreamers, harvesters and teachers. Instructing female children in survival skills was the domain of the grandmothers, and they counseled girls on their moral, social and spiritual responsibilities." According to Dakota elder Clifford Canku, Dakota women were "reared as young girls to be independent, spirited, humble, and to raise their own children with remarkable patience, love and kindness."[3]

Appendix 3:
Anglo-Dakota Daughters in
Nineteenth-Century Minnesota

Daybreak Woman's experiences as an Anglo-Dakota child and adolescent were unusual in that she was raised by both her parents until she was about five years old, then lived with her mother and grandmother for another eight years before going to live with her father in Canada until she married. Most Anglo-Dakota children were abandoned by their fathers (men who were British immigrants or Americans of British descent) and left with their Dakota mothers and kin. A small number of these Anglo-American men entered into marriages with Dakota or Euro-Dakota women, according to Dakota customs, and stayed in Dakota country, establishing large families. In early-nineteenth-century Minnesota the two most prominent examples of such families were those of Philander Prescott and Mary Keeiyah (Naġi Owiŋna) and of Martin McLeod and Mary Elizabeth Ortley (who was also the Anglo-Dakota daughter of a Scots trader who abandoned his Dakota family).[1]

Whereas an earlier generations of Scots fur traders such as James Aird, Daybreak Woman's grandfather, had come to the region in the late eighteenth century, married Dakota wives, and stayed for decades, after 1815—the end of the War of 1812, when the British were finally ousted from the fur trade in the region by the Americans—Anglo-American men increasingly left their Dakota wives and children after only a few months or years. After the United States established Fort Snelling at Bdote in 1820, many Anglo-American traders, soldiers, and government officials engaged in such short-term relationships (or simply used Dakota women sexually without establishing any relationship), and only some of them financially supported or showed an interest in their children with Dakota women. Between 1820 and 1840, examples of prominent Anglo-American men who left their Dakota wives and their children after only a few months or years included US Indian agent Lawrence Taliaferro, fur trader Henry

Sibley, and army officer Captain Seth Eastman. (Some men, such as Scots trader Daniel Lamont and army officer James McClure, did not intentionally abandon their families but died.) While a few men did take responsibility for financially supporting their children after they left, most just disappeared.[2]

Consequently, most Anglo-Dakota children were reared by their mothers and their Dakota kin. Some of these children came under the influence of Protestant missionaries who came into the region in the beginning in the 1830s, including the brothers Samuel and Gideon Pond, Thomas Williamson and his sister Jane Williamson, and Stephen Riggs and his wife, Mary. These missionaries often took Anglo-Dakota children (more often girls than boys) into their schools and households, teaching them to read and write in Dakota as well as English, working to convert them to Christianity, and impressing them with acculturation. Some Anglo-Dakota (and other Euro-Dakota) children lived for years in missionary households, while others had much shorter and more sporadic contact with missionaries.[3]

A few Anglo-Dakota daughters in Minnesota grew up to identify and live as Anglo-Americans as a result of missionary or other significant Anglo influence in their young lives. One such example was Jane Lamont, whose father was Daniel Lamont and whose mother was Hushes the Night (Haŋyetu Kihnaye Wiŋ), a daughter of Bdewakaŋtuŋwaŋ leader Cloud Man. Jane's mother placed her in the home of the Ponds as a child of about ten; she grew up to marry a Pond nephew and become a farmer's wife in white settler society. Another example is Henry Sibley's daughter, Helen, adopted by an Anglo-American family as a young girl after her mother, Red Blanket Woman, died. Rather than raise her himself with his family by his second wife, a white woman, Sibley placed Helen with another white family nearby. She was also raised as an Anglo-American woman, married an Anglo-American man, and lived as a doctor's wife in a small town in Wisconsin until her death in childbirth.

Unlike Helen Sibley and Jane Lamont, most Anglo-Dakota girls, even if heavily influenced by attending missionary schools or living with missionary families, continued to primarily identify themselves as Dakota people. Although they were very much aware of their Anglo heritage, knew who their fathers were, and in a few cases had direct contact with those fathers into adulthood, they saw themselves as more Dakota than not. Mary Taliaferro, whose mother was another daughter of Cloud Man, the Day Sets (Aŋpetu Inajiŋ Wiŋ), attended the Pond mission school at Lake Harriet on and off as a young girl. She married an Anglo-American man, Warren Woodbury, and lived with him and their children for a number of years in St. Paul. However, in the 1850s and early 1860s, Mary regularly took her children to the Dakota reservation on the Minnesota River to visit her relatives and to collect her annuity payments. They were visiting the reservation in August 1862, at the outbreak of the Dakota War. With many other Euro-Dakota families, Mary and her children were held captive by the Dakota war faction until their surrender at the end of the war. After her husband was killed in the Civil War in 1863, Mary and her children continued to live in St. Paul for several years. Eventually, however, they settled with their exiled Dakota relatives on the Santee Reservation in Nebraska.

Similarly, Mary's cousin, Nancy Eastman, the daughter of Captain Seth Eastman and another daughter of Cloud Man, Stands Sacredly (Wakaŋ Inajiŋ), grew up close to Fort Snelling and also attended the Pond missionary school. Nancy associated a great deal with the Anglo-Americans at the fort and even helped care for her half siblings after her father brought his second wife, a white woman, and their children back to Minnesota while he served as the fort commander. Nancy chose to marry a Dakota man, Many Lightnings, and live as a Dakota woman. She had four sons and a daughter before she died after giving birth to her youngest child in 1858. After the Dakota War, Many Lightnings' as well as Nancy's children adopted the Eastman name and made lives for themselves on various Dakota reservations in Nebraska and South Dakota. Nancy's youngest child, Charles Eastman, became a prominent Dakota doctor and educator; he wrote an account of his Dakota childhood titled *Indian Boyhood* and many other popular books.[4]

Like most Anglo-Dakota children's parents, Daybreak Woman's mother and father separated when she was quite young. However, her upbringing was in many ways more akin to the experiences of the McLeod and Prescott children, who grew up with both parents, than to those of Jane Lamont or Helen Sibley, who were fostered in Anglo-American families. Daybreak Woman's experience differed from the lives of most other Anglo-Dakota children because, although her parents separated, she lived for long periods of time with each of them.

Thomas Anderson was also unusual among Anglo-American men of this era who married Dakota women because when he decided to leave

Mni Sota Makoce, he asked his wife, Grey Cloud Woman, to join him. According to her grandson's memoir, Grey Cloud Woman was unwilling to leave her homeland and follow her husband to Canada. Thomas Anderson was a proud British Canadian who had fought against the Americans in the War of 1812. After the British defeat, he hated the thought of living under the US flag, and he refused to become an American citizen. He wanted to move north, just across the Canadian border, where he could continue to engage in the fur trade but not be governed by Americans. However, Grey Cloud Woman refused to leave.

There is a matrilineal heritage in this story that reflects the agency and independence of both mother and daughter in their marriages: Grey Cloud Woman refused to leave Mni Sota Makoce with her Anglo-American husband, and Daybreak Woman insisted that her Scots immigrant husband bring her back to Mni Sota Makoce as a condition of their marriage. In both instances, these women dictated the terms of their marriages and decided for themselves where and with whom they wanted to live.

Acknowledgments

Many thanks to Dakota history and culture teacher, consultant, and Daybreak Woman descendant Sisoka Duta (Joe Bendickson) for sharing his knowledge and time with me. Thanks also to descendant Tamara St. John, Archivist, Sisseton Wahpeton Tribal Archives and Collections, Sisseton Wahpeton Oyate, for her invaluable research assistance and generosity in sharing information vital to the book. Deep gratitude to Dakota orthography consultant Glenn Wasicuna for his timely contributions. I am also thankful to Jody Moore, another descendant, who provided important information that helped fill a gap in this family story. Thanks also to historian Lois Glewwe for generously sharing her knowledge and sources related to the Williamsons.

Thanks to the archivists and librarians at the Minnesota History Center in St. Paul, the Renville County Historical Society, the Rice County Historical Society, and the City of Faribault public library. Special thanks to archivist Peter Davis at the Huronia Museum in Ontario, Canada, for providing me with significant and essential sources related to Daybreak Woman's life in Canada. Thanks to cartographer Matt Kania of Map Hero for his excellent work creating the maps for the book.

The financial and institutional support of St. Catherine University has been essential to the research and writing of this book, especially the annual Faculty Scholars' Retreat and the Sister Mona Riley Endowed Fund in the Humanities. I am very grateful to be a faculty member at an institution that is for and about women, one which supports women scholars and women-focused scholarship.

A special thanks to my St. Catherine University faculty colleagues in my women's studies writing group, who read and reviewed parts of this book and provided their varied insights, support, and encouragement: Cecilia Konchar Farr, Cynthia Norton, Joanne Cavallaro, Lynne Gildensoph, and Gabrielle Civil. Thanks also to the Abigail Quigley McCarthy

Women's Center at St. Catherine University for its support of my scholarly endeavors in women's history over the past two decades.

Finally, thanks to all those at the Minnesota Historical Society Press who worked on the book for their excellence and professionalism, especially editor in chief Ann Regan, whose knowledge, wisdom, and editorial artistry have been invaluable in the creation of this book.

Notes

Notes to Introduction

Epigraph: Quoted in Westerman and White, *Mni Sota Makoce*, 13.

1. Robertson, "Reminiscences," *SDDHC*, 559–561; Woolworth, "Lives and Influences," 117; June Robertson Lehman, "Alexander Andrew and Jane (Anderson) Robertson," Robertson Family File; John H. Case, "Early Minnesota History" and "Jane Anderson Robertson," box 1, John H. Case Papers; Anderson, "Personal Narrative," 205; Folwell, *History of Minnesota*, 1:159–61, 270, 322–23, 483–86; February 1856, "Roll of Sioux Mixed-Bloods, Register of Names of Half-Breed or Mixed Bloods Now Living Who Claim Interests in Half-Breed Reservation on Lake Pepin Under the 1830 Treaty of Prairie du Chien," Library Records, Sibley House, Mendota, MN. Andrew Robertson also may have been attracted to Mni Sota Makoce by two financial prospects: Daybreak Woman's entitlement, as one-quarter Dakota, to a land claim under the Treaty of 1830 and to a payment from the pending 1837 Treaty.

2. Westerman and White, *Mni Sota Makoce*, 4 (quotation from Stephen Riggs), 13, 29.

3. Westerman and White, *Mni Sota Makoce*, 15, 19, 22; Oneroad and Skinner, *Being Dakota*, 60–61.

4. White, *The Middle Ground*, ix–xv, 316–45, 472–79; Peterson, "The People In Between"; Brown and Peterson, eds., *The New Peoples*.

5. White, "The Power of Whiteness," 181, 183; Carroll, "*Naginowenah*," 59–60.

6. In researching sources from the late eighteenth and early nineteenth centuries, Laurel Thatcher Ulrich observed that while women usually wrote about everyone, men typically wrote about themselves: Ulrich, *A Midwife's Tale*, 27–35.

7. See Westerman and White, *Mni Sota Makoce*, 6–9, on the challenges of writing Dakota history using non-Dakota sources.

8. Carroll, "Higgeldy-Piggeldy Assembly," "*Naginowenah*," and "Who Was Jane Lamont?" The primary Dakota expert consulted for this project is Sisoka Duta, Joe Bendickson, Dakota language and culture teaching specialist, University of Minnesota, instructor for a course in Dakota history and culture, spring 2019, University of Minnesota, in which I was enrolled as a student. Sisoka Duta is a descendant of Daybreak Woman. Also consulted for this project and instrumental in providing important data is Tamara St. John,

Tribal Historic Preservation Officer for the Sisseton Wahpeton Oyate and a descendant of Daybreak Woman.

9. Cultural values: Sisoka Duta, February 11, 2019; kinship defined by Dakota anthropologist Ella Deloria and quoted in Westerman and White, *Mni Sota Makoce*, 15.

10. White, "The Power of Whiteness," 180–83; Spickard, *Almost All Aliens,* 18–25; Carroll, "Higgeldy-Piggeldy Assembly," "*Naginowenah*," and "Who Was Jane Lamont?"

11. Spickard, *Almost All Aliens,* 79–90; White, "The Power of Whiteness," 180–81.

12. Carroll, "Higgeldy-Piggeldy Assembly," "*Naginowenah*," and "Who Was Jane Lamont?"

13. Spickard, *Almost All Aliens*, 5–14.

14. Cronon, *Changes in the Land*, 55–60, 78–80; White, "The Power of Whiteness," 180–81; Spickard, *Almost All Aliens*, 26.

15. Hyman, *Dakota Women's Work*, 133–135; Oneroad and Skinner, *Being Dakota*, 88–90.

16. Wahpetonwin, Carolyn Cavender Schommer, "Foreword," in Riggs, *A Dakota-English Dictionary*, vi.

Notes to Chapter 1: Mississippi River, 1812–1823

Epigraph: Thomas Robertson, "Reminiscences," 9, Dakota Conflict Manuscripts Collection (hereafter, DCMC).

1. Westerman and White, *Mni Sota Makoce*, 27, 130.

2. Gilman, "The Fur Trade in the Upper Mississippi Valley," 12–14. In the last forty years there has been significant scholarship produced on the fur trade in the Great Lakes and on the Upper Mississippi River region, including examinations of Euro-Indian families and their role in the fur trade and in fur trade society: Gilman, "The Fur Trade in the Upper Mississippi Valley"; Gilman, "The Last Days of the Upper Mississippi Fur Trade"; Gilman, *Henry Hastings Sibley*; Wingerd, *North Country*; Hyde, *Empires, Nations and Families*; Adelman and Aron, "From Borderlands to Borders"; Anderson, *Kinsmen of Another Kind*; Brown, *Strangers in Blood*; Brown and Peterson, eds., *The New Peoples*; Van Kirk, *Many Tender Ties*; Podruchny, *Making the Voyageur World*.

   The British defeated the French in the Seven Years' War (the French and Indian War) in 1763; they took over all the French territory in North America and took control of the fur trade as well, although most of the employees of the trade continued to be French or French-Indian. Although the Americans defeated the British in the American Revolution (1775–83), it was not until defeating the British again in the War of 1812 (1812–15) that they were finally able to push the British out of the interior and take control of the fur trade.

3. Gilman, "The Fur Trade in the Upper Mississippi Valley," 7–14; Alice Plehal,

"History of Prairie du Chien," 1–2; Scanlan, *Prairie du Chien*, vi–vii, 11, 20; Antoine de Julio, "The Vertefeuille House," 36–39.

4. Antoine de Julio, "The Vertefeuille House," 39–42.

5. Antoine de Julio, "The Vertefeuille House," 39–42; J. Lee, Agent for the United States, "Plan of the Settlement of Prairie du Chien, 1820," reproduced in Antoine de Julio, "The Vertefeuille House," 41–42.

6. Scanlan, *Prairie du Chien*, 168, 171–72, 180, 182–83. Zebulon Pike, on official expedition for the US government, was the 1805 visitor. Antoine de Julio, "The Vertefeuille House," 40–43; Shaw, "Personal Narrative," 226. Stephen Long, on expedition for the US government, provided this description. Historic American Buildings Survey, "Prairie du Chien" (HABS No. WI-302), 7.

7. Scanlan, *Prairie du Chien*, 171–73. Scanlan quotes directly from Boilvin's report to the Secretary of War. On territory and travel: Gilman, "The Fur Trade in the Upper Mississippi Valley," 7–12; Folwell, *History of Minnesota* 1:73–88; Anderson, *Kinsmen of Another Kind*, 58–76; see also Scanlan, *Prairie du Chien*; Kellogg, *The British Regime in Wisconsin*; and Meyer, *History of the Santee Sioux*. On marriage customs: Anderson, *Kinsmen of Another Kind*, ix–xvi, 51–54, 67–68; Carroll, "Who Was Jane Lamont?" and "Higgeldy-Piggeldy Assembly"; White, "The Power of Whiteness," 178–82.

8. Gilman, "The Fur Trade in the Upper Mississippi Valley," 14.

9. Carroll, "Who Was Jane Lamont?," 184–85; Hyman, *Dakota Women's Work*, 31, 44–45.

10. The United States established Fort Shelby in 1813; the British took the fort in 1814 and named it Fort McKay. The United States regained the fort after its victory in the War of 1812 and renamed it Fort Crawford in 1816. Evans and Earll, "Les Prairies des Chiens," 6–9; Scanlan, *Prairie du Chien*, 90, 178.
    Boilvin quote: Scanlan, *Prairie du Chien*, 171–72; Prairie du Chien mills: Keyes, "Documents," 3:354–56, 361–62, 4:443–50.

11. Hansen, "Prairie du Chien's Earliest Church Records, 1817"; Keyes, "Documents," 3:353–363, 4:443–58.

12. HABS, "Prairie du Chien," 7; Keyes, "Documents," 3:353, 356, 4:443–58; Anderson, "Journal of Captain Thomas G. Anderson," 248; Alan Woolworth, "James Aird, 1770–1819," box 22, Alan Woolworth Papers.

13. Keyes, "Documents," 3:353–54, 4:443, 452; Anderson, "Personal Narrative," 150.

14. Westerman and White, *Mni Sota Makoce*, 27; "Chief Wabasha III," *Sioux Research-Dakota, Lakota, Nakota*, Oyate1.proboards.com/thread/1547?page=2; Brisbois, "Recollections of Prairie du Chien," 285, 294, 296–97; Diedrich, *The Chiefs Wapahasha*, 30.

15. Anderson, *Kinsmen of Another Kind*, 50–54, 58–68. As most country marriages were not recorded, sources conflict as to the year of Grey Cloud Woman and Aird's marriage. Alan Woolworth suggests 1790 as the marriage

year but provides no specific source for this claim. John Case identifies the marriage year as 1793, but his source for that information is also unclear. Woolworth, "Lives and Influences"; Anderson, *Kinsmen of Another Kind,* 67–68; "Chief Wabasha III"; John H. Case, "Ayrd, Anderson, Robertson Family," John T. Case Papers; Gilman, "James Aird."

On location in Prairie du Chien: Woolworth, "Lives and Influences," 117; Case, "Ayrd, Anderson, Robertson Family" and "Early Minnesota History," Case Papers; John Case, "Grey Cloud Island and Vicinity."

16. On Aird property: Scanlan, *Prairie du Chien,* 44–45; Antoine de Julio, "The Vertefeuille House," 41–44; Keyes, "Documents," 3:361. In 1818, Aird purchased all of Joseph Rolette's land in the village for $9,000.

On the Aird home: Scanlan, *Prairie du Chien,* 166–68; Antoine de Julio, "The Vertefeuille House," 40–44. Pike noted in 1805 that the interior furnishings of the main village houses were "decent."

On their neighbors: Brisbois, "Recollections of Prairie du Chien," 294; "Claims at Prairie du Chien," American State Papers, 20th Congress, 1st and 2nd Sessions (1827–29), photocopy in Aird File, box 22, Woolworth Papers.

17. Gilman, "The Fur Trade in the Upper Mississippi Valley," 14; Gilman, "James Aird"; Scanlan, *Prairie du Chien,* 91–92; Woolworth, "James Aird," box 19, Woolworth Papers.

18. Keyes, "Documents," 3:361–62, 4:450–52; Evans and Earll, "La Prairie des Chiens," 12.

19. Antoine de Julio, "The Vertefeuille House," 43–44; HABS, "City of Prairie du Chien" (WI-302), 18. By 1819, Joseph Rolette owned land again in the village, having purchased J. B. Faribault's village lot.

20. Diedrich, *The Chiefs Wapahasha,* 30; Atkins, *Creating Minnesota,* 26–27; Denial, *Making Marriage,* 34–38. Grey Cloud Woman's sisters were Margaret, who first married Antoine DuBois and then Joseph Roulette, and Pelagie, who married Augustin Ange. Three other sisters are identified in various sources as the wives of Joseph LaRocque, Pierre LaPointe, and Amable Grignon (later François LaBathe). (I have been unable to ascertain the first names of these three women.) Grey Cloud Woman's father, Wapaha Śa, had more than one wife; the siblings did not all have the same mother.

The Rolettes, LaPointes, and Airds were all still listed as Prairie du Chien village lot owners in 1820. Augustin Ange, who married Grey Cloud Woman's sister Pelagie, was one of the first landowners in Prairie du Chien, although he was no longer a landowner by 1820. However, the Ange (often spelled as Anger) family was still prominent in the village's 1817 Catholic Church records, including Augustin, who served as godfather for several who were baptized. K., "Prairie du Chien," 107; Antoine de Julio, "The Vertefeuille House," 41–43; Hansen, "Prairie du Chien's Earliest Church Records"; Brisbois, "Recollections of Prairie du Chien."

21. Anderson, "Personal Narrative," 138–48.

22. Anderson, "Personal Narrative," 151–73, 191.

23. Sources conflict as to the year Grey Cloud Woman married Thomas Anderson. In his memoirs, Anderson says it was 1810; however, other sources suggest 1805, while others suggest 1808. Based on Anderson's trading locations, it seems most likely that it happened sometime between 1809 and 1810, the years that their first two children were born. Woolworth says it was fall of 1809, but provides no specific source for this claim. Angus was probably born in 1808 or 1809, and Daybreak Woman was born in August 1810 (although sources also conflict as to the year of her birth, this is the date and year she claimed in an interview late in her life and the one she passed on to her children). However, in the list of 1837 Treaty Claimants, Angus identifies himself in 1837 as twenty-seven and Jane identifies herself as twenty-five years of age, which would mean he was born in 1810 and she in 1812: "Official Register of Claims Under the 1837 Treaty," Library Records, Sibley House, Mendota, MN. It could be that she confused their birth years as she got older and continued to use Angus's birth year as her own. Angus died in 1840, and Grey Cloud Woman II died in 1850, so after that time there would have been none of Daybreak Woman's birth family members close by to verify birth years. Thomas Anderson seems not to have recorded the dates his children were born, and in his reminiscences he is very vague regarding Grey Cloud Woman and their children. If the marriage took place in 1808, Margaret was fifteen; if 1810, she was seventeen. Alan Woolworth, "Thomas G. Anderson," "Jane Anderson Robertson," "Margaret Aird Anderson Mooers," box 19, Woolworth Papers; Anderson, "Personal Narrative," 180–92; Case, "Grey Cloud Island and Vicinity"; Case, "Early Minnesota History," Case Papers; Robertson, "Reminiscences," *SDDHC*.

   References to the third child, Marion or Mary, are sparse and there is no reliable documentation related to when she was born or died. Anderson does not mention a third child in his narrative, but only recalls Jane and Angus, and says when he parted with Margaret she took their two children with her. It is possible she was pregnant with Marion when she left Anderson in spring 1814 and that the child died in the years between 1814 and 1825, when Margaret married for a second time. It's also possible that Mary was their first child, born before Angus, and she died before spring 1814. John Case lists Mary as a sibling based on his research and lists her first, which may indicate he thought she was the eldest. Much of his research was based on oral history of the Robertson and Mooers families. Thomas Robertson, Jane's (Daybreak Woman's) eldest surviving son, does not mention a Mary or Marion as one of his mother's siblings. He did recall that Angus was born at Prairie du Chien some years before his mother's birthday on August 4, 1810, on the Upper Minnesota River.

On Daybreak Woman's birth year: "Official Register of Claims Under the 1837 Treaty" and "Roll of Sioux Mixed-Bloods ... Who Claim Interests in ... Reservation on Lake Pepin Under the 1830 Treaty" (February 23, 1856), Library Records, Sibley House, Mendota, MN. Jane Robertson identifies herself as forty-seven years of age in this census.

24. Anderson, "Personal Narrative," 180, 192.

25. Gilman, "James Aird"; Curtiss-Wedge, *History of Renville County,* 1:544; Nute, "Posts in the Minnesota Fur Trading Era," 378; Robertson, "Reminiscences," *SDDHC,* 560; Case, "Jane Anderson Robertson," Case Papers; Anderson, "Personal Narrative," 181–92. The family story is that she was born there because her father was on his way to his wintering post at Lake Traverse, farther upriver. However, if this was the reason the family was at Patterson's Rapids in August, then Jane was born in 1809, because 1809–10 was the last winter Anderson spent trading on the Upper Minnesota. Anderson does recall going up the Minnesota River in the summer of 1811 to hunt buffalo at Big Stone Lake, at the river's source. Thus, it seems that if Daybreak Woman was born in 1810, 1811, or 1812 at Patterson's Rapids, it was because the family was on a hunting excursion with the Dakota.

26. Anderson, "Personal Narrative," 179, 181–84; Scanlan, *Prairie du Chien,* 87.

27. Anderson, "Personal Narrative," 150, 181–92; Woolworth, "Thomas G. Anderson," Woolworth Papers.

28. Anderson, "Personal Narrative," 192–201; Gilman, "The Fur Trade in the Upper Mississippi Valley," 12; Scanlan, *Prairie du Chien,* 174–77; Evans and Earll, "La Prairie des Chiens," 6–8; Kellogg, *The British Regime in Wisconsin,* 323–26.

29. Anderson, "Personal Narrative," 192–202; Lyman Draper, "Introduction" to Anderson's "Personal Narrative," 136–138; Scanlan, *Prairie du Chien,* 85–90, 91, 178–79; Diedrich, *The Chiefs Wapahasha,* 50–55; Milman, "Thomas Gummersall Anderson."

30. Anderson, "Personal Narrative," 192.

31. Anderson, "Journal of Thomas G. Anderson," 247–48.

32. Keyes, "Documents," 3:362–63; Scanlan, *Prairie du Chien,* 183; Case, "Jane Anderson Robertson," Case Papers.

33. Anderson, "Personal Narrative," 205.

34. Case, "Grey Cloud Island and Vicinity," 371; Case, "Early Minnesota History," Case Papers. Case notes that Grey Cloud Woman I died in 1844 at the age of 110. This claim that her age was 110 at time of death is improbable, because it would mean she had been born in 1734, twenty-three years earlier than Aird, who was born in 1757. She also would have been fifty at her marriage and sixty at the time their daughter was born.

35. Woolworth, "Margaret Aird Anderson Mooers," Woolworth Papers; Case, "Grey Cloud Island and Vicinity," 1–9; Case, "Early Minnesota History," Case Papers.

Notes to Chapter 2: Lake Huron, 1823–1837

Epigraphs: Jane Anderson to Secretary of the American Board of Commissioners for Foreign Missions, ca. February 1830, transcription in Widder, *Battle for the Soul*, 153–54; Robertson, "Reminiscences," DCMC, 1.

1. Osborne, "The Migration of Voyageurs from Drummond Island." Osborne notes that Michael LaBatte's account of growing up on Drummond Island was that the only languages spoken on the island were French and Indian. According to the Mackinaw Mission school records and information provided by Jane in her letter to the Missions Board, she did not attend the school until the fall of 1828 and she stayed there until 1831. Thus, she lived with her father and stepmother for five years prior to attending school. Widder, *Battle for the Soul*, 141, 153–54.

2. Although Jane Anderson Robertson told John Case in an interview late in her life that she attended the mission school on Mackinac beginning in 1823–24, the school's records, as well as other sources, indicate that she was not enrolled there until the fall of 1828. She probably recalled 1823 because it was the year she and Angus left Prairie du Chien to go to their father. It is clear from other sources, including correspondence Jane wrote herself, that she lived on Drummond Island with Anderson and his second family prior to going to the mission school and that she went back to Drummond Island during school vacations. Anderson, "Personal Narrative," 205; Letter of Eunice Osmer, Mackinac Island, to Elizabeth Anderson, Drummond Island, October 5, 1828 (transcription), Item # 2005-0009-0011, Thomas G. Anderson and Family Papers.

3. Cook, *Drummond Island*, 1–4; Brumwell, *Drummond Island*, 3–5; Anderson, "Personal Narrative," 202–5.

4. Milman, "Thomas Gummersall Anderson"; Anderson, "Personal Narrative," 202–4.

5. Cook, *Drummond Island*, 6–8, 10–11, 19; Anderson, "Personal Narrative," 202–5.

6. Cook, *Drummond Island*, 6.

7. Cook, *Drummond Island*, 1–3, 5, 9–10.

8. Elizabeth Hamilton was born September 14, 1795, at Niagara-on-the-Lake and died June 30, 1858, in Cobourg, Canada.

9. Armour, "David and Elizabeth," 19–23.

10. Baird, "Reminiscences of Early Days on Mackinac Island," 35–40; Armour, "David and Elizabeth," 27–29; McDowell, "Therese Schindler of Mackinac," 126; Armour, "David Mitchell."

11. Armour, "David and Elizabeth," 17–20; "Thomas Gummersall Anderson Timeline," Thomas G. Anderson and Family Papers; Armour, "David Mitchell"; Amanda Ferry to Elizabeth Anderson, September 13, 1827 (2005-0009-0006); Eunice Osmer to Elizabeth Anderson, October 5, 1828

(2005-0009-0011); Jane Anderson to Elizabeth Anderson, January 29, 1830; Amanda Ferry to Elizabeth Anderson, February 2, 1830 (2005-0009-0028)—all Thomas G. Anderson and Family Papers.

12. Jane Anderson to Secretary of American Board of Commissioners for Foreign Missions, ca. February 1830, transcription in Widder, *Battle for the Soul*, 153–54.

13. Hyde, *Empires, Nations and Families,* 9, 268; Wood, *Historic Mackinac,* 279–80; Lavender, *The Fist in the Wilderness,* 1, 5, 20; Widder, *Battle for the Soul,* 47–48.

14. Wood, *Historic Mackinac,* 279–80; Baird, "Reminiscences of Early Days on Mackinac Island," 20–35.

15. Keyes, "Documents," 3:346.

16. Baird, "Reminiscences of Early Days on Mackinac Island," 19, 23, 28–30, 34; Wood, *Historic Mackinac,* 279–80, 336, 663–64.

17. Widder, *Battle for the Soul,* iv, 16, 19–20, 49–55, 59.

18. Baird, "Reminiscences of Early Days on Mackinac Island," 19, 23, 28–30, 34, 46 (quote); McDowell, "Therese Schindler of Mackinac," 129; Martin, "Dr. William Beaumont," 267; Wood, *Historic Mackinac,* 279–80, 336, 663–64; Keyes, "Documents," 3:346; Widder, *Battle for the Soul,* xiii–xiv.

19. Wood, *Historic Mackinac,* 405; Widder, *Battle for the Soul,* xiv.

20. Widder, "Magdelaine Laframboise," 6.

21. Wood, *Historic Mackinac,* 399–417.

22. Widder, *Battle for the Soul,* xiv–xx. A very small number of students had no Indian heritage. They were from Euro-American families who lived on Mackinac Island, and they were day students.

23. Widder, *Battle for the Soul,* xix–xxi, 102–9.

24. Widder, *Battle for the Soul,* 141.

25. Widder, *Battle for the Soul,* 6, 110–14. The total number of students enrolled during each year Jane Anderson attended the school were 1828: 134; 1829: 104; 1830: 100; 1831: 130.

26. Anderson, "Personal Narrative," 205.

27. Eunice Osmer to Betsy Anderson, October 5, 1828 (2005-0009-0011), Thomas G. Anderson and Family Papers.

28. Anderson to Secretary of American Board of Commissioners for Foreign Missions, 1830.

29. Amanda Ferry to Betsy Anderson, February 2, 1830 (2005-0009-0028), Thomas G. Anderson and Family Papers.

30. Jane Anderson to Betsy Anderson, January 29, 1830, Thomas G. Anderson and Family Papers. The only letter Jane wrote that survives is a letter to the Board of Missions in the spring of 1830, found in Widder, *Battle for the Soul*, 153–54.

31. Anderson, "Personal Narrative," 205. In his memoir, Anderson says Jane had

three children, all boys. In fact, she had nine children, six boys and three girls.

32. Widder, *Battle for the Soul*, xv, 153–54.

33. Thomas says Betsy was a devout Episcopalian in his memoir: Anderson, "Personal Narrative," 205. In Minnesota Daybreak Woman and most of her children became Episcopalians and were closely associated with Reverend Samuel Hinman and Bishop Whipple: Lehman, *History of the Early Episcopal Church*, 3–4.

34. Cook, *Drummond Island*, 12–13; Osborne, "The Migration of Voyageurs from Drummond Island," 3; Gustavus Anderson to Lyman Draper, November 25, 1882, Letter 6 of 310, and Sophia Rowe Anderson to Lyman Draper, October 23, 1885, Letter 310—both Letters of Gustavus Anderson and Sophie Anderson Rowe to Lyman Draper, Wisconsin State Historical Society, Thomas G. Anderson and Family Papers. Gustavus Anderson confirms the arrival of the family at Penetanguishene in November 1828 in the 1882 letter.

35. Amanda Ferry told Betsy Anderson in a letter in early October 1828 that Jane would be bringing items to Betsy when she went home on vacation: Amanda Ferry to Betsy Anderson, October 5, 1828 (2005-0009-0011), Thomas G. Anderson and Family Papers; Cook, *Drummond Island*, 13.

36. Widder, *Battle for the Soul*, 153–54.

37. Lowery, "James Hamilton"; Sophia Rowe, "Twenty Years Gleanings," unpublished manuscript (2005-0009-0168), Thomas G. Anderson and Family Papers. On the outside of her manuscript Sophia notes that "JMH" lived only about six miles from Clayfields, the Anderson family home near Coldwater.

38. Milman, "Thomas Gummersall Anderson."

39. "Memories of the Late Mrs. Leonard Wilson," February 1929. The author was the daughter of Jacob Gill, the carpenter at the Indian agency who supervised the building of all structures. Rowe, "Twenty Years Gleanings" (quote).

40. Hunter, *A History of Simcoe County*.

41. "Thomas Gummersall Anderson Timeline," Thomas G. Anderson and Family Papers; Anderson, "Personal Narrative," 205–6; Rowe, "Twenty Years Gleanings." Angus appears regularly in the accounting records and as a witness to agreements or receipts of payments at the Coldwater Agency between March 1834 and March 1837: Vol. 55 (microfilm C-11018), Indian Affairs: Chief Superintendent's Office, Upper Canada, Correspondence, January-June 1834, p.58500; Vol. 56 (microfilm C-11018 and C-11019), Indian Affairs: Chief Superintendent's Office, Upper Canada, Correspondence, July-December 1834, p.58561; Vol. 57 (microfilm C-11020), Balance Sheet, December 1834, p.58997; Vol. 61 (microfilm C-11020 and C-11021), Balance Sheet, March 31, 1836, p.61104; Vol. 64 (microfilm C-11021 and C-11022), Balance Sheet, March 31, 1837, p.63227—all RG10, Library and Archives Canada.

42. Sophia Rowe, "Twenty Years Gleanings"; John H. Case, "The Building of the

Redwood and Yellow Medicine Indian Agencies on the Minnesota River in 1853–54," *Hastings Gazette*, July 1 and 8, 1921; Robertson, "Reminiscences," *SDDHC,* 559.

43. Thomas Anderson to Colonel Givens, Chief Superintendent of Indian Affairs, Toronto, February 3, 1836, Letterbook, Vol. 60, (microfilm C-11020), p.60655; Colonel Givens to Thomas Anderson, April 11, 1836, Letterbook, Vol. 501 (microfilm C-13342), 133—both RG10, Library and Archives Canada.

44. Vol. 54 (microfilm C-11018), Indian Affairs: Chief Superintendent's Office, Upper Canada, Correspondence, July-December 1833, p.57856, 58264, 59000; Vol. 58 (microfilm C-11020), Indian Affairs: Chief Superintendent's Office, Upper Canada, Correspondence, May-August 1835, p.59550, 59631, 59633; Vol. 59 (microfilm C-11019 and C-11020), Indian Affairs: Chief Superintendent's Office, Upper Canada, Correspondence, September-December 1835, p.59923, 59924, 59956, 59957, 60655, 61104—all RG10, Library and Archives Canada; Lehman, "Alexander Andrew and Jane (Anderson) Robertson," Robertson Family File; Robertson, "Reminiscences," *SDDHC,* 560–61; Flandrau, *The History of Minnesota,* 284–85.

45. Case, "Jane Anderson Robertson," Case Papers.

46. Despite their previous claims of affection for Andrew, by October 1836 the Coldwater Indians were again asking for a new teacher to replace him, although their reasons are not entirely clear. In response to their request, the chief superintendent told Anderson to tell them that, while he would nominate someone new for the position, to also say that, "from what the Lieutenant Governor had the opportunity of observing of the school when he visited at Coldwater, he had not only seen no reason to find fault with Mr. Robertson's conduct, but, on the contrary, to be well satisfied with it." Colonel Givens to Thomas Anderson, October 6, 1836, Letterbook, 191–93; Givens to Thomas Anderson, October 26, 1836, Letterbook, 201—both RG10, Library and Archives Canada. The latter indicated that Andrew would continue as teacher until March 31, 1837, when the Indians would take over their own affairs at Coldwater.

On Andrew Robertson's positions: Vol. 62 (microfilm C-11021), Indian Affairs: Chief Superintendent's Office, Correspondence, July-September 1836, p.61519, 61520, 61523, 61524; Vol. 66 (microfilm C-11022 and C-11023), Indian Affairs: Chief Superintendent's Office (Col. J. Givens), Correspondence, June-August 1837, p.63535, 63536; Vol. 67 (microfilm C-11023), Indian Affairs: Chief Superintendent's Office, Correspondence, September-December 1837, p.63959—all RG10, Library and Archives Canada.

Andrew Robertson appears numerous times in the Indian Agency Records from 1833 through June 1837. He appears in account books as an employee (schoolteacher); he is a witness to many agreements and account receipts; he also wrote several letters and received several letters while acting as superintendent of the agency in Anderson's absences in 1836 and 1837.

Vol. 501 (microfilm C-13342), Chief Superintendent's Letter Book, January 20, 1835–April 10, 1837, p. 73, 133, 147–48, 169; Vol. 54 (microfilm C-11018), Indian Affairs: Chief Superintendent's Office, Upper Canada (Col. J. Givens), Correspondence, July-December 1835; Vol. 55 (microfilm C-11018), Indian Affairs: Chief Superintendent's Office, Correspondence, January-June 1834, p.58264, 58498; Vol. 57 (microfilm C-11020), Indian Affairs: Chief Superintendent's Office, Correspondence, January-April, 1835, p.5900; Vol. 59 (microfilm C-11019 and C-11020), Indian Affairs: Chief Superintendent's Office, Correspondence, September-December 1835, p.59956; Vol. 60 (microfilm C-1120), Indian Affairs: Chief Superintendent's Office, Correspondence, January-March, 1836, p.60655—all RG10, Library and Archives Canada.

47. Gustavus Anderson to Lyman Draper, June 25, 1883, Letter 8, Letters from Sophia Rowe and Gustavus Anderson to Lyman Draper, Wisconsin Historical Society, Thomas G. Anderson and Family Papers. In this letter, Gustavus says his stepsister had written from Minnesota, where she was living with one of her sons on the Sisseton Agency.

Jane married Andrew Robertson in 1836. Their children were: James Wabasha, Thomas Anderson, Marion Wallace, Angus Malcolm, Gustavus Alexander, Francis Anderson, Mary Sophia, William Marshall, Martha Catherine. Lehman, "Alexander Andrew and Jane (Anderson) Robertson," Robertson Family File; Case, "Early Minnesota History" and "Jane Anderson Robertson," Case Papers.

Notes to Chapter 3: Mississippi River, 1837–1853

Epigraph: Robertson, "Reminiscences," *SDDHC,* 561.

1. Robertson, "Reminiscences," *SDDHC,* 561.

2. The last entry for Angus on the Indian Department account books for the Coldwater settlement was March 31, 1837, four months prior to the last entry for Andrew. This suggests that Angus left Coldwater and traveled back to the Upper Mississippi earlier than Jane and Andrew. Angus Anderson was Sibley's clerk from 1837 to 1839. Goodman and Goodman, *Joseph R. Brown,* 148–49.

3. George Featherstonehaugh, "Journal," microfilm frame 0054, George Featherstonehaugh and Family Papers; Anderson, *Kinsmen of Another Kind,* 140–41, 223; Goodman and Goodman, *Joseph R. Brown,* 149n55; Robertson, "Reminiscences," *SDDHC,* 561; Woolworth, "Hazen Mooers and John Mooers," Woolworth Papers.

4. Featherstonehaugh, "Journal," George Featherstonehaugh and Family Papers; "Register of Claims Under the 1837 Treaty," Library Records, Sibley House, Mendota, MN. Mary was born in 1825, Jane Anne in 1826, and Madeline in 1829.

5. Case, "Jane Anderson Robertson," Case Papers, 6.

6. Anderson, *Kinsmen of Another Kind,* 143–44; Carroll, "Who Was Jane Lamont?," 186.

7. Anderson, *Little Crow,* 25–35.

8. Jean Baptiste Faribault to Henry Dodge, August 15, 1837, Letters Received from the St. Peter's Indian Agency, 1837, Records of the Bureau of Indian Affairs, RG75, National Archives; "Official Register of Claims under the 1837 Treaty," Library Records, Sibley House, Mendota, MN. It is interesting to note that Jane's age is listed as twenty-five and Angus is twenty-seven, which indicates that she was born either in 1812 or 1813 and Angus either in 1810 or 1811, although Jane claimed later in her life to have been born in 1810.

9. Birk, "Grey Cloud Island," 20–22; Folwell, *History of Minnesota,* 1:160; Anderson, *Kinsmen of Another Kind,* 155–58; Case, "Jane Anderson Robertson," Case Papers. The Medicine Bottle who lived on the island and moved his band to Pine Bend was not the same man who was later executed for killings during the Dakota War of 1862. This Medicine Bottle was the brother of Grey Iron, chief of the Dakota band living in the village called Black Dog, located on the Minnesota River not far from its confluence with the Mississippi.

10. Case, "Medicine Bottle's Band" and "Jane Anderson Robertson," Case Papers; Robertson, "Reminiscences," *SDDHC,* 561; Goodman and Goodman, *Joseph R. Brown,* 149n55; Woolworth, "Hazen Mooers and John Mooers," Woolworth Papers.

11. Birk, "Grey Cloud Island," 1–2, 26; Goodman and Goodman, *Joseph R. Brown,* 149–51, 149n55, 160n57; Woolworth, "Jane Anderson Robertson" and "Hazen Mooers and John Mooers," Woolworth Papers. Susan was Brown's third wife. He first married and divorced Helen Dickson, then married and divorced Margaret McCoy, both Euro-Dakota women. He had three children by his first two wives.

12. Case, "Jane Anderson Robertson," Case Papers; Wingerd, *North Country,* 159. Angus died in St. Louis in 1841 or 1842: Robertson, "Reminiscences," *SDDHC,* 559–61; Goodman and Goodman, *Joseph R. Brown,* 149n55, 150, 160n57.

13. Case, "Jane Anderson Robertson," Case Papers; Robertson, "Reminiscences," *SDDHC,* 559–60.

14. Case, "Jane Anderson Robertson," Case Papers.

15. Andrew Robertson to Henry Hastings Sibley, Cave Spring, November 26, 1848, microfilm reel 5, Henry Hastings Sibley Papers; Folwell, *History of Minnesota,* 1:322–24.

16. Robertson, "Reminiscences," DCMC, 4; Case, "Jane Anderson Robertson," Case Papers; Case, "Redwood and Yellow Medicine Indian Agencies"; Robertson, "Reminiscences," *SDDHC,* 561–62.

17. Goodman and Goodman, *Joseph R. Brown,* 229; Woolworth, "Hazen Mooers," Woolworth Papers; Robertson, "Reminiscences," *SDDHC,* 561–62.

18. Trimble, "There Once Was a Kaposia Village"; Upham, *Minnesota Place Names*; Anderson, *Little Crow,* 11, 34.

19. Anderson, *Little Crow,* 10, 12–13.

20. Anderson, *Little Crow,* 13–15.

21. Anderson, *Little Crow,* 32–34, 55–56; Dakota County Historical Society, "Glimpses of Kaposia," 55–56.

22. Dakota County Historical Society, "Glimpses of Kaposia," 30–31; Trimble, "There Once Was a Kaposia Village."

23. Dakota County Historical Society, "Glimpses of Kaposia," 31–32, 42–46.

24. Robertson, "Reminiscences," DCMC, 164; Lois Glewwe Research File (shared with the author): Williamson mission.

25. Dakota County Historical Society, "Glimpses of Kaposia," 50–51.

26. "Schedule of School Kept at Kapoza," John Felix Aiton and Family Papers; Glewwe, "The Story of Jane Smith Williamson," Dakota Soul Sisters 7–11.

27. Thomas Williamson, "Report of Dakota Girls in Kapoza School taught by Jane Williamson," 1850 Annual Report to the Commissioner of Indian Affairs, Minnesota Historical Society; Glewwe Research File: US Department of Indian Affairs, St. Peter Agency, Agent Nathaniel McLean files, "The United States to Andrew Robertson for the Board of Missions," RG217E525, box 689; Jane Williamson to Nancy Aiton, October 28, 1851, John Felix Aiton and Family Papers; Glewwe, "The Story of Jane Smith Williamson."

28. Jane Williamson to Nancy Aiton, October 28, 1851, and Jane Williamson to Nancy Aiton, March 5, 1852, John Felix Aiton and Family Papers; Glewwe, "The Story of Jane Smith Williamson"; Glewwe Research File; Jane Williamson to Elizabeth Burgess, February 21, 1853, Thomas Williamson and Family Papers.

29. Atkins, *Creating Minnesota,* 26–33, 49–52.

30. Parker, ed., *The Recollections of Philander Prescott,* 213–14.

31. Woolworth, "Hazen Mooers," Woolworth Papers; Case, "Ayrd, Anderson, Robertson Family," Case Papers; "Official Register of Claims Under the 1837 Treaty," Library Records, Sibley House, Mendota, MN, shows Mary as age twelve, Jane Anne as age eleven, and Madeline as age eight in 1837.

32. Gilman, *Henry Hastings Sibley,* 118–20, 121–22.

33. Gilman, *Henry Hastings Sibley,* 120, 125.

34. Gilman, *Henry Hastings Sibley,* 124, 126. The "previous treaty" was the Treaty of 1825.

35. Gilman, *Henry Hastings Sibley,* 126; Anderson, *Kinsmen of Another Kind,* 183–89.

36. Gilman, *Henry Hastings Sibley,* 127–28.

37. Anderson, *Kinsmen of Another Kind,* 191–99, 205, 208.

38. Gilman, *Henry Hastings Sibley,* 130–33; Anderson, *Kinsmen of Another Kind,* 191–99, 205, 208.

39. Anderson, *Kinsmen of Another Kind,* 203–4.

Notes to Chapter 4: Minnesota River, 1853–1860

Epigraphs: Jared Daniels, "Yellow Medicine," 1–2, in Jared Daniels, "Reminiscences"; Anderson, *Kinsmen of Another Kind,* 230.

1. Lehman, "Alexander Andrew and Jane (Anderson) Robertson," Robertson Family File.
2. Case, "Redwood and Yellow Medicine Indian Agencies," 7–8.
3. Robertson, "Reminiscences," *SDDHC,* 563–64: "New Monument at Fort Ridgely," *Fairfax Standard,* undated clipping, Robertson Family File. This story also confirms that Jane's brother was older by two years. Woolworth, "Lives and Influences," 117; Lehman, "Alexander Andrew and Jane (Anderson) Robertson," Robertson Family File; Case, "Redwood and Yellow Medicine Indian Agencies," 9.
4. Case, "Redwood and Yellow Medicine Indian Agencies," 1–6. Ellen Laken was Hazen Mooers's third wife.
5. Anderson, *Kinsmen of Another Kind,* 205–8, 210–11; Daniels, "Yellow Medicine," 2–6.
6. Glewwe Research File: Thomas Williamson to Treat, March 3, 1855, and Thomas Williamson to Treat, January 13, 1855, box 7, ABCFM Correspondence.
7. Glewwe Research File: Thomas Williamson to Treat, March 3, 1855, and Thomas Williamson to Treat, January 13, 1855, box 7, ABCFM Correspondence; box 189, 489, Northwest Missions Papers.
8. Daniels, "Yellow Medicine," 1.
9. Daniels, "Yellow Medicine," 2, 6–7.
10. Daniels, "Yellow Medicine," 5–7.
11. Daniels, "Yellow Medicine," 1–2.
12. "Record of Payment" to Thomas Robertson, for interpreter from July 1 to September 30, 1856, November Correspondence, 1856; "List of Persons Employed at the Yellow Medicine Agency in the First Quarter in 1857," Correspondence, 1857—both Charles E. Flandrau and Family Papers.
13. Flandrau, *The History of Minnesota,* 284–86.
14. Flandrau, *The History of Minnesota,* 285.
15. "February Monthly Report from the Sioux Agency to the Office of Indian Affairs," March 4, 1847, microfilm M686; "February 1857 Monthly Report to the Office of Indian Affairs"—both Charles E. Flandrau and Family Papers.
16. Anderson, *Little Crow,* 79–80; Andrew Robertson to Charles Flandrau, November 25, 1856; January 23, 1857; March 30, 1857; March 31, 1857; April 1, 1857; April 4, 1857; April 18, 1857; April 20, 1857—all Correspondence Files, 1856–57, Charles E. Flandrau and Family Papers.
17. Andrew Robertson to Charles Flandrau, April 4, 1857, Correspondence, Charles E. Flandrau and Family Papers.

18. Folwell, *History of Minnesota*, 1:353–61.

19. Folwell, *History of Minnesota*, 1:324–25; 1856 Mixed Blood Claimants Roll, Grey Cloud Collection, Minnesota Historical Society.

20. Robertson, "Reminiscences," DCMC, 18–19; Glewwe Research File: Thomas Williamson to Treat, November 1857, ABCFM Correspondence; Jane Williamson, Mission School Report, March 31, 1862.

21. Robertson, "Reminiscences," *SDDHC*, 564–67; Woolworth and Woolworth, "The Treaty of Mendota," 50–64; Robertson, "Reminiscences," DCMC, 5–6; Lois Glewwe, interview, June 1, 2020; Diedrich, *Little Paul*, 137.

22. Case, "Redwood and Yellow Medicine Indian Agencies," 9; Michno, *Dakota Dawn*, Map F, "Lower Redwood Agency."

23. Atkins, *Creating Minnesota,* 50–52; Anderson and Woolworth, *Through Dakota Eyes*, 44, 47, 51–52, 54–55.

24. Carroll, "*Naginowenah*"; Anderson, *Kinsmen of Another Kind,* 205–8.

25. Faribault, "The Story of Nancy McClure," 439–46.

26. Celia Campbell Stay, in Anderson and Woolworth, *Through Dakota Eyes*, 44–45.

27. William Robertson married (Marie/Maria) Augusta Brown; Martha Robertson married J. R. Brown Jr.

28. Woolworth and Woolworth, "The Treaty of Mendota" and "The Treaty of Traverse des Sioux," 34–47; Michno, *Dakota Dawn*, 55–57; Anderson, *Little Crow,* 90–92; Chief Wabasha, in Anderson and Woolworth, *Through Dakota Eyes*, 27–28.

29. Anderson, *Kinsmen of Another Kind,* 209–10, 224–25.

30. Nairn, "A History of the Sioux Massacre," 3; Wingerd, *North Country*, 272–73.

31. Wingerd, *North Country*, 274.

32. Diedrich, *Little Paul,* 77, 84.

33. Wingerd, *North Country*, 274–75; Anderson, *Kinsmen of Another Kind,* 227–32.

34. Anderson, *Kinsmen of Another Kind,* 227–31; Wingerd, *North Country*, 276.

35. Case, "Redwood and Yellow Medicine Indian Agencies," 9; Anderson, *Little Crow,* 94–98, 104–5; Lehman, "Andrew Alexander and Jane (Anderson) Robertson," Robertson Family File.

36. Anderson, *Kinsmen of Another Kind,* 227–31; Wingerd, *North Country*, 276, 277, 278.

37. Anderson, *Little Crow,* 103; Wingerd, *North Country*, 277–78; Anderson, *Kinsmen of Another Kind,* 227–31.

38. Wingerd, *North Country*, 292; Big Eagle, in Anderson and Woolworth, *Through Dakota Eyes*, 23; Anderson, *Little Crow,* 108.

39. Big Eagle, in Anderson and Woolworth, *Through Dakota Eyes*, 26–27.

40. Wingerd, *North Country*, 271–72, 293–94.

41. Wingerd, *North Country*, 279; Anderson, *Kinsmen of Another Kind,* 233–36.

42. Wingerd, *North Country*, 290–91.

43. Wingerd, *North Country*, 271; Anderson, *Kinsmen of Another Kind,* 242–43.

44. Anderson, *Kinsmen of Another Kind,* 241–43.

45. Anderson, *Kinsmen of Another Kind,* 245.

46. Michno, *Dakota Dawn*, 65. Seabury school is referred to in Samuel Brown's reminiscences of being in Camp Release and with Frank (see Anderson and Woolworth, *Through Dakota Eyes*); James Dobbin, "Shattuck School, Seabury Mission," brochure, 1897, Minnesota Historical Society; Allen, *And the Wilderness Shall Blossom*, 54.

47. Robertson, "Reminiscences," DCMC, 8–9.

48. Woolworth and Woolworth, "The Treaty of Mendota," 59–64; Robertson, "Reminiscences," DCMC, 168.

49. J. R. Brown, "Report of the Lower Sioux Agency," September 6, 1859, St. Peter Agency, Office of Indian Affairs, RG75, National Archives.

50. June Robertson Lehman and James Weatherstone, researchers, John H. Case, "An Account of the Redwood and Yellow Medicine Agencies," reprinted in the *Hastings Gazette,* July 1 and July 8, 1921.

Notes to Chapter 5: Minnesota River, 1860–August 17, 1862

Epigraph: Robertson, "Reminiscences," DCMC, 42.

1. Woloch, *Women and the American Experience*, 216–53.

2. That Thomas saw himself as head of the family after Andrew died is evident in various accounts in which he describes the family home at Beaver Creek as his house rather than his mother's house or the family's house. As another example, in court testimony Thomas gave in 1901, he described his mother as "living with him" at Beaver Creek, as though it was his household. In addition, in his accounts of his role in the Dakota War, it is clear that he considered himself as the head of the family, seeing it as his responsibility, as the eldest son, to protect his mother and siblings. US Army Court of Claims, *The Sisseton and Wahpeton Bands of Dakota or Sioux Indians vs. the United States*, 135; Robertson "Reminiscences," DCMC, 12–13.

    Andrew discusses the process of applying for the scrip in his correspondence in 1857 with agent Charles Flandrau: Correspondence, 1857, Charles E. Flandrau and Family Papers; Tamara St. John, "Jane Anderson Robertson" (shared with the author), 3.

    On land scrip: Entries 878, 879, 880, "Original Land Entries: Part 1 and Part 2, Mixed Blood Indian Scrip," *Minnesota Genealogical Journal* 17–18, in St. John, "Jane Anderson Robertson"; June Robertson Lehman, "Robertson Family," 3, Robertson Family File. The family's land claims were not officially registered until April 1861, although they moved to Beaver Creek in 1860.

Robertson, "Reminiscences," DCMC, 10; Glewwe Research File: Jane Williamson, Mission School Report on Sophie Robertson, March 31, 1862.

3. Curtiss-Wedge, *History of Renville County*, 1:549; Neill, *History of the Minnesota Valley*, 798–800; Michno, *Dakota Dawn*, Maps E and F.

4. Ezmon Earle, "Reminiscences of the Sioux Massacre of 1862," Dakota Conflicts Manuscript Collection (hereafter, DCMC), 3.

5. Lehman, "Robertson Family," Redwood Agency Map, 4, Robertson Family File; Glewwe Research File: "Marion Robertson"; A. J. Ebell, "Latest Indian War News," *St. Paul Daily News*, September 11, 1862, reprinted in Woolworth and Bakeman, eds., *Camera and Sketchbook*, 97–99.

6. George Tanner, "History of the Schools in Faribault," file 1, box 21, 58–62, George Tanner Papers.

7. Whipple, *Lights and Shadows*, 61–65, 110; Tanner, "History of Faribault Schools," 60–62.

8. June Robertson Lehman, "A History of the Early Episcopal Church of St. John's Mission," manuscript, map 4, 1999, Renville County Historical Society; Anderson, *Kinsmen of Another Kind*, 247; Diedrich, *The Chiefs Wapahasha*, 115. Chief Wapahasa III (1812–76) was Daybreak Woman's relative; he was Grey Cloud Woman II's first cousin. He was born in 1812, so he and Daybreak Woman were almost the same age. Anderson, *Gabriel Renville*, 88–92; Daniels, "Reminiscences," 18.

9. Lehman, "A History of the Early Episcopal Church of St. John's Mission," manuscript; Whipple, *Lights and Shadows*, 61–65, 110; Robertson, "Reminiscences," *SDDHC*, 567.

10. Glewwe Research File: Thomas Williamson to Treat, October 29, 1861, box 7, ABCFM Correspondence, and box 1, 726, Thomas Williamson and Family Papers; Monjeau-Marz, *Dakota Indian Internment*, 145–46.

11. Neill, *History of the Minnesota Valley*, 798; Martin J. Severance, interview with Thomas Hughes, November 27, 1903, manuscript, William Watts Folwell Papers (cited in Folwell, *History of Minnesota*, 2:222n15); Big Eagle, in Anderson and Woolworth, *Through Dakota Eyes*, 25.

12. Anderson, *Kinsmen of Another Kind*, 247–48; Holcombe, *Minnesota in Three Centuries*, 3:281–283; Wingerd, *North Country*, 296–97.

13. Wingerd, *North Country*, 294–95.

14. Wingerd, *North Country*, 296; Big Eagle, in Anderson and Woolworth, *Through Dakota Eyes*, 24.

15. Anderson and Woolworth, *Through Dakota Eyes*, 12; Chief Wabasha, in Anderson and Woolworth, *Through Dakota Eyes*, 30.

16. Good Star Woman, in Anderson and Woolworth, *Through Dakota Eyes*, 38.

17. Wingerd, *North Country*, 296–97.

18. Carrie Zeman, "Introduction," in Renville, *Dispatches from the Dakota War*,

56–57; Nancy Faribault, in Anderson and Woolworth, *Through Dakota Eyes*, 80–81.

19. Anderson, *Massacre in Minnesota*, 79; Anderson and Woolworth, *Through Dakota Eyes*, 20.

20. Wingerd, *North Country*, 301; White, "Captivity Among the Sioux," 396; Robertson, "Reminiscences," DCMC, 10.

21. Wakefield, *Six Weeks in the Sioux Teepees*, 62, 64.

22. Holcombe, *Minnesota in Three Centuries*, 3:290–91; Anderson, *Kinsmen of Another Kind*, 248.

23. Holcombe, *Minnesota in Three Centuries,* 3:290–92.

24. Diedrich, *Little Paul*, 93.

25. Holcombe, *Minnesota in Three Centuries,* 3:294–98; Anderson, *Kinsmen of Another Kind,* 248–50; Dietrich, *Little Paul*, 93.

26. Diedrich, *Little Paul*, 93; Holcombe, *Minnesota in Three Centuries,* 3:295–96; Anderson, *Kinsmen of Another Kind,* 249–50; Wingerd, *North Country*, 302–3.

27. Holcombe, *Minnesota in Three Centuries,* 3:296–97; Anderson, *Kinsmen of Another Kind,* 249–50; Diedrich, *Little Paul*, 93–94.

28. Robert Hakewaste, in Anderson and Woolworth, *Through Dakota Eyes*, 32; Diedrich, *Little Paul*, 92; Wingerd, *North Country*, 302; Anderson, *Kinsmen of Another Kind*, 251.

29. Wingerd, *North Country*, 303; Diedrich, *Little Paul*, 94.

30. According to Emily West, the mission teacher at Redwood Agency, Galbraith attended the Episcopal service that ended early Sunday evening on August 17 and stayed to talk afterward, so he did not leave on August 15 or 16 as other historians have claimed. He probably left that evening and stayed in New Ulm that night. "Emily West's Account of the Events at the Redwood Agency, August 17–18, 1862," box 22, George Tanner Papers; Diedrich, *Little Paul*, 94.
    On Galbraith's decision: Holcombe, *Minnesota in Three Centuries,* 3:298–99; Anderson, *Kinsmen of Another Kind,* 248–50; Robert Hakewaste, in Anderson and Woolworth, *Through Dakota Eyes*, 31–32.

31. Anderson, *Kinsmen of Another Kind*, 252; Wingerd, *North Country*, 303.

32. Nairn, "A History of the Sioux Massacre," 2; "Emily West's Account," George Tanner Papers.

33. DeCamp Sweet, "Mrs. J. E. DeCamp Sweet's Narrative," 356–58.

34. The Shakopee and Red Middle Voice bands were located on the Redwood River and Rice Creek, two to five miles upriver from Beaver Creek: Michno, *Dakota Dawn*, Map Gallery. Anderson, *Kinsmen of Another Kind*, 253.

35. Little Crow to Henry Sibley, September 7, 1862, in *Executive Documents of the State of Minnesota for … 1862,* 444, quoted in Renville, *Dispatches from the Dakota War*, 202.

36. Paul Maza Kute Mani to Alexander Ramsey, September 2, 1862, in Renville,

Dispatches from the Dakota War, 199–200; Bakeman and Richardson, eds., *Trails of Tears*, 103n8.

37. Robertson, "Reminiscences," DCMC, 41; Wingerd, *North Country*, 303–4; Big Eagle and Good Star Woman, in Anderson and Woolworth, *Through Dakota Eyes*, 35–39.

38. Anderson, *Massacre in Minnesota*, 83; Robertson, "Reminiscences," DCMC, 41–42; Wingerd, *North Country*, 303–4.

39. Anderson, *Kinsmen of Another Kind*, 253–54; Anderson, *Little Crow*, 132; Little Crow, in Anderson and Woolworth, *Through Dakota Eyes*, 39–42.

Notes to Chapter 6: Minnesota River, August 18–August 26, 1862

Epigraph: Esther Wakeman, in Anderson and Woolworth, *Through Dakota Eyes*, 53–55.

1. Robertson, "Reminiscences," DCMC, 11–13; Thomas Robertson, Testimony in Case #62, *U.S. v. Katpantpanoo*, US Army Military Commission, Sioux War Trials, 1862, trial transcripts, file P1423, microfilm M262, reel 1, Minnesota Historical Society.

2. Wingerd, *North Country*, 304–5; Michno, *Dakota Dawn*, 399.

3. Michno, *Dakota Dawn*, 58.

4. The evidence is contradictory as to whether Myrick's mouth was actually stuffed with grass. Big Eagle's account, given three decades after the war, is the first eyewitness account to say that Myrick's mouth was stuffed with grass; however, the earliest accounts of the Redwood Agency attack and the statements of those who actually encountered or retrieved Myrick's body fail to say anything about grass in his mouth. Of course, another possibility is that his mouth was stuffed with grass and then it fell out or was removed by the time his body was encountered by later witnesses: Anderson, *Little Crow*, 222n3. Webb, *Redwood*, 75–76.

5. Anderson, *Little Crow*, 135; Webb, *Redwood*, 78–79; Robertson, "Reminiscences," DCMC, 42.

6. The Prescotts had another daughter, Sophia, age nineteen, who was not with them when the attack on the Redwood Agency occurred: Carroll, "*Naginowenah*." The name "Keeiyah" is not recognizable to speakers of Dakota.

7. Webb, *Redwood*, 78–79; Anderson and Woolworth, *Through Dakota Eyes*, 30, 43.

8. Webb, *Redwood*, 78–79.

9. Carroll, "*Naginowenah*"; Anderson, *Little Crow*, 136; Webb, *Redwood*, 79; Robertson, "Reminiscences," DCMC, 34; Lehman and Weatherstone, researchers, John Case, "An Account of the Redwood and Yellow Medicine Indian Agencies."

10. Whipple, *Lights and Shadows*, 111.

11. Nairn, "A History of the Sioux Massacre," 4.

12. Esther Wakeman, in Anderson and Woolworth, *Through Dakota Eyes*, 53–55n10, 66.

13. Nairn, "A History of the Sioux Massacre," 4.

14. Nairn, "A History of the Sioux Massacre," 4. Alexander Hunter's assailant is identified in the trial proceedings as Hinhanshoonkoyagmane (He Who Walks Clothed with an Owl's Tail): Isch, *The Dakota War Trials*, 45–46.

15. Neill, *History of the Minnesota Valley*, 799–800; Michno, *Dakota Dawn*, 97.

16. Earle, "Reminiscences," DCMC, 1.

17. Robertson, "Reminiscences," DCMC, 11–13; Robertson Testimony, Case #62.

18. Katpaŋtpaŋ U's use of the term "niece" does not necessarily indicate that he was related by blood to Daybreak Woman. Among the Dakota this term was also used to indicate a special, close relationship. Robertson, "Reminiscences," DCMC, 10–12.

19. Robertson, "Reminiscences," DCMC, 10–12; Isch, *The Dakota War Trials*, Case #63, 105–6; Folwell, *Court Proceedings*, 29.

20. Robertson Testimony, Case #62; Robertson, "Reminiscences," DCMC, 11–13.

21. Robertson, "Reminiscences," DCMC, 12–13.

22. Anderson, *Massacre in Minnesota*, 89–92.

23. Robertson, "Reminiscences," DCMC, 12–13; Robertson, "Reminiscences," *SDDHC*, 568–70; Webb, *Redwood*, 84.

24. Samuel J. Brown, in Anderson and Woolworth, *Through Dakota Eyes*, 78, 130–33; Anderson and Woolworth, "At Little Crow's Village," *Through Dakota Eyes*, 130–34, 143–44n1.

25. Anderson, *Little Crow*, 138–40, 144–46; Anderson and Woolworth, *Through Dakota Eyes*, 51, 93. For Dakota and Euro-Dakota accounts of these battles, see Anderson and Woolworth, *Through Dakota Eyes*, 146–67; Wingerd, *North Country*, 307; Anderson, *Little Crow*, 144–46. Robertson, "Reminiscences," *SDDHC*, 568–70. Thomas was present at the second battle of Fort Ridgely on August 22 and the second battle of New Ulm on August 23.

26. Ebell, "Latest Indian War News," 97–98.

27. Robertson, "Reminiscences," DCMC, 12–13.

28. Thomas Robertson, deposition, Testimony Given in the US Army Court of Claims, No. 22524, *The Sisseton and Wahpeton Bands of Dakota or Sioux Indians vs. United* States, 133–36.

29. Ebell, "Latest Indian War News," 98.

30. Glewwe Research File: "Sophie Robertson," Jane Williamson, School Report, March 31, 1862.

31. Woolworth and Bakeman, eds., *Camera and Sketchbook,* 47; Riggs, *Mary and I*, 155–57; Anderson and Woolworth, *Through Dakota Eyes*, 102–3.

32. Riggs, *Mary and I*, 149–50, 154–57, 158–59, 171–72, 173–74; Folwell, *History of Minnesota*, 2:118–20; Kirsten Delegard, "Adrian Ebell, People Escaping from Violence in the U.S.–Dakota War, 1862," Plate #96, in Wingerd, *North*

Country; Woolworth and Bakeman, eds., *Camera and Sketchbook*, 48–49. The photograph is also reprinted in Folwell, *History of Minnesota*, 2:121.

33. Glewwe, "The Story of Jane Smith Williamson," 11n1; Riggs, *Mary and I*, 159–60; Woolworth and Bakeman, eds., *Camera and Sketchbook*, 50–51, 121; Anderson, *Kinsmen of Another Kind*, 264–65.

34. Riggs, *Mary and I*, 161–62, 176; Woolworth and Bakeman, eds., *Camera and Sketchbook*, 50–51, 121; Folwell, *History of Minnesota*, 2:120–21.

35. Wingerd, *North Country*, 311; Michno, *Dakota Dawn*, 399–403. Michno puts the total number of civilians killed (whites killed outside of battles) at 331. Curtis Dahlin says the total for civilian deaths is between 400 and 500: Curtis Dahlin, "Words vs. Actions," in Bakeman and Richardson, eds., *Trails of Tears*, 37. Anderson, in *Massacre in Minnesota*, ix, says "more than 600 settlers" were killed. Michno, *Dakota Dawn*, Appendix A; Dahlin, "Words vs. Actions," 37; Carley, *The Sioux Uprising of 1862*, 1; Anderson and Woolworth, *Through Dakota Eyes*, 1; Robertson, "Reminiscences," DCMC, 27.

36. Anderson and Woolworth, "At Little Crow's Village," in Anderson and Woolworth, *Through Dakota Eyes*, 129; Webb, *Redwood*, 96–99.

37. Samuel Brown, in Anderson and Woolworth, *Through Dakota Eyes*, 134; Carroll, "Who Was Jane Lamont?," 191.

38. Celia Campbell Stay, in Anderson and Woolworth, *Through Dakota Eyes*, 136–37; Snana, in Anderson and Woolworth, *Through Dakota Eyes*, 141, 143.

39. Nancy Faribault, in Anderson and Woolworth, *Through Dakota Eyes*, 138–39.

40. White, "Captivity Among the Sioux," 403–8, 410–11; Tarble, *The Story of My Capture*, 31–34.

41. Tarble, *The Story of My Capture*, 35–42.

42. DeCamp Sweet, "Mrs. J. E. Decamp Sweet's Narrative," 365–70.

43. Webb, *Redwood*, 98; Gilman, *Henry Hastings Sibley*, 172–76, 178–80; Anderson, *Little Crow*, 154–55; Wingerd, *North Country*, 309–11.

44. Esther Wakeman, in Anderson and Woolworth, *Through Dakota Eyes*, 53–55; Big Eagle, in Anderson and Woolworth, *Through Dakota Eyes*, 55–56.

45. White, "Captivity Among the Sioux," 401–4.

46. Anderson, *Little Crow*, 142; Ebell, "Latest Indian War News," 97.

47. Robertson Testimony, Case #62.

Notes to Chapter 7: Minnesota River, August 26–October 5, 1862

Epigraph: Wakefield, *Six Weeks in the Sioux Teepees*, 64.

1. Anderson, *Kinsmen of Another Kind*, 254; Robertson, "Reminiscences," SDDHC, 568–70.

2. Renville, *Dispatches from the Dakota War*, 75.

3. Renville, *Dispatches from the Dakota War*, 67, 275n233.

4. Webb, *Redwood*, 99; Standing Buffalo quoted in Wingerd, *North Country*, 311; Anderson and Woolworth, *Through Dakota Eyes*, 168.

5. Gilman, *Henry Hastings Sibley,* 181; Anderson, *Little Crow,* 151; Diedrich, *Little Paul,* 103.

6. Anderson, *Little Crow,* 151–53.

7. Gabriel Renville, in Anderson and Woolworth, *Through Dakota Eyes,* 189–90.

8. Robertson, "Reminiscences," *SDDHC,* 570–71.

9. Anderson and Woolworth, *Through Dakota Eyes,* 177–79; Anderson, *Little Crow,* 155–56.

10. Anderson, *Little Crow,* 156.

11. T. Robertson, in Anderson and Woolworth, *Through Dakota Eyes,* 181; Wakefield, *Six Weeks in the Sioux Teepees,* 102.

12. T. Robertson, in Anderson and Woolworth, *Through Dakota Eyes,* 183.

13. T. Robertson, in Anderson and Woolworth, *Through Dakota Eyes,* 183–85.

14. T. Robertson, in Anderson and Woolworth, *Through Dakota Eyes,* 183–85; Wingerd, *North Country,* 311; Renville, *Dispatches from the Dakota War,* 75.

15. Anderson, *Massacre in Minnesota,* 212–13; Derounian-Stodola, *The War in Words,* 69–70, 104–15; Paul Mazakutemani, in Anderson and Woolworth, *Through Dakota Eyes,* 197–98.

16. Diedrich, *Little Paul,* 115.

17. Robertson, "Reminiscences," DCMC, 40; Ebell, "Latest Indian War News," 99; Thomas A. Robertson to Marion Satterlee, March 26, 1923, Marion P. Satterlee Papers.

18. Bachman, *Northern Slave, Black Dakota,* 169.

19. Anderson, *Massacre in Minnesota,* 198–204. Several young women who were captured and initially held in Wakute's house suffered rape by multiple men over several days in Wakute's absence. One of these young women was Mary Schwandt, whom Snana and Good Thunder rescued afterward and took in. Another young woman in the house, Mattie Williams, was abused similarly before being claimed by her original captor, Laying Up Buffalo, who took her to his tipi. Williams was one of the two women who charged Dakota men with rape at the military commission trials.

20. White, "Captivity Among the Sioux," 403, 411; Isch, *The Dakota War Trials,* Trial of Te Tay Hde Don, Trial #279, 291.

21. Both Nancy Faribault and Mary Ann Dalton Campbell received requests for shelter from white women captives: Anderson, *Massacre in Minnesota,* 201–2; Nancy Faribault, "Account," in Anderson and Woolworth, *Through Dakota Eyes,* 247.

22. Joseph Coursolle, "Joseph Coursolle's Story," in Anderson and Woolworth, *Through Dakota Eyes,* 241.

23. Coursolle, "Joseph Coursolle's Story," 161–65.

24. Robertson, "Reminiscences," DCMC, 39–40; Renville, *Dispatches from the Dakota War,* 65–67.

25. Renville, *Dispatches from the Dakota War,* 67–68.

26. Nancy Faribault, in Anderson and Woolworth, *Through Dakota Eyes*, 248; Isch, *The Dakota War Trials*, 31n74. Return Holcombe, a historian who interviewed many former captives in the 1890s, confirms Mooers's role in helping them and says he was admired: Return Holcombe to Samuel Brown, April 13, 1899, Joseph R. and Samuel J. Brown Family Papers.

27. Gabriel Renville, in Anderson and Woolworth, *Through Dakota Eyes*, 189.

28. Samuel Brown, in Anderson and Woolworth, *Through Dakota Eyes*, 176.

29. Celia Campbell Stay, in Anderson and Woolworth, *Through Dakota Eyes*, 250–51.

30. Renville, *Dispatches from the Dakota War*, 77; Dahlin, *A Pictorial History*, 10.

31. Isch, *The Dakota War Trials*, 305. Thomas testified at the trial of Zoo Yay Sa that "this old man came to my brother and myself and others of the half breeds before the last battle and said we must go, or they would come around again."

32. Anderson and Woolworth, *Through Dakota Eyes*, 219.

33. Anderson, *Little Crow*, 156–59; Webb, *Redwood*, 103.

34. Anderson, *Little Crow*, 160–61; Renville, *Dispatches from the Dakota War*, 273n224, puts the number of captives at sixteen.

35. Renville, *Dispatches from the Dakota War*, 73, 179–81; White, "Captivity Among the Sioux," 417–22.

36. Nancy Faribault, in Anderson and Woolworth, *Through Dakota Eyes*, 244–49.

37. Nancy Faribault, in Anderson and Woolworth, *Through Dakota Eyes*, 247.

38. Anderson, *Little Crow*, 161; Wingerd, *North Country*, 312; Webb, *Redwood*, 104.

39. Big Eagle, in Anderson and Woolworth, *Through Dakota Eyes*, 235, 237.

40. Renville, *Dispatches from the Dakota War*, 273n224; Riggs, "A List of White Persons and Half Breeds," 24–26.

41. Robertson, "Reminiscences," DCMC, 23–24.

42. Wingerd, *North Country*, 313; Renville, *Dispatches from the Dakota War*, 87; Bachman, *Northern Slave, Black Dakota*, 170; Samuel Brown, in Anderson and Woolworth, *Through Dakota Eyes*, 226–27.

43. Nancy Faribault, in Anderson and Woolworth, *Through Dakota Eyes*, 246.

44. As quoted in Lois Glewwe, "The Journey of the Prisoners Convoy to South Bend," in Bakeman and Richardson, eds., *Trails of Tears*, 86–87.

45. Stephen Osman, "Sibley's Army in November 1862," in Bakeman and Richardson, eds., *Trails of Tears*, 22.

46. Waziyatawin, *What Does Justice Look Like?*, 43–45; Sibley letter quoted in Osman, "Sibley's Army in November 1862," in Bakeman and Richardson, eds., *Trails of Tears*, 23.

47. Robertson, "Reminiscences," DCMC, 26. As Marion testified in court on October 5 against the man accused of killing her husband, they would not have

left earlier than October 6, even though Thomas places their departure at the same time as the camp moving down to Yellow Medicine, on October 4.

48. Nancy Faribault, in Anderson and Woolworth, *Through Dakota Eyes*, 248–49.

49. Isch, *The Dakota War Trials*, Trial of Hinhanshoonkoyagmane, Trial #6, 46, 162–77, Cases #131–39; Chomsky, "The U.S.–Dakota War Trials," 13. The names of the other men were Louis Frenier, Antoine Provencalle, Francis Roy, David Faribault Jr., Charles Crawford, Joe Provencalle, Baptiste Campbell, and Louis LaBelle.

Notes to Chapter 8: Minnesota River, October 6–November 4, 1862

Epigraph: Daniels, "Reminiscences."

1. Bachman, *Northern Slave, Black Dakota*, 177. Mary Woodbury was a Euro-Dakota woman, although Bachman lists her among the released white captives who testified at the trials. She was the daughter of Indian agent Lawrence Taliaferro and a daughter of Bdewakaŋtuŋwaŋ chief Cloud Man. Carroll, "Who Was Jane Lamont?" In the first twenty-nine trials held at Camp Release, when the commission was still focused on those charged with specific crimes against whites, five Dakota men testified against other Dakota men in seven cases and ten Euro-Dakota people testified in fourteen cases.

   Isch, *The Dakota War Trials*, 534–52. The Euro-Dakota men who stood trial were Jo Allard, Joseph Rouillier, Antoine Reyer, Hypolite Auge, Joseph Frenier, John Frenier, Thomas Frenier, Augustus Frenier, Joseph Godfrey, Charles Crawford, Henry Millard (Milord), Louis Frenier, Antoine Provencalle, Francis Roy, David Faribault Jr., Thomas Robertson, Joe Provencalle, Baptiste Campbell, and Louis LaBelle. Hypolite Auge, Baptiste Campbell, and Henry Milord were executed at Mankato on December 26, 1862. Bachman, *Northern Slave, Black Dakota*, Appendix: Whiting-Ruggles Report, 1862, 352–56.

2. Haymond, *The Infamous Dakota War Trials*, 59–83.

3. Bachman, *Northern Slave, Black Dakota*, 124–26; Isch, *The Dakota War Trials*, 1–6, 10–13; Samuel Brown, "Recollections," in Anderson and Woolworth, *Through Dakota Eyes*, 225–27.

4. Bachman, *Northern Slave, Black Dakota*, 123–30, 182–83; Samuel Brown, in Anderson and Woolworth, *Through Dakota Eyes*, 225.

5. Bachman, *Northern Slave, Black Dakota*, 185; Chomsky, "The U.S.-Dakota War Trials," 22–24; Anderson, *Massacre in Minnesota*, 229.

6. Bachman, *Northern Slave, Black Dakota*, 190–91.

7. Bachman, *Northern Slave, Black Dakota*, 190–91; Isch, *The Dakota War Trials*, Case #135, 169.

8. Robertson, "Reminiscences," DCMC, 24. Taju (Tazoo) or Red Otter was

hanged at Mankato on December 26, 1862. Isch, *The Dakota War Trials*, 169; Thomas Robertson, deposition, US Army Court of Claims, *The Sisseton and Wahpeton Bands of Dakota or Sioux Indians v. United States*, 136–37.

9. Isch, *The Dakota War Trials*, 534–85.

10. Isch, *The Dakota War Trials*, 169–70.

11. Isch, *The Dakota War Trials*, Case #249, 266; Case #298, 305.

12. Isch, *The Dakota War Trials*. At five of the forty-nine trials for which his testimony was recorded, Thomas had no information about the defendant. At most of the other trials his testimony was very short, often limited to only one or two sentences. In four of the cases in which he was listed as a witness, the defendants were found not guilty. The four cases in which defendants were found not guilty and at which Thomas was a witness were #27, #55, #265, and #346. Thomas was listed as a witness in eight of the trials of the thirty-eight Dakota men who were executed at Mankato. In two of those cases, his testimony was not recorded, so it is not clear whether he testified or not. In one of the cases, he said he had no information about the defendant. Isch, *The Dakota War Trials*; Robertson, "Reminiscences," DCMC, 10–13. On Katpaŋtpaŋ U, see Isch, *The Dakota War Trials*, Case #63, 105–6.

13. Isch, *The Dakota War Trials*, Case #178, 211; Bachman, *Northern Slave, Black Dakota*, 279n24.

14. Isch, *The Dakota War Trials,* 147–50.

15. Isch, *The Dakota War Trials*, 39–42, 45–46. Both trials were on November 2 at Redwood.

16. Isch, *The Dakota War Trials*, 527–28.

17. Chomsky, "The U.S.–Dakota War Trials," 24–27; Anderson, *Massacre in Minnesota*, 224–27.

18. Chomsky, "The U.S.–Dakota War Trials," 13, 28, 37; Webb, *Redwood*, 105–7; Gilman, *Henry Hastings Sibley*, 190; Isch, *The Dakota War Trials*, 26; Bachman, *Northern Slave, Black Dakota*, 193.

19. Chomsky, "The U.S.–Dakota War Trials," 14–15, 46–50, 90; Isch, *The Dakota War Trials*, 1–6, 16–17.

20. Bachman, *Northern Slave, Black Dakota*, 183.

21. Robertson, "Reminiscences," DCMC, 26; Monjeau-Marz, *Dakota Indian Internment,* 138.

22. Gabriel Renville, in Anderson and Woolworth, *Through Dakota Eyes*, 233.

23. John Poage Wiliamson to S. B. Treat, November 5–6, 1862, as quoted in Monjeau-Marz, *Dakota Indian Internment,* 29. Jane Williamson's letter is cited in Lois Glewwe's blog, Dakota Soul Sisters; Jane Williamson to Stephen Riggs, October 27, 1862, box 1, Stephen Riggs Family Papers.

24. Robertson, "Reminiscences," DCMC, 26.

25. Robertson, "Reminiscences," DCMC, 27.

Notes to Chapter 9: Mississippi and Missouri Rivers, 1862–1866

Epigraph: As quoted in Monjeau-Marz, *Dakota Indian Internment,* 29.

1. Bachman, *Northern Slave, Black Dakota,* 182; Folwell, *History of Minnesota,* 2:194–95; Diedrich, *Little Paul,* 116; Gilman, *Henry Hastings Sibley,* 187–88; Robertson, "Reminiscences," DCMC, 25–26.

2. Osman, "Sibley's Army in 1862," in Bakeman and Richardson, eds., *Trails of Tears,* 27; Mary Bakeman and Alan Woolworth, "The Family Caravan," in Bakeman and Richardson, eds., *Trails of Tears,* 62.

3. Bakeman and Woolworth, "The Family Caravan," in Bakeman and Richardson, eds., *Trails of Tears,* 61.

4. While sources indicate there were wagons in the caravan for the women and children, it is not entirely clear how many wagons (or horses) were provided or available to the Dakota prisoners in the family caravan. Historian Folwell says there were not enough wagons for all the women and children: Folwell, *History of Minnesota,* 2:200.

5. Gilman, *Henry Hastings Sibley,* 187–88; Anderson, *Massacre in Minnesota,* 233; Sam Brown quoted in Bakeman and Woolworth, "Family Caravan," in Bakeman and Richardson, eds., *Trails of Tears,* 66–67; Robertson, "Reminiscences," DCMC, 27–28.

6. Walt Bachman, "Colonel Miller's War," Curtis Dahlin, "Words vs. Actions," Lois Glewwe, "The Journey of the Prisoners Convoy to South Bend," Stephen Osman, "Sibley's Army in November, 1862," and Bakeman and Woolworth, "Family Caravan"—all in Bakeman and Richardson, eds., *Trails of Tears.*

7. Good Star Woman, in Anderson and Woolworth, *Through Dakota Eyes,* 263.

8. Angela Cavender Wilson, "Grandmother to Granddaughter: Generations of Oral History in a Dakota Family," in Mihesuah, ed., *Natives and Academics,* 32–33.

9. Wilson, "Grandmother to Granddaughter," in Mihesuah, ed., *Natives and Academics,* 32.

10. As quoted in Bakeman and Woolworth, "Family Caravan," in Bakeman and Richardson, eds., *Trails of Tears,* 70.

11. Brown does not explain the source of this number and there was no official census recorded at Redwood prior to the march to Fort Snelling. Some historians have suggested the difference in Brown's number and the census at Fort Snelling could be largely explained by the fact that many Euro-Dakota captives who had already left the camps had been included in the total of 1,658. However, most of those who had already left had done so back in late September and early October, so why they would have been included as part of the count at Redwood in early November when they had not been present for over a month is not clear (assuming there was a *new* count taken at Redwood and Brown was not relying on numbers from late September). Samuel Brown, in Anderson and Woolworth, *Through Dakota Eyes,* 227.

12. Monjeau-Marz and Osman, "About the Fort Snelling Indian Camps," 114.

13. Members of the Renville family and some children of scouts were allowed to go live with families in Mendota and St. Anthony: Renville, *Dispatches from the Dakota War*, 87.

14. Monjeau-Marz, *Dakota Indian Internment*, 38, 42–43; Robertson, "Reminiscences," DCMC, 28.

15. Robertson, "Reminiscences," DCMC, 28.

16. Monjeau-Marz, *Dakota Indian Internment*, 40, 66, 70, and "Census of Indian Camp at Fort Snelling," 138; Monjeau-Marz and Osman, "About the Fort Snelling Indian Camps," 128.

17. Dahlin, *A Pictorial History*, 84–87; Good Star Woman, in Anderson and Woolworth, *Through Dakota Eyes*, 264; Monjeau-Marz, *Dakota Indian Internment*, 71.

18. Zeman, "Introduction," in Renville, *Dispatches from the Dakota War*, 86–87; Monjeau-Marz and Osman, "About the Fort Snelling Indian Camps," 127, 128. Euro-Dakota residents who still had scrip could also sell it: Millikan, "The Great Treasure of the Fort Snelling Prison Camp," 11–12.

19. John Williamson quoted in Monjeau-Marz and Osman, "About the Fort Snelling Indian Camps," 114; Whipple, *Lights and Shadows*, 133; other reports: Monjeau-Marz and Osman, "About the Fort Snelling Indian Camps," 127.

20. As quoted in Monjeau-Marz, *Dakota Indian Internment*, 130.

21. Monjeau-Marz, *Dakota Indian Internment*, 38–39.

22. John Williamson to Thomas Williamson, November 17, 1862, as quoted in Monjeau-Marz, *Dakota Indian Internment*, 38; Monjeau-Marz, *Dakota Indian Internment*, 43; *Mankato Weekly Record*, March 28, 1863, as quoted in Monjeau-Marz, *Dakota Indian Internment*, 44.

23. Bachman, *Northern Slave, Black Dakota*, 291; Monjeau-Marz, *Dakota Indian Internment*, 53–58.

24. Good Star Woman, in Anderson and Woolworth, *Through Dakota Eyes*, 264.

25. Gabriel Renville, as quoted in Monjeau-Marz, *Dakota Indian Internment*, 59.

26. Bishop Henry Whipple to Cordelia Whipple, January 13, 1863, as quoted in Monjeau-Marz, *Dakota Indian Internment*, 59; Riggs quoted in Monjeau-Marz, *Dakota Indian Internment*, 59–60.

27. Renville, *Dispatches from the Dakota War*, 271–72n203, 280n292.

28. Renville quoted in Monjeau-Marz, *Dakota Indian Internment*, 72; Anderson, *Gabriel Renville*, 41–42.

29. Diedrich, *Little Paul*, 120–22; Dahlin, *A Pictorial History*, 84–87; Monjeau-Marz, *Dakota Indian Internment*, 97–100; Zeman, "Introduction," in Renville, *Dispatches from the Dakota War*, 86–87, 96; Monjeau-Marz and Osman, "About the Fort Snelling Indian Camps," 120.

30. Monjeau-Marz, *Dakota Indian Internment*, 99, 106; Werner, "Dakota Diaspora," 39–40; Gilman, *Henry Hasting Sibley*, 191.

31. Monjeau-Marz, *Dakota Indian Internment,* 107; Diedrich, *The Chiefs Wapa-hasa,* 131–33.
32. Robertson, "Reminiscences," DCMC, 34–35.
33. Diedrich, *The Chiefs Wapahasa,* 131–33; Werner, "Dakota Diaspora," 50–51.
34. Robertson, "Reminiscences," DCMC, 35–37.
35. Henry Whipple to Commissioner of Indian Affairs, P825, box 4, 3–4, Bishop Henry Whipple Papers.
36. Good Star Woman, in Anderson and Woolworth, *Through Dakota Eyes,* 264.
37. Werner, "Dakota Diaspora," 51–64; Hyman, *Dakota Women's Work,* 100–106.
38. Meyer, *History of the Santee Sioux,* 146–55; Hyman, *Dakota Women's Work,* 104–6.
39. Diedrich, *The Chiefs Wapahasa,* 133–34.
40. Bishop Henry Whipple Account Book, June 13, 1864, Episcopal Diocese of Minnesota Account Books, box 43, Whipple Papers.

Notes to Chapter 10: Cannon and Straight Rivers, 1862–1868

Epigraph: Jane Anderson Robertson to Superintendent of Indians, 1862, Andrew Robertson file.

1. Glewwe, Dakota Soul Sisters 11; Glewwe Research File: correspondence of Jane Williamson.
2. Samuel D. Hinman to Bishop Henry Whipple, October 17, 1862, box 3, Whipple Papers; Carroll, *"Naginowenah."*
3. Neill and Bryant, *History of Rice County,* 1:269–70.
4. Neill and Bryant, *History of Rice County,* 2:318–23; Curtiss-Wedge, *History of Rice and Steele Counties,* 1:86–87, 216–17, 218; *Faribault Central Republican,* October 24, 1866.
5. Hoisington, *A Splendid Little Town,* 6–13.
6. Diedrich, *Old Betsey,* 70–78; *Faribault Central Republican,* June 10, 1863.
7. Jane Anderson Robertson to Superintendent of Indians, 1862, Andrew Robertson file.
8. The nature and opportunities for women's work in the nineteenth century has been extensively covered by historians of women in the United States. For example, see DuBois and Dumenil, *Through Women's Eyes.* For an account of the kind of work educated middle-class white women did in this era, see Louisa May Alcott's account of her own employment, as documented in her book titled *Work.*
9. Robertson, "Reminiscences," DCMC, 36–37; Episcopal Diocese of Minnesota Account Books, box 43, Whipple Papers; June Robertson Lehman, "Gustavus Robertson," Robertson Family File.
10. Minnesota State Census: Rice County (Faribault), 1865; US Census: Faribault, Rice County, Minnesota, 1870.
11. *Faribault Republican,* June 8, 1870, July 20, 1870, and March 5, 1871.

12. "First Will Was Signed with an X," *Redwood Gazette,* 1869–1939, Grey Cloud Woman Notebooks, June Robertson Lehman Files.

13. Henry Whipple to Commissioner of Indian Affairs, June 22, 1866, box 4, Whipple Papers; Wingerd, *North Country,* 337–38; Diedrich, *Old Betsey,* 80–94.

14. Diedrich, *Old Betsey,* 70–78.

15. Diedrich, *Old Betsey,* 70–89; Meyer, *History of the Santee Sioux,* 259–60; Neill and Bryant, *History of Rice County,* 2:325.

16. Diedrich, *Old Betsey,* 82–83.

17. Curtiss-Wedge, *History of Rice and Steele Counties,* 86–87; Diedrich, *Old Betsey,* 70–89; Allen, *And the Wilderness Shall Blossom,* 54, 121. In 1866 the government recorded 374 Dakota in Minnesota: 65 at Faribault, 158 at Yellow Medicine, 12 at Wabasha, and 139 at Big Stone Lake. In 1867 most of these went to the Santee Reservation, but not all. Folwell, *History of Minnesota,* 2:264.

18. Frink, *A Short History of Faribault.*

19. Robertson Genealogy, Sisseton Wahpeton Oyate Tribal Archives, Lake Traverse Reservation, provided by Historic Preservation Officer Tamara St. John. According to these records, Angus's first wife was Emma Shortfoot and his second wife was Nancy Shortfoot. Thomas is listed as marrying two Shortfoot women, the first Lydia and the second Ida, who is listed as the mother of all his children. St. John thinks Lydia was Ida's mother, however, not a sister.

    Case, "Early History of Minnesota," Case Papers. The cause of the boy's death is not documented, but in the nineteenth century the mortality rate of young children was high, and they frequently succumbed to diseases that later would be prevented by vaccines or treated with antibiotics, including scarlet fever, diphtheria, measles, and whooping cough. In the early 1860s the Faribault newspaper reported regularly on the deaths of children from diphtheria and measles.

20. Genealogical Records, Sisseton Wahpeton Oyate Tribal Archives, provided by Historic Preservation Officer Tamara St. John; June Robertson Lehman Files.

Notes to Chapter 11: Minnesota River and Lake Traverse, 1868–1904

Epigraph: *Inter Lake Tribune* (Browns Valley, MN), March 17, 1904.

1. Jo Bennett, "History of Brown's Valley and Its Environs" (1881), Minnesota Historical Society; Renville, *Dispatches from the Dakota War,* 110–12.

2. Gilman, *Henry Hasting Sibley,* 204.

3. Diedrich, *Little Paul,* 156; Allen, *And the Wilderness Shall Blossom,* 140.

4. Bennett, "History of Brown's Valley," 14.

5. Robertson, "Reminiscences," DCMC, 37–38.

6. Robertson Genealogical Records, provided by Historic Preservation Officer

Tamara St. John. St. John says that Lydia may not be the correct name of Thomas's first wife; Lydia may have been his mother-in-law. Robertson, "Reminiscences," DCMC, 31.

7. Sterling, "Bishop Henry Whipple," 240–45.

8. Robertson, "Reminiscences," DCMC, 37–38; Daniels, "Reminiscences," ch. 9, 1–5. The original census showed 1,314 people on the reservation.

9. Daniels, "Reminiscences," ch. 9, 7–16; Sisseton Dakota Indian Reservation Jubilee Committee, *History of the Sisseton-Wahpeton Indian Reservation*, 1–4.

10. The 1870 US Federal Census shows Sophie Weatherstone living in the home of their next-door neighbor, a single man; she is listed as a housekeeper. She may have had the job for some time, and it may be how she met Henry initially. Frank is listed as a clerk in the post office in the 1870 census; he was living in Faribault.

11. Will says Dessie was an infant when Lawrence died. In addition, a Prescott descendant says the information in the family was that he died early in January 1869, but that was not possible; it could have been early January 1870. William Robertson, notarized letter re: Ephraim Prescott, March 31, 1941, and additional information provided to author by Prescott descendant Jody Moore via email, July 22, 2013.

12. The 1875 Minnesota State Census shows Frank and Clara (Claire) still living with her family in Winona. However, by 1880, according to the federal census, Frank and Clara had their own home in Winona with their two children.

   Beaver Falls Gazette, April 26, 1870, lists Sophie as a landowner and the taxes due on her property. This land was not the same forty acres claimed in her name with scrip in 1861, which the family had lived on before the war. In 1869 Sophie sold that land and purchased other land in the vicinity to farm. It is not entirely clear whether Gustavus remained in Faribault through 1871 prior to moving to Beaver Falls. He is not listed on the 1870 federal census as living in Faribault, but he could just have been away from home at the time. According to his descendant June Robertson Lehman, "the entire family left Faribault in 1871," but the entire family was not there in 1870. Daybreak Woman, Thomas, Angus, Gustavus, William, and Martha do not appear anywhere on the 1870 federal census, which means they must have all been on the reservation. The land sale and description of Sophie as an "Indian woman" is from Ethel Greenslet, "Pioneer Life in Renville County," *Olivia Times Journal*, 1958, 1.

13. In 1887, William was living on the Pine Ridge Reservation: Indian Census Rolls, Federal Census Collection, Ancestry.com.

14. There are references in the correspondence between the Brown and Robertson families to Daybreak Woman's midwifery and nursing activities: Brown Family Papers.

15. Jane A. Robertson to Samuel Brown, March 10, 1873, Brown Family Papers.

16. Although a number of the Robertson family genealogies and other accounts indicate that Marion died in 1871, according to the *Iapi Oaye Vital Statistics, 1871–1939*, at the Minnesota Historical Society, Marion Prescott died on June 7, 1873. These statistics are gathered from information in Dakota-language newspapers on the various Dakota reservations. This 1873 date is confirmed by Will's letter: William Robertson to Samuel Brown, May 24, 1873, Brown Family Papers.

17. See all correspondence, 1871–98, Brown Family Papers.

18. William Robertson to Sam Brown, April 14, 1876, Brown Family Papers.

19. Samuel Brown to William Robertson, May 5, 1876, Brown Family Papers.

20. William Robertson to Samuel Brown, October 13, 1876; William Robertson to Sam Brown, January 24, 1877; Augusta Brown to Sam Brown, September 19, 1876—all Brown Family Papers.

21. William Robertson to Samuel Brown, October 13, 1876; William Robertson to Sam Brown, January 24, 1877; Augusta Brown to Sam Brown, September 19, 1876—all Brown Family Papers.

22. Renville, *Dispatches from the Dakota War*, 97–100.

23. The genealogical records related to the marriages of Thomas and Angus to the four sisters in the Shortfoot family are inconsistent and confused, but it appears, based on the birth dates of their children, that they did not practice polygyny, but rather serial marriage. Thomas first married Lydia Shortfoot, with whom he had two sons in 1866 and 1867; then he married Ida Short-foot, with whom he had seven children, the first born in 1873. Angus married Emma Shortfoot, with whom he had four children, all born in the 1870s. His second wife was Nancy Shortfoot, with whom he had three children, the first born in 1890. Genealogical records provided by Tamara St. John, Tribal Historic Preservation Officer, Sisseton Wahpeton Oyate Tribal Archives.

24. Robertson, "Reminiscences," DCMC, 45.

25. Daniels, "Reminiscences," ch. 9, 17–18.

26. Diedrich, *Little Paul,* 176–79; Daniels, "Reminiscences," ch. 9, 18.

27. Diedrich, *Little Paul,* 178–88.

28. Anderson, *Gabriel Renville,* 121–24; Robertson, "Reminiscences," DCMC, 39.

29. Diedrich, *Little Paul,* 190; Robertson, "Reminiscences," DCMC, 186–87.

30. Angus Brown to Samuel Brown, April 26, 1879, and Joe Brown to Samuel Brown, May 8, 1879—both Brown Family Papers.

31. In letters written to Sam Brown in early 1879 from the Sisseton Agency, it is said that diphtheria was rampant and killing many young children on the reservation: Brown Family Papers. Will Robertson to Sam Brown, January 18, 1879, and March 4, 1879, Brown Family Papers.

32. Michael Haines, "Fertility and Mortality in the United States: Infant Mortality Rates," Economic History online, EH.net; "Infant Mortality," *Encyclopedia of Children and Childhood in History and Society* (2004), online.

33. Will Robertson to Sam Brown, September 23, 1879, Brown Family Papers.

34. Angus Brown to Sam Brown, December 1, 1879, and January 10, 1880, Brown Family Papers.

35. 1880 Federal Census; Joseph R. Brown Testimony, State of South Dakota, In Re Heirship to the Estate of Mrs. Jane A. Robertson, January 3, 1918.

36. Jane Robertson to Sam Brown, February, 1883, and Will Robertson to Sam Brown, February 6, 1883—both Brown Family Papers.

37. 1888, 1890, 1891 Lake Traverse Tribal Censuses, Indian Census Rolls, Federal Census Collection, Ancestry.com. The 1895 Minnesota State Census shows Daybreak Woman living with the Weatherstones at Beaver Falls. Although in their testimony to the probate court Thomas Robertson and J. R. Brown said that Sophie took care of Daybreak Woman continuously from the time Mattie died, the evidence says otherwise. Likely they were trying to make a stronger case for Sophie to inherit her mother's estate, which was being contested because Daybreak Woman's will left all of her property to her young grandson. Jubilee Committee, *History of the Sisseton-Wahpeton Indian Reservation*, 4, 23.

38. Jane A. Robertson to Samuel Brown, August 1885, Brown Family Papers.

39. Joe Brown to Sam Brown, February 25, 1888, Brown Family Papers.

40. Brian Altonen, "The 1890 Census Disease Maps," https://brianaltonenmph.com; "The 1889–1890 Flu Pandemic," www.flutrackers.com; Graber, ed., *Sister to the Sioux*, 45–46; Federal Census Collection, Indian Census Rolls, Ancestry.com. Neither Dessie nor Ephraim Prescott appear in the Indian Census Rolls in the 1880s, in contrast to the other members of the family. It is possible that they spent at least some of their years as younger children visiting or living with Prescott relatives in Minneapolis, which would explain their absence from the Indian Census Rolls until 1888. However, neither appear on the Minnesota State Census of 1885, so their whereabouts during this decade remain a mystery.

41. "Beaver Falls, the Beginning of the County," 1, 15–17, Beaver Falls History.

42. "Beaver Falls," 1–8.

43. Diedrich, *Old Betsey*, 125–26; interview with Mary Myrick Hinman LaCroix, February 1980, Rapid City, SD, by Betty Paukert Derrick, p4, Oral History Collection, Minnesota Historical Society.

44. Lehman, *History of the Early Episcopal Church*, 8, 11, 17.

45. Webb, *Redwood*, 113–14; Hinman file, box 24, George Tanner Papers.

46. Will Robertson to Samuel Brown, August 19, 1894, Brown Family Papers.

47. Brown Testimony In Re: Heirship of the Estate of Mrs. Jane A. Robertson; Jane Anderson Robertson documents file, provided by Tamara St. John, Tribal Historic Preservation Officer, Sisseton Wahpeton Oyate. Although she outlived her grandmother Daybreak Woman by a year, Augusta, Mattie's daughter, like her cousin Berthe, died in childbirth in 1905.

48. Thomas Robertson Testimony, State of South Dakota, In Re: Heirship of the Estate of Mrs. Jane A. Robertson, January 28, 1918, provided by Tamara St. John, Tribal Historic Preservation Officer, Sisseton Wahpeton Oyate.

49. *Inter Lake Tribune* (Browns Valley, MN), March 17, 1904.

50. Jane Anderson Robertson, Will, and Report of Heirship, Mrs. Jane A. Robertson, Sisseton Indian Agency, SD, provided by Tamara St. John, Tribal Historic Preservation Officer, Sisseton Wahpeton Oyate; Robertson Testimony In Re: Heirship of the Estate of Mrs. Jane A. Robertson.

51. *Inter Lake Tribune* (Browns Valley, MN), March 17, 1904.

Notes to Epilogue

Epigraph: T. Robertson, "Reminiscences," DCMC, 27.

1. Thomas Robertson Testimony In Re: Heirship to the Estate of Mrs. Jane A. Robertson.

Notes to Appendix 2

Epigraph: *The Dakota Friend,* April 1, 1852.

1. Wilson, *Beloved Child,* 86–87.

2. Penman, ed., *Honor the Grandmothers,* 34–35, 37–39, 54–56, 88, 117.

3. Sisoka Duta, "Dakota History and Culture," lecture, University of Minnesota, February 6, 2019; Oneroad and Skinner, *Being Dakota,* 96–98; Anderson, *Kinsmen of Another Kind,* 17–18, 169–70, 182–83; Penman, *Honor the Grandmothers,* 3, 34–35; Canku quoted in Wilson, *Beloved Child,* 86–87.

Notes to Appendix 3

1. Anglo-Dakota people were those of Dakota and British or British-American heritage. Carroll, "'Higgeldy-Piggeldy Assembly," 219–33, and "*Naginowenah,*" 58–68.

2. James Aird was Jane Anderson Robertson's grandfather; his story is told in Chapter One. For more on Archibald Campbell and family, see Atkins, *Creating Minnesota,* 26–33.

3. Carroll, "Who Was Jane Lamont?"

4. Carroll, "Who Was Jane Lamont?"; Wilson, *Ohiyesa,* 12–16; Dietrich, "A Good Man in a Changing World," 7.

Bibliography

This bibliography is divided into primary and secondary sources. Primary sources are the fundamental pieces of evidence used by historians to re-create and explain the past. They include letters, diaries, journals, memoirs in written or oral form, interviews, newspaper articles or other publications, and government, business, church, or organizational records created in a past time period. Secondary sources are analyses or interpretations based on primary and other sources. Examples of secondary sources are history monographs, biographies, articles, essays, documentary films, and physical or virtual exhibits.

Primary Sources

Manuscript Collections, Minnesota Historical Society

Aiton, John Felix, and Family. Papers.

Babcock, Willoughby, and Family. Papers.

Bailly, Alexis. Papers.

Bloomington, Minnesota. Manuscripts.

Boutwell, William T. Papers.

Brown, Joseph R., and Samuel J. Family. Papers.

Brown, William R., and Family. Papers.

Case, John. Papers.

Dakota Conflict Manuscripts Collection.

Daniels, Jared. "Reminiscences."

Derrick, Betty P. Interview with Mary Myrick Hinman LaCroix, Oral History Collection.

Evans, Constance, and Ona Earll. "La Prairie des Chiens: A Short Narrative of Events at Prairie du Chien, Wisconsin From 1673." Unpublished manuscript. Prairie du Chien, 1937.

Featherstonehaugh, George, and Family. Papers.

First Presbyterian Church of Minneapolis. Records.

First Presbyterian Church of St. Paul. Parish Record Books.

Flandrau, Charles E., and Family. Papers.

Folwell, William Watts. Papers.

Garrioch, Peter. Diary.

Garrioch, Peter. Papers.

Hinman, Samuel D., and Family. Papers.

Marsh, John. Papers.

McLeod, Martin, and Family. Papers.

Nairn, John. "A History of the Sioux Massacre: The Personal Recollection of John Nairn." Microfilm M582, reel 3, 3, Dakota Conflict Manuscripts Collection.

Northwest Missions. Papers.

Oral History Collection, American Indian History.

Pond Family. Papers.

Prairie Island Indian Community. Papers.

Prescott, Philander. Papers.

Riggs, Stephen, and Family. Papers.

Robertson, Andrew. File.

Satterlee, Marion P. Papers.

Sibley, Henry Hastings. Papers.

Stevens, J. D. Papers.

Stevens, John H. Papers.

Taliaferro, Lawrence. Papers.

Tanner, George. Papers.

Whipple, Bishop Henry. Papers.

Williams, J. Fletcher. Papers.

Williamson, Thomas, and Family. Papers.

Woolworth, Alan. Papers.

Collections at Other Archives

Anderson, Thomas G., and Family. Papers. Huronia Museum, Midland, Ontario, Canada.

Beaver Falls History. Renville County Historical Society, Morton, MN.

Faribault, David, and Nancy McClure Faribault. Sibley House Library, Mendota, MN.

History of Faribault. Rice County Historical Society, Faribault, MN.

Robertson Family File. Renville County Historical Society, Morton, MN.

Sibley, Helen Hastings. Sibley House Library, Mendota, MN.

Sisseton Wahpeton Oyate Tribal Archives and Collections. Lake Traverse Reservation, SD.

Published Primary Sources

Anderson, Gary C., and Alan Woolworth. *Through Dakota Eyes: Narrative Accounts of the Minnesota Indian War of 1862*. St. Paul: Minnesota Historical Society Press, 1988.

Anderson, Thomas G. "Journal of Captain Thomas G. Anderson." *Collections of the State Historical Society of Wisconsin* 9 (1882): 208–61.

Anderson, Thomas G. "Personal Narrative of Captain Thomas G. Anderson." *Collections of the State Historical Society of Wisconsin* 9 (1882): 137–206.

Baird, Elizabeth Therese. "Reminiscences of Early Days on Mackinac Island." *Collections of the State Historical Society of Wisconsin* 14 (1898): 17–64.

Barrett, J. O. "History of Traverse County, Brown's Valley and Environs." 1881. Reprint, *Minneapolis Star Tribune*, 1966, Minnesota Historical Society.

Blackford, John, and V. Wickman, comp. *Historic Red Rock Camp Meeting.* Minnesota Historical Society.

Brisbois, Bernard. "Recollections of Prairie du Chien." *Collections of the State Historical Society of Wisconsin* 9 (1882): 282–302.

Canku, Clifford, and Michael Simon. *The Dakota Prisoner of War Letters: Dakota Kaskapi Okicize Wowapi.* St. Paul: Minnesota Historical Society Press, 2013.

Daniels, Asa. "Reminiscences of Little Crow." *Minnesota Historical Society Collections* 12 (1908): 513–30.

Daniels, Jared W. "Reminiscences." *Minnesota Historical Society Collections* 14 (1912): 1–11.

DeCamp Sweet, J. E. "Mrs J. E. DeCamp Sweet's Narrative of Her Captivity in the Sioux Outbreak of 1862." *Minnesota Historical Society Collections* 6 (1894): 354–80.

Eastman, Charles. *Indian Boyhood.* 1902. Reprint, New York: Dover Publications, 1971.

Eastman, Mary. *Dahcotah, or Life and Legends of the Sioux.* 1849. Reprint, Minneapolis, MN: Ross and Haines, 1962.

Faribault, Nancy. "The Story of Nancy McClure." *Minnesota History Collections* 6 (1894): 439–60.

Featherstonehaugh, George W. *A Canoe Voyage Up the Minny Sotar.* St. Paul: Minnesota Historical Society Press, 1970.

Flandrau, Charles. "Reminiscences of Minnesota During the Territorial Period." *Minnesota Historical Society Collections* 9 (1901): 197–222.

Folwell, William W. *The Court Proceedings in the Trial of Dakota Indians Following the Massacre in Minnesota in August 1862.* Minneapolis: Saterlee Printing Company, 1927.

Hinman, Samuel, missionary, and Thomas Robertson, interpreter. *Episcopal Book of Common Prayer in Dakota.* Faribault, MN, 1862.

Keyes, Willard. "Documents: A Journal of Life in Wisconsin 100 Years Ago." *Wisconsin Magazine of History* 3, no. 3–4 (1919–20): 339–63, 443–58.

Larpenteur, Auguste. "Recollections of St. Paul." *Minnesota Historical Society Collections* 9 (1901): 363–94.

McClure, Nancy. "The Story of Nancy McClure." *Minnesota Historical Society Collections* 6 (1894): 439–60.

Parker, Donald, ed. *The Recollections of Philander Prescott*. Lincoln: University of Nebraska Press, 1966.

Penman, Sarah. *Honor the Grandmothers: Dakota and Lakota Women Tell Their Stories*. St. Paul: Minnesota Historical Society Press, 2000.

Pond, Samuel. "The Dakotas or Sioux in Minnesota as They Were in 1834." *Minnesota Historical Society Collections* 12 (1908): 319–501.

——. *Two Volunteer Missionaries Among the Dakota*. Boston: Congregational Sunday School Publications, 1893.

Prescott, Philander. "Autobiography and Reminiscences of Philander Prescott." *Minnesota Historical Society Collections* 6 (1894): 475–91.

Renville, Mary Butler. *Dispatches from the Dakota War: A Thrilling Narrative of Indian Captivity*. Edited by Carrie Zeman and Kathryn Derounian-Stodola. Lincoln: University of Nebraska Press, 2012.

Riggs, Mary. *A Small Bit of Bread and Butter: Letters from the Dakota Territory, 1832–1869*. Prairie Village, KS: Ash Grove Press, 1996.

Riggs, Stephen. *A Dakota-English Dictionary*. Edited by James Owen Dorsey. St. Paul: Minnesota Historical Society Press, 1992.

——. "The Dakota Mission." *Minnesota Historical Society Collections* 3 (1880): 115–28.

——. *Mary and I: Forty Years with the Sioux*. Boston: Congregational Sunday School Press, 1880.

Riggs, Stephen, comp. "A List of the White Prisoners and Half Breeds Delivered at Camp Release, October, 1862." Transcribed by Alan Woolworth. *Minnesota's Heritage* 5 (January 2012).

Riggs, Stephen R. "Protestant Missions in Minnesota." *Minnesota Historical Society Collections* 6 (1894): 117–88.

Robertson, Thomas. "Reminiscences of Thomas Robertson." *South Dakota Department of History Collections* 20 (1940): 559–601.

Shaw, John. "Personal Narrative of Colonel John Shaw." *Wisconsin Historical Collections* 2 (1856): 197–226.

Sibley, Henry. "Reminiscences Historical and Personal." *Minnesota Historical Society Collections* 1 (1850–56): 457–85.

Sibley, Henry H. "Memoir of J. B. Faribault." *Minnesota Historical Society Collections* 3 (1880): 168–79.

——. "Reminiscences of the Early Days of Minnesota." *Minnesota Historical Society Collections* 3 (1880): 242–82.

Taliaferro, Lawrence. "Autobiography of Lawrence Taliaferro, Indian Agent at Fort Snelling." *Minnesota Historical Society Collections* 6 (1894): 189–256.

Tarble, Helen Mar Carrothers. *The Story of My Capture and Escape During the Minnesota Indian Massacre of 1862*. St. Paul, MN: Abbott Printing Co., 1904.

Upham, Warren, comp. "Jared Waldo Daniels." *Minnesota Historical Society Collections* Biographies, 1655–1919.

Van Cleve, Charlotte. "A Reminiscence of Fort Snelling." *Minnesota Historical Society Collections* 3 (1880): 76–81.

———. *"Three Score Years and Ten": Lifelong Memories of Fort Snelling, Minnesota and other Parts of the West.* Minneapolis, MN: Harrison and Smith, 1888.

Wakefield, Sarah. *Six Weeks in the Sioux Teepees: A Narrative of Indian Captivity.* Edited with Introduction by June Namias. Norman: University of Oklahoma Press, 1997.

Walsh, William, comp. *Journal of the Reverend S. D. Hinman, Missionary to the Santee Sioux Indians and Taopi by Bishop Whipple.* Philadelphia: McCalla and Stavely, 1869.

Whipple, Henry B. *Lights and Shadows of a Long Episcopate.* New York: Macmillan and Co., 1912.

White, Urania. "Captivity Among the Sioux." *Minnesota Historical Society Collections* 9 (1898–1900): 395–426.

Williams, Meade C. "The Old Mission Church of Mackinac Island: An Historical Discourse Delivered at the Re-opening on July 28, 1895." Detroit: Wilton-Smith Company, 1895.

US Government Records

US Army Court of Claims. *The Sisseton and Wahpeton Bands of Sioux Indians vs. the United States.* (1901–07) (Case #22524). Washington, DC: Government Printing Office, 1907.

US Army Military Commission. *Sioux War Trials, 1862.*

US Department of Interior. "Report on the Sisseton and Wahpeton Bands of Dakota." Washington, DC: Government Printing Office, 1898.

US Department of Interior. "The Santee Sioux of Nebraska and Flandreau, South Dakota." Washington, DC: Government Printing Office, 1898.

US Department of Interior, National Park Service, Historic American Buildings Survey. "City of Prairie du Chien" (HABS WI-302). Washington, DC.

US Office of Indian Affairs (OIA) at the Minnesota Historical Society
    Affidavit of Mary Woodbury (1888)
    Annuity Payroll (1890)
    Annuity Payroll (1900)
    Annuity Rolls (Mdwekanton Dakota) (1849–61)
    Census of Mdewakanton Sioux (1899)
    Correspondence of Walter McLeod to Commissioners
    Letters Received from the St. Peter's Agency.
    List of Sioux Scouts (1892)
    Reservation Census, Santee Agency (1885–1916)

US Senate. *Affidavits and Petitions of Santee Sioux* (1896).

Government of Canada Records: Library and Archives Canada

Indian Affairs: Central Toronto Superintendency Records, Coldwater Account Book and Audits, 1833–36, RG10, vol. 654 (microfilm reel C-13400).

Indian Affairs: Chief Superintendent's Office, Upper Canada (Col. J. Givins) Correspondence, 1833–37, RG10, vol. 54–67 (microfilm reels C-11018–23).

Indian Affairs: Chief Superintendent's Office Letterbook, 1835–38, RG10, vol. 501–2 (microfilm reel C-13342).

Secondary Sources

Manuscript Collections, Minnesota Historical Society

Bean, William. "Eastman, Cloud Man, Many Lightnings: An Anglo-Dakota Family." 1989.

Belliveau, Walter. "The Life of Alexis Bailly, Minnesota Pioneer." 1928.

Birk, Douglas. "Grey Cloud Island: An Archeological Approach." 1972.

Coash, John. "Leo Francis Rocque: Half-Breed, A Family History." 2000.

Ford, John. "Biographical Notes on William R. Brown." 1874.

Lynch, Sister Claire, OSB. "Reverend William Thurston Boutwell, 1803–1890." 1983.

Munson, Don. "Prairie du Chien during the American Revolution." 1974.

Plehal, Alice. "History of Prairie du Chien, 1760–1800." 1924.

Articles and Books

Ackerman, Gertrude. "Joseph Renville of Lac qui Parle." *Minnesota History* 12, no. 3 (1931): 231–46.

Adams, Moses. *History of the Dakota Presbytery.* Goodwill, SD: Presbytery of the Dakota, 1892.

Adelman, Jeremy, and Stephen Aron. "From Borderlands to Borders: Empires, Nation-States and the Peoples in Between in North American History." *American Historical Review* 4, no. 3 (June 1999): 814–41.

Addicks, Duke. "Zebulon Pike and James Aird: The Explorer and the Scottish Gentleman." *Ramsey County History* 40, no. 2 (Summer 2005): 17–18.

Albers, Patricia. "Autonomy and Dependency in the Lives of Dakota Women." *Review of Radical Political Economics* 17, no. 3 (1985): 109–34.

Allen, Anne B. *And the Wilderness Shall Blossom: Henry Benjamin Whipple, Churchman, Educator, Advocate for the Indians.* Afton, MN: Afton Historical Society Press, 2008.

Allen, Clifford, et al. *History of the Flandreau Santee Tribe.* Flandreau, SD: Tribal History Program, 1971.

Anderson, Gary C. *Gabriel Renville: From the Dakota War to the Creation of the Sisseton-Wahpeton Reservation, 1825–1892.* Pierre: South Dakota Historical Society Press, 2018.

——. "Joseph Renville and the Ethos of Biculturalism." In *Being and Becoming Indian: Biographical Studies of North American Frontiers*, edited by James A. Clifton, 59–81, Chicago: Dorsey Press, 1989.

——. *Kinsmen of Another Kind: Dakota-White Relations in the Upper Mississippi Valley, 1650–1862*. Lincoln: University of Nebraska Press, 1984.

——. *Little Crow: Spokesman for the Sioux*. St. Paul: Minnesota Historical Society Press, 1986.

——. *Massacre in Minnesota: The Dakota War of 1862, the Most Violent Ethnic Conflict in American History*. Norman: University of Oklahoma Press, 2019.

Anderson, Peter. *Charles A. Eastman, Physician*. Chicago: Children's Press, 1992.

Andrews, C. C. *Minnesota and Dacotah*. Washington, DC: Robert Farham, 1857.

Antoine de Julio, Mary. "The Vertefeuille House of Prairie du Chien: A Survivor from the Era of French Wisconsin." *Wisconsin Magazine of History* 80, no. 1 (Autumn 1996): 36–56.

Armour, David. "David Mitchell." *Dictionary of Canadian Biography Online*. University of Toronto/Université Laval, 2003.

Armour, David A. "David and Elizabeth: The Mitchell Family of the Straits of Mackinac." *Michigan History* 64, no. 4 (July 1980): 17–29.

Atkins, Annette. *Creating Minnesota: A History from the Inside Out*. St. Paul: Minnesota Historical Society Press, 2010.

Atwater, Isaac, and John H. Stevens, eds. *History of Minneapolis and Hennepin County, Minnesota*. New York: Munsell Company, 1895.

Babcock, Willoughby. "A Pioneer Indian Agent at Fort Snelling." *Minnesota Alumni Weekly* 31, no. 25 (1932): 407–8, 419.

Badt, Karin. *Charles Eastman: Sioux Physician*. New York: Chelsea House, 1995.

Bachman, Walt. *Northern Slave, Black Dakota: The Life and Times of Joseph Godfrey*. Bloomington, MN: Pond Dakota Press, 2013.

Bakeman, Mary H., and Antona Richardson, eds. *Trails of Tears: Minnesota's Dakota Indian Exile Begins*. Roseville, MN: Prairie Echoes (Park Genealogical Books), 2008.

Bakeman, Mary H., and Alan R. Woolworth, eds. *Camera and Sketchbook: Witnesses to the Sioux Uprising of 1862*. Roseville, MN: Prairie Echoes Press, 2004.

Barton, Winifred. *John P. Williamson: A Brother to the Sioux*. New York: Fleming Revell Company, 1919.

Beaumont, Deborah. "Doctor William Beaumont: His Life in Mackinac and Wisconsin, 1820–1834." *Wisconsin Magazine of History* 4, no. 3 (March 1921): 263–80.

Birk, Douglas. *Survey of Grey Cloud Island*. St. Paul: Minnesota Historical Society, 1972.

Blegen, Theodore. "The Pond Brothers." *Minnesota History* 15, no. 3 (1934): 273–81.

———. "Two Missionaries in the Sioux Country." *Minnesota History* 21, no. 1 (1940): 15–32, 158–75, 272–83.

Bray, Edmund, and Martha Bray, trans. and eds. *Joseph N. Nicollet on the Plains and Prairies: The Expeditions of 1838–9 with Journals, Letters, Notes on the Dakota Indians.* St. Paul: Minnesota Historical Society Press, 1976.

Brown, Jennifer S. H. *Strangers in Blood: Fur Trade Company Families in Indian Country.* Vancouver: University of British Colombia Press, 1980.

Brown, Jennifer S. H., and Jacqueline Peterson, eds. *The New Peoples: Being and Becoming Métis in North America.* Lincoln: University of Nebraska Press, 1985.

Brumwell, Jill. *Drummond Island: History, Folklore and Early People.* Drummond Island, MI: Black Bear Press, 2003.

Buffalohead, Priscilla. "Farmers, Warriors, Traders: A Fresh Look at Ojibway Women." *Minnesota History* 48, no. 6 (Summer 1983): 236–44.

Carley, Kenneth. *The Sioux Uprising of 1862.* St. Paul: Minnesota Historical Society Press, 1976.

Carroll, Jane Lamm. "This Higgeldy-Piggeldy Assembly: The McLeods, an Anglo-Dakota Family." *Minnesota History* 60, no. 6 (Summer 2007): 219–33.

———. "*Naginowenah*, Lucy Prescott and the Wizard of Cereal Foods: Three Generations of an Anglo-Dakota Family." *Minnesota History* 63, no. 2 (Summer 2012): 58–68.

———. "'Who Was Jane Lamont?': Anglo-Dakota Daughters in Early Minnesota." *Minnesota History* 59, no. 5 (Spring 2005): 184–96.

Case, John. "Historical Notes of Grey Cloud Island and Vicinity." *Minnesota Historical Society Collections* 15 (1909–14): 371–78.

Cavendar, Chris. "The Dakota People of Minnesota." *Hennepin County History* 47, no. 3 (Summer 1988): 11–15.

Chomsky, Carol. "The U.S.–Dakota War Trials: A Study in Military Injustice." *Stanford Law Review* 43, no. 1 (November 1990): 13–97.

Christgau, John. *Birch Coulie: The Epic Battle of the Dakota War.* Lincoln: University of Nebraska Press, 2012.

Collier, Julius. *History of Shakopee Minnesota.* Shakopee, MN: Shakopee Print Company, 1933.

———. *The Shakopee Story.* Shakopee, MN: Lakewood Press, 1960.

Cook, Samuel F. *Drummond Island: The Story of British Occupation, 1815–1828.* Lansing, MI: R. Smith Printing Company, 1896. Published online at "Roger Peters' Home Page," www.wissensdrang.com.

Copeland, Marion. *Charles Alexander Eastman.* Boise, ID: Boise State University, 1978.

Cronon, William. *Changes in the Land: Indians, Colonists, and the Ecology of New England.* New York: Hill and Wang, 1983.

Curtiss-Wedge, Franklyn, comp. *History of Dakota and Goodhue Counties, Minnesota.* Vol. 1. Chicago: Copper Company, 1910.

——. *History of Renville County, Minnesota*. Vol. 1. Chicago: H. C. Cooper, Jr. and Co., 1916.

——. *History of Rice and Steele Counties of Minnesota*. Vol. 1. Chicago: H. C. Cooper, Jr. and Co., 1910.

Dahlin, Curtis. *The Fort Sisseton Dakota Scouts and Their Camps in Eastern Dakota Territory*. Roseville, MN: Dahlin Publication, 2017.

——. *A Pictorial History of the Dakota Uprising*. Roseville, MN: Dahlin Publication, 2012.

——. *Renville County in the Dakota Uprising*. Roseville, MN: Dahlin Publication, 2012.

——. *Stories and Final Resting Places of Notable Friendly Dakota and Mixed Bloods on the Sisseton-Wahpeton Indian Reservation*. Roseville, MN: Dahlin Publication, 2010.

——. *Victims of the Dakota Uprising*. Roseville, MN: Dahlin Publication, 2012.

Dakota County Historical Society, "Glimpses of Kaposia—The Village of Little Crow." *Over the Years* 26, no. 3 (1986): 1–10.

Danziger, Edmund. "The Crow Creek Experiment: An Aftermath of the Sioux War of 1862." *North Dakota History* 37, no. 2 (Spring 1970): 105–23.

Deloria, Ella. *The Dakota Way of Life*. Sioux Falls, SD: Mariah Press, 2007.

Denial, Catherine. *Making Marriage: Husbands, Wives and the American State in Dakota and Ojibwe Country*. St. Paul: Minnesota Historical Society Press, 2013.

Derounian-Stodola, Kathryn. *The War in Words: Reading the Dakota Conflict through Captivity Literature*. Lincoln: University of Nebraska Press, 2009.

Devens, Carol. *Countering Colonization: Native American Women and Great Lakes Missions, 1630–1900*. Berkeley: University of California Press, 1992.

Diedrich, Mark. *The Chiefs Wapahasha: Three Generations of Dakota Leadership*. Rochester, MN: Coyote Books, 2004.

——. "A Good Man in a Changing World: Cloud Man, the Dakota Leader, and His Life and Times." *Ramsey County History* 36, no. 1 (2001): 4–24.

——. *Little Paul: Christian Leader of the Dakota Peace Party*. Rochester, MN: Coyote Books, 2010.

——. *Old Betsey: The Life and Times of a Famous Dakota Woman and Her Family*. Rochester, MN: Coyote Books, 1995.

Driving Hawk Sneve, Virginia. *Sioux Women: Traditionally Sacred*. Pierre: South Dakota Historical Society Press, 2016.

DuBois, Ellen, and Lynn Dumenil. *Through Women's Eyes: An American History*. Boston: Bedford St. Martin's, 2016.

Durand, Paul. *Where the Waters Gather and the Rivers Meet: An Atlas of the Eastern Sioux*. Prior Lake, MN: P. C. Durand, 1994.

Ebell, Adrian. "The Indian Massacres and War of 1862." *Harper's Monthly Magazine* 27 (June 1863).

Flandrau, Charles E. *The History of Minnesota and Tales of the Frontier.* St. Paul, MN: E. W. Porter, 1900.

Folsom, William. *Fifty Years in the Northwest.* St. Paul, MN: Pioneer Press Company, 1888.

Folwell, William W. *A History of Minnesota.* 4 vols. 1921. Reprint, St. Paul: Minnesota Historical Society, 1956.

Frink, F. W. *A Short History of Faribault and Some of Its People.* Faribault, MN: Faribault Republican, 1901.

Frye, Kermit. *The Old Bloomington Cemetery.* Roseville, MN: Park Genealogical Books, 1999.

Gates, Charles. "The Lac qui Parle Mission." *Minnesota Historical Society Collections* 16 (1935): 133–51.

Gibbon, Guy. *The Sioux: The Dakota and Lakota Nations.* Malden, MA: Blackwell Press, 2003.

Gilman, Rhoda. "The Fur Trade in the Upper Mississippi Valley, 1630–1850." *Wisconsin Magazine of History* 58, no. 1 (Autumn 1974): 2–18.

——. *Henry Hastings Sibley: Divided Heart.* St. Paul: Minnesota Historical Society Press, 2004.

——. "James Aird." *Dictionary of Canadian Biography Online.* University of Toronto, 2000. www.biographi.ca.

——. "The Last Days of the Upper Mississippi Fur Trade." *Minnesota History* 42, no. 4 (Winter 1970): 122–40.

Glewwe, Lois A. Dakota Soul Sisters: Stories of the Women of the Dakota Missions. www.dakotasoulsisters.com.

Goodman, Nancy, and Robert Goodman. *Joseph R. Brown: Adventurer on the Minnesota Frontier.* Rochester, MN: Lone Oak Press, 1996.

Graber, Kay, ed. *Sister to the Sioux: The Memoirs of Elaine Goodale Eastman.* Lincoln: University of Nebraska Press, 2004.

Green, Rayna. *Women in American Indian Society.* New York: Chelsea House, 1992.

Gunn, G. H. "Peter Garrioch at St. Peter's." *Minnesota History* 20, no. 2 (1939): 119–28.

Hansen, James. "Prairie du Chien's Earliest Church Records, 1817." *Minnesota Genealogical Journal* 4 (November 1985): 329–42.

Hansen, Marcus. *Old Fort Snelling.* Minneapolis, MN: Ross and Hanson, 1958.

Haymond, John. *The Infamous Dakota War Trials of 1862.* Jefferson, NC: McFarland and Company, 2016.

Heilbron, Bertha, ed. *With Pen and Pencil on the Frontier in 1851: The Diary and Sketches of Frank Blackwell Mayer.* St. Paul: Minnesota Historical Society Press, 1932.

Hendricks, Judith, ed. *Bloomington on the Minnesota.* Bloomington, MN: Bloomington Bicentennial Committee, 1976.

Hobart, Chauncey. *The History of Methodism in Minnesota*. Red Wing, MN: Red Wing Printing, 1887.

Hoisington, Daniel J. *A Splendid Little Town: A History of Faribault, Minnesota*. Faribault, MN: Faribault Heritage Commission, 1994.

Holcombe, Return. *Minnesota in Three Centuries, 1655–1908. Vol. 3: Minnesota as a State, 1858–1870*. New York: Publishing Society of Minnesota, 1908.

Hughes, Thomas. *Indian Chiefs of Southern Minnesota*. Mankato, MN: Free Press, 1927.

Hunter, Andrew. *A History of Simcoe County*. 1909. Reprint, Barrie, ON: Simcoe County Historical Society, 1948.

Hyde, Anne. *Empires, Nations and Families: A History of the North American West, 1800–1860*. Lincoln: University of Nebraska Press, 2011.

Hyman, Colette. *Dakota Women's Work: Creativity, Culture, and Exile*. St. Paul: Minnesota Historical Society Press, 2012.

——. "Survival at Crow Creek, 1863–1866." *Minnesota History* 61, no. 4 (2009): 148–61.

Isch, John. *The Dakota Trials: The 1862–1864 Military Commission Trials*. New Ulm, MN: Brown County Historical Society, 2012.

Jones, Evan. *Citadel in the Wilderness: The Story of Fort Snelling and the Northwest Frontier*. New York: Coward-McCann, 1966.

——. *The Minnesota: Forgotten River*. New York: Holt, Rinehart and Winston, 1962.

K., M. A. "Prairie du Chien." *Wisconsin Domesday Book*, 107–10. Madison: State Historical Society of Wisconsin, c. 1925.

Kane, Lucille. *The Falls of St. Anthony: The Waterfall That Built Minneapolis*. St. Paul: Minnesota Historical Society Press, 1987.

Kellogg, Louise. *The British Regime in Wisconsin*. Madison: University of Wisconsin Press, 1935.

——. *The French Regime in Wisconsin and the Northwest*. Madison: University of Wisconsin Press, 1925.

Landis, Ruth. *The Mystic Lake Sioux: Sociology of the Mdewakanton Santee*. Madison: University of Wisconsin Press, 1968.

Lass, William. "Histories of the U.S.–Dakota War of 1862." *Minnesota History* 63, no. 2 (Summer 2012): 44–57.

Lavender, David. *The Fist in the Wilderness*. New York: Doubleday, 1964.

Lawrence, Elden. *The Peace Seekers: Indian Christians and the Dakota Conflict*. Sioux Falls, SD: Pine Hill Press, 2005.

Lehman, June Robertson. *A History of the Early Episcopal Church of the St. John's Mission*. Morton, MN: Renville County Historical Society, 1999.

Letterman, Edward J. *From Whole Log to No Log: A History of the Indians Where the Mississippi and Minnesota Rivers Meet*. Minneapolis, MN: Dillon Press, 1969.

Lorbiecki, Marybeth. *Painting the Dakota: Seth Eastman at Fort Snelling*. Afton, MN: Afton Historical Society, 2000.

Lowery, Carol. "James Hamilton." *Dictionary of Canadian Biography Online.* University of Toronto/Université Laval, 2003.

Mahan, Bruce. *Old Fort Crawford and the Frontier.* Iowa City: State Historical Society of Iowa, 1926.

Martin, Deborah Beaumont. "Dr. William Beaumont: His Life in Mackinac and Wisconsin 1820–1834." *Wisconsin Magazine of History* 4, no. 3 (March 1921): 263–80.

McDowell, John E. "Therese Schindler of Mackinac: Upward Mobility in the Great Lakes Fur Trade." *Wisconsin Magazine of History* 61, no. 2 (Winter 1977–78): 125–43.

Meyer, Roy. *History of the Santee Sioux.* Lincoln: University of Nebraska Press, 1967.

———. "The Prairie Island Community: A Remnant of Minnesota Sioux." *Minnesota History* 37, no. 7 (Fall 1961): 271–82.

Michno, Gregory. *Dakota Dawn: The Decisive First Week of the Sioux Uprising, August 1862.* New York: Savis Beatie, 2011.

Mihesuah, Devon, ed. *Natives and Academics: Researching and Writing About American Indians.* Lincoln: University of Nebraska Press, 1998.

Millikan, William. "The Great Treasure of the Fort Snelling Prison Camp." *Minnesota History* 62, no. 1 (Spring 2010): 4–17.

Milman, T. R. "Thomas Gummersall Anderson." *Dictionary of Canadian Biography Online.* University of Toronto, 2000. www.biographi.ca.

Minnesota Historical Society. *The Fur Trade in Minnesota Country.* St. Paul: Minnesota Historical Society, 1967.

Monjeau-Marz, Corinne. *The Dakota Indian Internment at Fort Snelling, 1862–64.* St. Paul: Prairie Smoke Press, 2005.

Monjeau-Marz, Corinne, and Stephen Osman. "What You May Not Know About the Fort Snelling Indian Camps." *Minnesota's Heritage* 7 (January 2013): 112–33.

Munson, Dan. *Prairie du Chien During the American Revolution.* N.p.: Don Munson Publishing, 1974.

Neill, Edward D. "Dakota Land, Dakota Life." *Minnesota Historical Society Collections* 1 (1850–56): 205–40.

———. "Early Days at Fort Snelling." *Minnesota Historical Society Collections* 1 (1850–56): 420–38.

———. *History of the Minnesota Valley.* Minneapolis, MN: North Star, 1882.

———. *History of Washington County and the St. Croix Valley.* Minneapolis, MN: North Star, 1881.

———. "A Sketch of Joseph Renville." *Minnesota Historical Society Collections* 1 (1850–56): 196–206.

Neill, Edward D., and Charles S. Bryant. *History of Rice County.* Minneapolis: N.p., 1882–83.

Nute, Grace Lee. "The Diary of Martin McLeod." *Minnesota History* 4, no. 7–8 (1921–22): 351–439.

——. "Posts in the Minnesota Fur Trading Era, 1660–1855." *Minnesota History* 11, no. 4 (1930): 353–85.

——. *The Voyageur.* St. Paul: Minnesota Historical Society Press, 1931.

——. "Wilderness Marthas." *Minnesota History* 8, no. 3 (1927): 247–59.

Oak Grove Presbyterian Church. *The Heritage of Oak Grove.* Bloomington, MN: Oak Grove Presbyterian Church, 1976.

——. *Oak Grove Mission: 150 Years.* Bloomington, MN: Oak Grove Presbyterian Church, 1993.

O'Meara, Frank. *Daughters of the Country: The Women of the Fur Traders and Mountain Men.* New York: Harcourt, Brace and Co., 1968.

Oneroad, Amos E., and Alanson B. Skinner. *Being Dakota: Tales and Traditions.* Edited by Laura L. Anderson. St. Paul: Minnesota Historical Society Press, 2003.

Osborne, A. C. "The Migration of Voyageurs from Drummond Island to Penetanguishene in 1828." *Ontario Historical Society Papers* 3 (1901): 123–66.

Parker, Donald. *Lac qui Parle: Its Missionaries, Traders and Indians.* Brookings: South Dakota State College, 1964.

Podruchny, Carolyn. *Making the Voyageur World: Travelers and Traders in the North American Fur Trade.* Lincoln: University of Nebraska Press, 2006.

Prucha, Francis Paul. "Army Sutlers and the American Fur Company." *Minnesota History* 40, no. 1 (1966): 22–31.

——. *Broadax and Bayonet: The Role of the U.S. Army in the Development of the Northwest.* Lincoln: University of Nebraska Press, 1953.

——. *Lewis Cass and American Indian Policy.* Detroit, MI: Detroit Historical Society, 1967.

——. *The Sword of the Republic: The U.S. Army on the Frontier.* Lincoln: University of Nebraska Press, 1969.

Relf, Francis. "The Removal of the Sioux Indians from Minnesota." *Minnesota History Bulletin* 6 (May 1918): 420–25.

Rich, E. E. *The Fur Trade and the Northwest to 1857.* Toronto: McLelland and Stewart, Ltd., 1967.

Robinson, Doane. *History of the Dakota.* Minneapolis, MN: Ross and Haines, 1904.

Rowe, Mrs. Anderson. "Record from 1699 to 1896." *Ontario Historical Society Papers and Records* 6 (1905): 111–12.

Rubenstein, Mitchell, and Alan Woolworth. "The Dakota and Ojibway." In *They Chose Minnesota: A Survey of the State's Ethnic Groups,* edited by June Holmquist, 17–35, St. Paul: Minnesota Historical Society Press, 1981.

Satterlee, Marion. *Outbreak and Massacre by the Dakota Indians in Minnesota in 1862*. Minneapolis, MN: Marion Satterlee, 1923.

Scanlan, Peter. *Prairie du Chien: French, British, American*. Menasha, WI: Collegiate Press, 1937.

Sheppard, Betty P., and Rev. Edward Sheppard. *The Bishop Whipple Mission*. Morton, MN: Lower Sioux Community: Episcopal Diocese of Minnesota, 1981.

Sibley, Henry H. *Iron Face: The Adventures of Jack Frazier*. Chicago: Caxton Club, 1950.

Sisseton Dakota Indian Reservation Jubilee Committee. *History of the Sisseton-Wahpeton Indian Reservation*. Sisseton, SD: The Committee, 1967.

Sleeper-Smith, Susan. *Indian Women and French Men: Rethinking Cultural Encounters in the Western Great Lakes*. Amherst: University of Massachusetts Press, 2001.

Spickard, Paul R. *Almost All Aliens: Immigration, Race, and Colonialism in American History and Identity*. New York: Routledge, 2007.

Sterling, Everett W. "Bishop Henry Whipple: Indian Agent Extraordinary." *Historical Magazine of the Protestant Episcopal Church* 26, no. 3 (September 1957): 239–47.

Stevens, John H. *Early History of Hennepin County*. Minneapolis, MN: Northwestern Democrat, 1856.

Swanberg, L. E., ed. *Then and Now: A History of Rice County, Faribault and Its Communities*. Faribault, MN: Rice County Bicentennial Commission, 1976.

Tanner, Helen H. *The Ojibwas: A Critical Bibliography*. New York: Chelsea House, 1992.

Trimble, Steve. "There Once Was a Kaposia Village." *St. Paul Historical* app. St. Paul, MN: Historical St. Paul, 2020. http://saintpaulhistorical.com/items/show/115.

Ulrich, Laurel Thatcher. *A Midwife's Tale: The Life of Martha Ballard, Based on Her Diary, 1785–1812*. New York: Vintage Books, 1990.

Upham, Warren. *Minnesota Place Names: A Geographical Encyclopedia*. St. Paul: Minnesota Historical Society Press, 2001.

Van Kirk, Sylvia. *Many Tender Ties: Women in Fur-Trade Society in Western Canada, 1670–1870*. Winnipeg: Watson and Dwyer, 1980.

Vizenor, Gerald. *The People Named the Chippewa: Narrative Histories*. Minneapolis: University of Minnesota Press, 1984.

Warner, George, and C. Foote, eds. *History of Hennepin County*. Minneapolis, MN: North Star Publishing, 1881.

——. *History of the Minnesota Valley*. Minneapolis, MN: North Star Publishing, 1882.

Waziyatawin. *What Does Justice Look Like?: The Struggle for Liberation in Dakota Homeland*. St. Paul, MN: Living Justice Press, 2008.

Webb, Wayne. *Redwood: The Story of a County*. Redwood County Board of Commissioners, 1964.

Werner, Robert. "Dakota Diaspora After 1862." *Minnesota's Heritage* 6 (July 2012): 38–59.

Westerman, Gwen, and Bruce White. *Mni Sota Makoce: The Land of the Dakota*. St. Paul: Minnesota Historical Society Press, 2012.

White, Bruce. "The Power of Whiteness: The Life and Times of Joseph Rolette, Jr." In *Making Minnesota Territory, 1849–1858,* edited by Anne Kaplan, 178–197, St. Paul: Minnesota Historical Society Press, 1998.

White, Bruce, and Helen White. *Fort Snelling in 1838*. St. Paul: Turnstone Historical Research, 1998.

White, Richard. *The Middle Ground: Indians, Empires and Republics in the Great Lakes Region, 1650–1815.* Cambridge, UK: Cambridge University Press, 1991.

Widder, Keith. *Battle for the Soul: Métis Children Encounter Evangelical Protestants at Mackinaw Mission, 1823–1837.* East Lansing: Michigan State University Press, 1999.

——. "Magdelaine Laframboise: The First Lady of Mackinac Island." *Mackinac History* 4, no. 1 (2007): 2–11.

Willand, Jon Lee. *Lac qui Parle and the Dakota Mission*. Madison, MN: Lac qui Parle Historical Society, 1964.

Williams, John F. *History of the City of St. Paul*. St. Paul: Minnesota Historical Society, 1983.

Wilson, Diane. *Beloved Child: A Dakota Way of Life*. St. Paul, MN: Borealis Books, 2011.

——. *Spirit Car: Journey to a Dakota Past*. St. Paul, MN: Borealis Books, 2006.

Wilson, Raymond. *Ohiyesa: Charles Eastman, Santee Sioux*. Urbana: University of Illinois Press, 1983.

Wilson, Waziyatawin Angela. *Remember This! Dakota Decolonization and the Eli Taylor Narratives*. Lincoln: University of Nebraska Press, 2005.

Wilson, Waziyatawin Angela, ed. *In the Footsteps of Our Ancestors: The Dakota Commemorative Marches of the 21st Century*. St. Paul, MN: Living Justice Press, 2006.

Wingerd, Mary. *North Country: The Making of Minnesota*. Minneapolis: University of Minnesota Press, 2010.

Woloch, Nancy. *Women and the American Experience*. New York: McGraw-Hill, 2006.

Wood, Edwin O. *Historic Mackinac*. New York: Macmillan and Co., 1918.

Woolworth, Alan. "Dakota Indian Scouts on the Minnesota/Dakota Territory Frontier, 1863–1866." *Minnesota's Heritage* 6 (July 2012): 60–77.

——. "The Lives and Influences of the Andrew Robertson Family." *Minnesota's Heritage* 1 (January 2010): 114–20.

Woolworth, Alan, ed. *The Flandrau Papers: Treasure Trove for Mixed Blood Dakota Indian Genealogy*. Roseville, MN: Park Genealogical Society Books, 1997.

Woolworth, Alan, and Nancy Woolworth. "Treaty of Mendota, 1851." White Bear Lake, MN: Woolworth Research Associates, 1982.

——. "The Treaty of Traverse des Sioux of 1851." White Bear Lake, MN: Woolworth and Associates, 1982.

Wozniak, John W. *Contact, Negotiation and Conflict: An Ethnohistory of the Eastern Dakota, 1819–1839*. Washington, DC: University Press of America, 1978.

Dissertations and Documentaries

Anderson, Carolyn. "Dakota Identity in Minnesota, 1820–1995." PhD diss., University of Minnesota, 1997.

Beane, Katherine. "*Wokakapi Kin Ahdipi* 'Bringing the Story Home': A History within the *Wakpa Ipaksan Dakota Oyate*." PhD diss., University of Minnesota, 2014.

Dakota Exile. Twin Cities Public Television/PBS, 2019.

Dakota 38. Smooth Feather, 2012.

Jorstad, Erling. "The Life of H. H. Sibley." PhD diss., Indiana University, 1957.

Peterson, Jacqueline. "The People In Between: Indian-White Marriage and the Genesis of Métis Society and Culture in the Great Lakes Region, 1680–1830." PhD diss., University of Illinois, 1981.

WACIPI—Powwow. Twin Cities Public Television/PBS, 1995.

Index

Page numbers in *italics* indicate illustrations or maps.